I0837278

GUARDING A GREAT CITY

BY

WILLIAM McADOO

POLICE COMMISSIONER
NEW YORK CITY
1904-1906

HARPER & BROTHERS PUBLISHERS
NEW YORK AND LONDON
MCMVI

Published May, 1906.

CONTENTS

PREFACE

BOTH before and since leaving the Police Department, I have been asked so often to address various social and other organizations on the subject of the police, or to write articles dealing with some particular phase of police work, that many friends have urged me to put my experience and views on this important subject in the more permanent form of a book, to which inquiries, so far as I am concerned, could be referred. If these opinions of mine have any value, they will thus at least be accessible in permanent form. The subject itself is one which concerns not only the citizens of New York, but the vast army of visitors and sojourners in the metropolis, and is one to which the country at large gives a great deal of attention. Every advance in adding to the efficiency and honesty of police administration in New York is sure, sooner or later, to be followed by the other great cities in the United States. The example of this mighty city is far-reaching.

I have undertaken this work with no little hesitancy because of the frankness and candor which the treatment of the subject demands if it is to make for the public good. I have tried, wherever possible, to avoid the personal equation whether in speaking of myself or others, and I can truthfully say that I have honestly and conscientiously endeavored to speak the truth impartially, judicially, and I trust I may be allowed to say courageously and without regard to consequences so far as I am personally concerned. If this publication will lead to an earnest, honest, and unselfish effort to reform existing abuses, to make the police of New York what they should be, and what they are capable of being—a respected and self-respecting, honest, intelligent, courageous, and efficient body of men—I will have been more than repaid for any labors undergone or any pains and penalties exacted in the performance of official duties or individual and independent effort.

GUARDING A GREAT CITY

GUARDING A GREAT CITY

I

INTRODUCTION TO POLICE HEADQUARTERS AND MULBERRY STREET

EARLY in the month of December, 1903, and after the first election of the present Mayor of New York, I was walking down Park Row on my way to the Elevated Railroad station in company with a distinguished citizen, who turned to me and suddenly said, "You ought to be Police Commissioner, and I have heard your name most favorably mentioned in that connection." I am not exaggerating when I say that if he had said to me that I ought to be in Sing Sing for the term of my natural life, I could not have been more surprised or alarmed. The larger part of my official career had been spent in Washington—in Congress and at the Navy Department—and from that point of view and the impression which one gets from reading the newspapers about police affairs in New York, I looked upon the office of Police Commissioner with wonder that any man of character and reputation would have the courage to assume its responsibilities and hope to retain the confidence and respect of his friends and fellow-citizens. That an honest man should walk into what appeared to be such a muck-heap of scandal, corruption, and conspiracy might argue great courage, but a total lack of discretion and good judgment. Could any man, however honest and able, solve the police problem in New York? Was he prepared to suffer an ordeal of criticism, abuse, and gross misrepresentation, to which the self-inflicted torture of a Sioux Indian undergoing trial for admission into the ranks of the warriors would seem restful and soothing? Filled with a vague horror of the possibilities of the situation, I hastened to beg of this gentleman, in writing, that he discountenance and discourage any talk of my going to the Police Commissioner's office; that both my heart and my head were positively against it. In reply to this, he and other friends struck me on a tender spot. Plainly speaking, they charged me with cowardice and shrinking from what they said was a call of duty, and that if I did not accept this office they would lose their respect for me and their belief in me as a man of courage, with a proper regard for the betterment of the public service in its most important branch. I have always had a foolish disinclination to take a "dare," and to this day carry with me sundry bodily scars, souvenirs of attempts more or less dangerous, to follow schoolboy leaders in unsafe but attractive enterprises. It was, therefore, with a weakened resolution that I met the present Mayor in the Ways and Means Committee-room of the House of Representatives at Washington, a short time before the Christmas holidays of 1903, and with assurance of undeviating friendship, support, and unrestricted confidence, and that no one in or out of any political organization should come between us, and that all our dealings should be open and candid as between friends and gentlemen, I agreed to accept the office.

I must confess it was with a heavy heart that I turned my face towards that antique and shabby palace, that sepulchre of reputations, that tomb of character, that morgue of political ambition, that cavern of intrigue and dissimulation—the Police Headquarters at Mulberry Street. Through the stained and malodorous snow-heaps of Little Italy I wended my way on January 1, 1904, armed with the Mayor's warrant, to the high stone steps of No. 300 Mulberry Street, and into the then dingy, unattractive, and not overclean quarters of the head of the New York police force.

Mulberry Street is one of those thoroughfares of which the smallest percentage of the people of New York have any actual knowledge. It represents to them a vague and mystic crime-land, a quagmire of corruption, a chamber of horrors. They have no knowledge of the rather picturesque and attractive features of the neighborhood. They have never heard the Italian band, which must attend the funerals of the members of ever so many Italian societies under their rules, and which, therefore, is sure to have at least one funeral for every day in the year. How many citizens have seen them, as I have, marching in the blizzards of winter leading the procession to some Long Island cemetery in picturesque and multicolored uniforms begotten on the shores of the Mediterranean, with icicles six inches long formed at the end of their brass horns, and yet going forward through slush two feet deep with all the courage, determination, and heroism of their ancient Roman forebears?

Even the sweat-shops in the vicinity, when you come to know them, offer most interesting studies in sociology, politics, and economic science. The call of the boy selling the newspapers is not disturbing, as the papers sold there in the evening in large numbers are mostly in Yiddish; so that one is in blissful ignorance of their criticism or praise.

Then there is always about the neighborhood the dominating police influence, and the interesting colony of resident members of the press, who occupy several floors in the buildings opposite. From their vantage-point they could watch the Commissioner wash his hands or drink his Croton or bottled spring-water, as his taste might lead him, take note of his visitors, and, in hot summer days, if they were unkind enough to listen, might possibly hear him swear. This relationship between the Commissioner and the press was delightfully *al fresco*, and had a democratic flavor of the town-meeting. If the Commissioner ever grew weary of his task, a glance from his windows assured him of the support of his faithful and never-tiring guardians. Many of them were prophets in Mulberry Street when the very name of the thoroughfare itself was unknown to him. They had seen long processions of Commissioners come and go; they had witnessed the rise and fall of mighty monarchs; they had seen the uncrowned kings depart with saddened steps and chastened spirits, with much experience and many sorrows; and not a few, under vast suspicion, leave these mildewed halls and bid farewell forever to this untidy and dilapidated seat of power. They had lived long lives in these whispering galleries of scandal, gossip, and suspicion. The Commissioner who flatters himself that he can long impose on these trained and sleepless gentlemen is certainly unwise in his day and generation. The first thing, therefore, that one finds on going to Mulberry Street as Commissioner is that his relations with the press and its representatives are most important. Police Headquarters is a manufactory of news. It is expected to turn out a sufficient output daily to meet the wants of its steady customers. The old saying that no news is good news does not apply here.

No news is bad news for the representatives of the press. The members of the press are not wholly to blame in this matter. Police news is a steady article every day in the year on the menu of the average citizen. He wants it and he must have it. He comes in closer contact with the police in all relations, as individual and citizen, than with any other institution, and very naturally he wants to know about them.

On the whole, I had no fault to find with these young men who represent the newspapers. If there was any fault it was with the newspaper itself, and with those who directed its policy. These are but the trusty scouts sent out on the firing-line under orders of the commanding officers. Very often they know that the orders are unjust and improper, and I am quite sure they are heartily ashamed of being the instruments to carry them out; so that they are sometimes entitled more to sympathy than to bitterness and hatred. The first impression of this powerful factor in the management of the police is that the newspapers, especially the leading ones, are at fault in the way they treat Police Headquarters. It is no disparagement of those who represent the various journals there to say that, if this subject is to be treated seriously, the newspapers should be represented in Mulberry Street by their very ablest men — men of experience, good judgment, discretion, and ability, and who should command respectable salaries for the work they do.

Above all, as I said in my address to the newspaper men on leaving Headquarters, it would be greatly to the advantage of a newspaper to be represented continuously by the same man, so that he would gain a knowledge from experience and long-continued observation of the workings of the police machine, and therefore could write intelligently and discriminatingly on what was happening. Nothing was more discouraging to me than to have a newspaper send up a new man on some question of the hour, who probably had never until then been assigned to police work. Before he could be made to understand the question itself, it was necessary to acquaint him with the elementary phases of the subject in hand in order that any intelligent reply could be made to his inquiries. No newspaper could render a greater service to the people of New York than by sending a man of high grade every day to Police Headquarters, an able and intelligent gentleman, impartial and unrestricted in the liberty given him to tell the truth as he saw it. Whatever the policy or history of his newspaper, he should be allowed to state the facts intelligently and fearlessly, and give the public the information to which it is entitled. Such a man would at once get the respect and confidence of an honest Police Commissioner, and his criticism would be received as worthy of consideration and not in an unfriendly spirit. There were, among the men at Police Headquarters, those with whom I found I could talk in unreserved confidence, and I can testify that they were never guilty of a betrayal of this trust.

At the very outstart the measure of the Police Commissioner is taken by the press, and will continue to be a more or less lasting impression. His mode, therefore, of meeting these men at the first is of vast importance and will make for his success or failure. The Commissioner who really, in the nature of things, may know very little about the police of New York, and who goes there with an assumption of knowledge, will at once be written down as destined for destruction. The attitude of such a Commissioner is to exact no confidence, seek no information, and assume a knowledge which these bright fellows see at once he does not possess. In their own language, the whole thing is a bluff.

Between nothing to say and everything to say there is a wide range of country, in which one may sojourn with relative degrees of happiness and contentment. Many reporters are deplorably cynical for men so young in years, and they are constantly scratching the Russian to look for the Tartar. With his great opportunities, they are constantly asking themselves and others, "Is the Commissioner straight or otherwise?" Whether he is able, wise, and courageous they will find out for themselves, and will tell it if the big men who own and manage the newspapers will let them.

It is rather unfortunate that the large majority of the police look upon the press as unfriendly, and if a Commissioner creates the impression that he is in the hands of a newspaper cabinet, he is in great danger of losing the support and sympathy of the police force. They know that, at times, it will be his duty to stand up for the force, individually and collectively, sometimes against the entire newspaper press. If a policeman is unjustly accused, and if the Commissioner knows him to be an honest and able man, he must be prepared to shield and protect him, with all the powers of his office and personality if necessary, against every newspaper in New York. He must never sacrifice the interests of the police, collectively or individually, for his personal advantage. If he does, he commands a distrustful if not a mutinous army. No commander-in-chief could rely upon such troops in the day of strife. No Police Commissioner, under such circumstances, can expect loyal and earnest support from the officers and men of the police.

The best news, from the newspaper stand-point, is that which makes for destructive criticism, which cracks somebody over the head, which condemns unsparingly, and which is served piping-hot and with a great deal of red pepper in it. A Commissioner who could serve out a dish of this every day might, for a time, get a good standing in Park Row, but the things the police would say about him in the back rooms of the station-houses would not be fit to print; and the thoughts which they would think of him, and very rightly at that, would certainly not flatter him if they found expression.

The first speech I made to the newspaper men was as follows: "I won't tell you all I know, and I won't always know all that you think I know, but I will never deceive or mislead you, and I will have no favorites. All will be treated alike." I am proud to say that that pledge was kept to the letter. Once let one newspaper suspect that the Police Commissioner or those under him are allowing "beats" and distributing inside information to another newspaper, then the end is not far off. Indeed, this is as it should be. Nothing would be more dangerous to the public than an agreement on the part of the newspapers to a conspiracy of silence or an understanding to support a weak or wicked administration of the police — the whole press making itself an echo or a chorus, suppressing some facts and exaggerating others. This would be fatal to good government. The newspaper press is entitled to all the legitimate news of the police; it has a right, under reasonable restrictions, to have access to the Commissioner and to propound such inquiries as are reasonable and fair and are not impertinent, and not calculated to interfere with the police in suppressing crime or pursuing criminals.

If a newspaper is grossly unfair and persistently misrepresents, and its representative, in addition, is treacherous and untruthful, just quietly declare it out of the game. In any event it is better to laugh at a liar than to argue with him. Many a liar will quail before a laugh at his expense who would, on the other hand, face the Supreme Court at Washington, and not take back a word in the face of proof to the contrary. Lies travel faster than truth, but they don't live as long.

It certainly does seem reasonable that in the intercourse between the Commissioner and the representatives of the press there should be some happy medium between a secret society and a free parliament. If he is constantly saying he will not tell, the press will soon begin to say he doesn't know, and not to know is the cardinal sin. If a Commissioner is thoroughly independent of everybody, from the Mayor down and up, and has nothing to conceal, he can, without losing his dignity or injuring the service, speak with a certain degree of frankness on any subject appertaining to the police. If he is a bossed man or a consenting tool, with a string tied to his leg from the City Hall or a political headquarters, he is naturally afraid to say anything, for what he says to-day he will be asked to unsay to-morrow, and what he promised to do on Monday he will have to undo on Tuesday. He will not be sure, if he threatens a vice, but that a strong hand will pull the cord and he will have to face about, pelted by questions from the press which he cannot answer. If he makes a single unfair transfer or withdraws his hand from a crooked policeman or unjustly smites an honest one, he will be on the defensive and asked if he has not heard voices in the night, or whether he is following his own good judgment and conscience or is a puppet in other hands. If he has no settled policy, but is a mere opportunist, he will be naturally afraid to state his line of conduct because he has to change it so often. The four questions which his press guardians will be constantly asking themselves are:

First: Is the Police Commissioner a free man, or is he being influenced by others either for politics, personal gain, or other ulterior motives?

Second: Is he absolutely temptation-proof and an aggressively honest man?

Third: Has he a high order of ability and the power to command?

Fourth: Will he get the confidence and respect of the men under him, and has he a well-defined police policy of his own, cast on big public lines to get beneficial and lasting results and to leave the force better than when he found it?

The Mayor who appoints him, after all, invariably looks to the newspapers to see what reception his

Commissioner is getting, and to draw from them what the public estimate of the man is. No matter how intimate the relations are, the Mayor will surely be influenced by the trend of opinion as expressed in the newspapers unless he is a man of large caliber, big-minded, and of independent thought, and has the courage to stand by a Commissioner whom he knows to be right in face of any opposition, no matter how vociferous and united.

A public man of the widest reputation is known personally to a comparatively few in a great city like New York. The impression of him will be largely that which they gather from the newspapers. If he is the victim of continuous and what might be called artistic misrepresentation, he, of course, will be misunderstood and misjudged, and he must rely solely on the approbation of his own conscience and wait for the vindication of time. If he were to ask my advice I would tell him not to read the newspapers, or to read very little of them, and to confine himself to those positive statements which allege facts with regard to police conditions and make specific charges as to criminal occurrences or a prevalence of vice by collusion with the police. If he has not the capacity to discriminate between what is news and what is not news, what is essential and what is political and for effect, he had better delegate the reading of the newspapers to his subordinates. If he is going to shift his policy with every change in the editorials, it will be the old fable of the two men who rode the donkey and then carried the donkey, and then finally threw the donkey in the stream—only in this instance he will be playing the rôle of donkey.

Before I left the Police Department I had trained myself so thoroughly that I couldn't see a scarehead with type six inches long. A friend subscribed for and had sent to me a conservative and influential family newspaper, published in one of the oldest districts in this country, where I found the poet's corner, the household hints and social visits immensely instructive, and I eked out my other reading by renewing acquaintance with those weekly compendiums that sum up the world's news in a sort of book-keeping style, giving you the facts and letting you draw your own conclusions.

Very early in my official career my family limited my choice to one or two of the daily papers, and these had a tenure of office as slight as my own; for when the domestic censor concluded they had passed into that hopeless and impossible region which precluded their being further read, they were denied entrance and others taken on probation, the probationary period being generally short, and the rejection of the candidate being something in the nature of a continuous performance. This gave a diversity to our reading and an intimate knowledge of metropolitan journalism.

Your friends are always calling your attention to those "fine" editorials which praise you, and your enemies will be sure to send you, under separate cover, those which, to say the least, are not flattering. I am now prepared to agree with the statement which Colonel George Harvey made at a recent public dinner, in speaking of this subject: That, after all, the newspapers cannot make or unmake a public officer—that is, for any great length of time. They can help him and they can hurt him; they can aid him to get opportunity, but he must have the stuff in himself or he won't be able to walk the tight-wire successfully over the roaring falls beneath him; they cannot save him from a serious stumble, and they cannot supply him for any great length of time with brains, courage, and moral stamina. If he goes right ahead in the middle of the road, doing every day's work thoroughly and zealously, he will get to his destination in spite of any number of scareheads, scurrilous abuse, back-door whisperings, unjust innuendoes, sneers, or jeers. The measure of his work in the end will be what he has accomplished in actual results. His work will be tested as all other work, by wear and tear and weather, by time and circumstance. The acid must go on the brick. The acid will tell whether the brick, however highly polished and ornamental, is gold or clay. In any event, if the Commissioner really wishes to succeed, his course must be in the middle of the road. His official life must be an open book, and all his aims the public good.

If all the newspapers of New York should to-morrow begin a united effort to better police conditions in New York by encouraging the honest men on the force, by demanding proper and lasting reforms, by separating the good from the bad, by intelligent and impartial discussion of police administration, by holding the Mayor as well as the Police Commissioner to the strictest accountability for whatever is wrong, a new era would have been begun in the history of police conditions in this city.

The attitude at present of the public towards the police, as evidenced by the organs and mouth-pieces in press, pulpit, and forum of so-called public opinion, is so indiscriminating in its criticism, is based on so many false assumptions, and is so unjust to the honest and deserving policemen, that I do not wonder there are so many unfaithful, dishonest, and unfit members of the force, but rather that there is such a large number of faithful, upright, and intelligent men among them. If the public assert and believe that the whole police force is dishonest, brutal, lawless, and ignorant, and only fit to put down riots and big turbulences in a savage way, what incentive and encouragement does this give to the individual member to be otherwise?

II

THE POLICE ESTABLISHMENT

THE average citizen has a just horror of a public document—long lines of figures and cut-and-dried phrases filled with all the formalism of officialdom. The official world and the newspaper world which is compelled to take note of these publications goes on the assumption that the facts therein stated are known to everybody. In the official world here in New York and in the newspaper offices everybody could tell you off-hand how many inspectors there are and how many captains, and give you an accurate statement as to the outlines of the New York police force; but stop the first man you meet on the streets, or the first one hundred men, and ask them for the same information, and I am much mistaken if one out of a hundred could give you a half-wise intelligent answer. The higher-class citizens know less, of course, by actual contact about the police than the baser and rougher elements who know them by sad experience. The citizens down in the East-Side quarters are better informed on police matters in the concrete than the rich, comfortably housed inhabitants of the upper residential parts of the city. More people in his district knew Inspector Schmittberger on the East Side in proportion to the population than those, for instance, who would know Inspector Sweeney or Inspector Walsh in the upper and residential parts of New York. It is, therefore, necessary to give a short outline of the police machinery as it actually is in order that one may intelligently understand its workings. It is created somewhat on military lines. The Commissioner, of course, is the Commander-in-chief, and under him the Deputies, three in number. If I were back again in the Navy Department I would look upon the First Deputy as the executive officer on the ship, the Second Deputy as a sort of navigating officer through the unexplored regions of Brooklyn and Queens, and the Third Deputy as a judge advocate. The First Deputy-Commissioner, and, indeed, all the Deputy-Commissioners, are just what the Commissioner makes them. They may be very close to him and have influence, or they may be mere figure-heads. Their duties may be eminently confidential or they may be entirely formal. The stereotyped definitions of duty generally allotted by each Commissioner to his subordinates may be carried out in the letter or in the spirit. It has been customary hitherto for the Third Deputy to try the cases in the large Borough of Manhattan, and the Second Deputy to try those for Brooklyn and Queens. The trial of these cases is one of the most important duties conferred upon the Commissioner. His administration will be judged by the conduct of these trials and the punishments meted out. The police and the public demand fairness, firmness, impartiality, intelligence, and judicial discrimination. They are, unfortunately, so accustomed to such practices that they look for back-door influence and political "pull." They will demand consistency and a square deal, and that the trial be conducted with dignity and propriety. Above all else, substantial justice must be done to the increasing of the discipline and efficiency of the police force. These trials, moreover, are reviewable by the higher courts of this State. When prepared in printed form they must stand the tests of the courts of law. Slap-dash judgments will there be promptly overturned. Whether wisely or not, these trials are not in the nature of courts-martial. The Commissioner is bound in bonds of iron by the law. His decisions are not personal; they must be judicial. He can designate any of the Deputies to try cases, the first, second, or third. I used all of the Deputies in these trials. No sentence goes into effect until he has approved it, and he can lower or raise punishments or disregard the recommendations of his subordinates. Once he signs his name, however, he cannot change his decision. He can try the cases himself if he wishes. For many reasons I do not consider it wise for him to do so unless on extraordinary occasions. To the police force he is the court of last resort; he stands between them and the trial Deputies. He is supposed to review the record coolly and impartially, without being heated by the frictions of the trial-room. He can temper the undue severity of the trial Commissioner; he can check him when he is too lax or easy-going, and if he has anything to say he can put it as an indorsement on the papers. Moreover, his duties are so multifarious that unless the case involves one of deep and far-reaching policy he will have to depend to a great extent on his subordinates.

An ideal administration of the police force would be a well-balanced staff of Deputies, all able men, with common sympathies and actuated by disinterested and honest motives. The salaries of these men, as well as that of the Commissioner, are totally inadequate to the requirements of the place. Very rich men may be incapable, and poor men who are able have to make too great a sacrifice to leave any successful business or profession and go through the hard work and drudgery and assume the responsibility and accept the criticisms which the place entails for the salary allowed by law. If the Police Commissioner is dishonest he will not bother about the salary. If he is an honest man and a poor man the public are asking sacrifices from him which are almost cruel. It is against the genius of our institutions to say that only a rich man should hold an office because he alone could afford it. This would put honest and able men, if they are poor, out of the public service. Any Police Commissioner in Mulberry Street who is corrupt can get rich, and the chances are that he will not be found out, and will suffer nothing worse than the suspicions of the knowing ones. He will work harder than any life-insurance president; he has a millionfold more responsibility; must have great executive capacity, and be prepared to suffer daily and hourly criticism. Haggling over such salaries has always seemed to me absurd. If the right man were found to be Police Commissioner no salary could be too high. New York wants the best, and the people will be perfectly willing to pay for it. They pay $17,500 a year to a Supreme Court Justice, and does any one pretend that the Police Commissioner's work isn't as hard, that his responsibilities are not at least as great, and that his office is not just as important?

When I left the Department each borough had an inspector, and at Headquarters there was a chief inspector and an inspector for the Borough of Manhattan. The others were District Inspectors. There is no uniform rule as to the number of precincts which comprise an inspection district. The lines are drawn by the Commissioner arbitrarily. It would be hard to exaggerate the importance of the office of police inspector in this city. It has immense powers and possibilities. An intelligent and courageous inspector who knows his business is a dominating force in the district over which he rules. The people and the politicians all want to be in his good graces. He personifies the law in that district. The crooked and criminal elements, the vicious and the corrupt, will, of course, hate him if he is an honest and fearless man. If the inspector is a strong man he will command his captains. He sets the pace and gives the tone to every precinct in the district. An honest inspector begets honest captains; a dishonest inspector will render futile the efforts of the honest captains in the whole district.

The duties of captain and sergeant are generally well understood, and of roundsmen we speak in another place.

While the police force to be at its best must always maintain the essential features of a more or less military establishment, yet the individual policeman on his post is at once soldier, watchman, detective, lawyer, judge, public censor of morals, and general regulator of human conduct, from spitting on the sidewalk to committing homicide, from the capturing of unlicensed dogs to giving builders and general contractors the free use of the public streets.

III

POLICE CONDITIONS AS I FOUND THEM

UNLIKE the army or navy, what would be equivalent to the commissioned officers in the police without exception rise from the ranks, from the Chief Inspector to the lowest man on the list of roundsmen. It would seem impossible to devise any other scheme, as a policeman's training, after all, is mainly practical experience. Moreover, to get the best out of the force the incentive to promotion must always be held before them. It would be impossible to create a police Annapolis or West Point and graduate the officers from such a school. On the other hand, the recruiting of all officers from the ranks has visible drawbacks, as for instance, in the case of the roundsmen. The patrolman of yesterday is the roundsman of to-day. He has naturally shared all the prejudices of the rank and file against a roundsman who would be deemed by them severe and over-vigilant. He may himself have been tried several times on the complaint of roundsmen for infraction of the rules. Up to this time he has looked at everything concerning the police from the patrolman's point of view. He is quite likely to be put to duty as a roundsman in the same precinct and among the same men where he has served as a patrolman. If he enters on a fearless execution of his duty there will be plenty of whisperings from his former comrades as to his own delinquencies; but beyond this there is not sufficient distinction between the two grades in the Police Department. The new roundsman, for instance, is not apt to demand the respect due his rank, and is likely to be too familiar with the men under him and they with him. This lack of distinction is even more marked now under civil service rules than under the old system. Under the old system it required men of nerve and dominating personality to fight their way up and then pay to get in. As a general rule the officers commanding the police do not exact proper respect from their subordinates, and do not insist, as they should, upon the recognition due their rank and authority. They forget to drop good-fellowship and friendly acquaintance when they put on their uniform to perform official duty.

The roundsman is the most important police officer in the Police Department. If he doesn't do his duty faithfully and thoroughly the patrol is bound to be inefficient, and an honest patrol is the basis of all good police work. Indeed, it is the foundation for successful police administration. With human nature as it is, the men, if left entirely to themselves, and not properly supervised, will very naturally not give the patrol to which the city is entitled. Many of them will become lazy, and some of them will shirk, and a large number of them are inclined to long conversation with fellow-officers or citizens. The policeman, among all human beings, is singularly gregarious. His conversational qualities are unlimited. He dislikes to be by himself, and he loves to talk to some one or to something. I am quite sure that some of these men would talk to the lamp-posts if they could find no human company. The citizens who find opportunity of conversing with the men on post are apt to be pleased with them. They have had much experience, and are generally good story-tellers; and, besides, they know all of the gossip of the neighborhood, and are standard authorities on the political situation in the city and the State. I do not mean to imply by this that there are not a vast number of honest and painstaking policemen whose inclinations are all towards a strict performance of their duty, and who are men of high character and exemplary habits, but I do mean to insist that the patrol cannot be left to itself, and that therefore the roundsman, whether of the precinct or of Headquarters, or of both, is essential to that degree of police protection to which the citizens are entitled.

I tried many expedients, but after several months found, to my regret, the Headquarters roundsmen, or "shoo-flies," as they are called, a necessity. The so-called "shoo-fly" roundsmen are an old feature of police work. When the force is run for politics this is called a "spy system," and degrading, and the men are "put on honor" to patrol faithfully, which is easier than being put on trial for not doing so; and then the thing sounds good anyway. If I had found a better way to insure an honest and faithful patrol, I would probably have joined the "statesmen" in denouncing the "spy system"; but it is the thing itself, not the label, that is essential. In every precinct there are a number of roundsmen who go out on tours of inspection to see that the men are on post and doing their duty. The details of these tours of inspection are known to the men themselves, and often in individual cases the patrolman knows the exact route that the uniformed man will take. Friendly citizens who take note of the uniformed roundsman can warn the patrolman of his approach; his uniform advertises his presence everywhere. A kindly motorman running a car who passes a roundsman can farther on signal the patrolman that the "rounds" is coming, and at night those characters in a great city who never sleep can sound the warning word if there is any danger to a patrolman who is off his post, conversing, or probably in-doors. Then, too, many roundsmen are constitutionally opposed to making complaints. They like to be considered good fellows with the men; they are too apt to take it out in a little talk instead of in a trial. Then the whole tone and temper of some precincts may be in favor of laxity, from the captain down, and this might go on for years and the Commissioner be in entire ignorance of the situation except, possibly, by the increase of preventable crimes in the district. It has therefore been found necessary by Police Commissioners heretofore to have a Headquarters staff of roundsmen in plain clothes whose range was the whole city, who might turn up in Staten Island to-night and to-morrow night in Flushing, to-day in Central Park, next day in the Tenderloin, in the heart of Brooklyn, or the Battery, and always wherever not looked for. On January 1st, this year, there were only five of these men, and that was the same number that had been doing this work under the Commissioner who preceded me, and they were the same men. As a matter of fact, I at one time tried to add to the number, but a call for volunteers elicited no response. These five men were veterans in this business. They had literally made thousands of complaints, and in almost every instance their complaint led to a conviction. Of course they had a host of most bitter and malignant enemies, and probably there were no five men on the police force so thoroughly hated. I had great respect and sympathy for these five men. While they may not at all times have been faultless, and while they differed individually as to their character, ability, and methods, yet they were, as a whole, always able to well and clearly state their case before the trial Commissioner. Their work was hard and exacting, and utterly thankless; and, generally speaking, they were cut off from all chances of preferment, and every day added to the number of their enemies and critics. I do not hesitate to say that if I had had the opportunity I would have been glad to reward them by promotion, which they richly deserved, because I never heard any substantial accusation that they had abused the great trust reposed in them, and it is quite certain that if they had been corrupt the army of enemies who camped on their trail would have been quick to find it out. They therefore must be looked upon as men of unusual integrity under painful circumstances and more than usual temptations. I tried last year various systems as a substitute for the "shoo-flies," and it is possible that some better way may be devised.

I became convinced towards the latter part of my term as Police Commissioner that the present status of the roundsman should be entirely changed. He does not, as it is now, carry with him sufficient authority, nor that atmosphere of command to which his rank and duties ought to entitle him. His uniform should be distinctly different from that of the patrolman. He is something more than a sergeant in the army, and every army officer knows what a good sergeant means. In my opinion, his uniform should be made more distinctive; and I think it would be best to create him as a sergeant of police, junior grade, or divide the sergeants into first and second divisions, and put the roundsmen in the second division. If you go down the steps of responsibility, holding the inspectors responsible for the captains, and the sergeants in turn responsible for the enforcement of the laws and the protection of property, they will all in the end point to the roundsmen. The police operate as individual units, and are not, therefore, under the eye of their commanding officer. The officer who comes nearest to them, and whose duty it is to supervise them personally in the closest way, is the roundsman. If the roundsmen in a precinct are doing their full duty and maintaining their position between the captain and the men the police efficiency will be good. If they are over-friendly, familiar, slipshod, lazy, indifferent, or worse, the men will shirk their patrol, evade their duties, dodge responsibility, and the police conditions in the precinct will be bad. Theoretically, it sounds well to say that the captain can remedy all this. Strictly speaking, that is not true. If it is true he should be allowed the full control of the roundsmen, and his requests as to those assigned to his precinct should be honored unless there are good reasons at Headquarters for doing otherwise. Moreover, and this is always to be remembered, the courts have laid it down strictly and clearly that convictions of officers will not stand unless the evidence, the same as in any criminal trial, brings home to them a guilty knowledge and omission to act, and this beyond the reasonable doubt, which is the cardinal feature of criminal jurisprudence. Trials and convictions which will not stand the test of a judicial review under the existing laws by the courts of the State are worse than useless. They will be promptly reversed, and the results are demoralizing. I have advocated a change of law with reference to such trials, and I believe the powers of the Commissioner could with safety be augmented into something akin to that which prevails in the army and navy, but as the law now stands the judges of the higher courts are compelled to review the case on the written record with the same care and scrupulosity that they would a trial in one of the criminal courts for penal offences, and it must appear from the record that the trial was judicially conducted with due regard to the laws of evidence prevailing in the courts of this State. Dealing with things as they are, the trials must be conducted with judicial propriety and with that regard to the forms of law which prevail in the other courts and tribunals of this State. On my entrance to the office of Commissioner I was met with the return of a large number of officers of all ranks, the findings in whose cases by the former Commissioners had been set aside by the Courts of Appeal, and it was very embarrassing to readjust these returned officers to the changed conditions in the personnel occasioned by the vacancies created and promotions made at the time of their dismissal. The singular uniformity of all the courts as to the rules governing these trials made it quite plain that it is useless to put officers, especially of the higher grades, on trial unless the case against them will stand in a court of law. The Commissioner may go through the forms of a trial, inconveniencing and punishing an officer against whom he maintains a reasonable degree of suspicion as to his character, conduct, and efficiency, but if the evidence doesn't warrant the finding, or the trial has been improperly conducted, the inevitable overturning of the results by the higher courts will only add to his discomfiture, and in addition beget in the minds of the reviewing authorities a grave doubt as to his fairness in the conduct of the trial, which will withdraw from him that judicial support and sympathy to which he is entitled.

If the police were recruited like the army, housed in barracks remote from their homes, subject at all times to personal scrutiny and supervision, performing their duties in numbers and not individually, and widely separated and divested of all political power as citizens, the subject of dealing with them would be much simplified; but the policeman, while a quasi-soldier, is a citizen with a home, family, and standing in the community, and entitled to the same active participation as all other citizens in its political affairs.

A suggestion of the introduction of arbitrary and court-martial methods at once begets an opposition of nearly ten thousand citizens on the police force, each one of whom is able to muster possibly ten other votes, or in all one hundred thousand voters. This is very far from an ideal condition, if it is not a dangerous one, but in dealing with this subject we should look the facts in the face. And then there is growing up within the Police Department associations in all the grades which are supposed to be on the surface for merely social and benevolent purposes, but benevolence in this case is closely allied to protection, and protection means the guarding of the rights and interests of a class as against all others. These agents are potent for good or evil. They are found not only in the police but among the letter-carriers and many other classes of government employés. It is within their power if they act unitedly and determinedly by voluntary contributions to protect their interests with large sums of money, and they are almost sure to be appealed to by politicians for their united support in behalf of this candidate or that. Indeed, nothing is so common as for the policeman-citizen to receive numbers of printed appeals about election time from various candidates for the Legislature telling him how much they have done for the police as a class in the way of legislation at former sessions, and appealing to his sense of gratitude and self-interest to again support them. These police organizations must not be thought to convey the idea of large meetings at frequent intervals in halls or assembly-rooms. The organization on paper is but a skeleton one. Full meetings of its members are practically impossible, but they can act very quickly and efficiently for their purposes through delegates and station-house conferences. Indeed, there is a sort of telepathy throughout the Department by which police opinion becomes organized at once as for or against a man or a measure; so that it would be practically impossible for a Police Commissioner to break up such united effort. In addition to this the Police Commissioner has to recognize at once that there is a public opinion within the service itself which may make or mar his administration, and that sometimes it may be used for good as well as evil. The Commissioner is obliged to have the confidence, respect, and, to some extent at least, the good-will of the men under him if he is to get the best results from them. If he is arbitrary, unjust, and given to bullying, and combines this with obvious ignorance of police affairs, the officers and men will give him just his pound of flesh so far as he can take it, and absolutely nothing more. A commander-in-chief who is hated and despised will not win many battles. On the other hand, an able and masterful man will be forgiven much even of harshness or severity provided the men under him do not doubt his sense of justice or his capacity to meet the situation. President Roosevelt as a Commissioner was strict, and a good disciplinarian, but just, fair, square, and manly, and he is revered by the police to this day.

I succeeded a Commissioner who represented an administration elected on the platform of reform and non-partisanship. I gladly accepted all of those things which he had inaugurated, and which I believed to be for the public good, and took pleasure in acknowledging my obligation to him for their initiation. I changed no rule of his unless convinced by experience and investigation that a change would add to the efficiency of the force, and those officers to whom he had given an unusual degree of confidence I accepted as recommended by one honest man to another, and some of them retained my confidence and respect until the day I left the Department, thus confirming his original judgment. He had striven as I did after him to bring new blood into the higher grades of the force, and showed a partiality for the younger men. This I believed to be a wise course, and some of these younger captains did him infinite credit, and are to-day most excellent commanding officers.

In the campaign which preceded the first election of the present Mayor the electorate had been thoroughly aroused by most unusual methods and by reiterated charges to a belief that the election would be followed by a return to most evil and dangerous police conditions, and an open and audacious revival of the practice of the worst vices under police protection; in fact, that the open town and a corrupt police force were the only things possible. This, it will be admitted by the severest critics, was a difficult condition for the new Police Commissioner to face. The force itself was stirred by the worst apprehensions and demoralized with the idea that it was to be ruthlessly prostituted to political purposes and made the mere adjunct to the dominating partisan organization. This is one of the cruelest things in connection with police work. The police force and its powers have so often been made the football of personal and political interests, honest officers driven into exile and dishonest ones elevated into positions of trust and responsibility, crooks resurrected from oblivion and again placed in the front ranks, faithful officers disdainfully swept aside for incompetent time-servers, merit discounted and punished and incompetency promoted, and the whole Department so permeated with an odor of corruption, "pull," petty politics, intrigue, conspiracy, and malice, that it must be revolting to any citizen to witness the effects which these shifts of administration and changes in politics produce in the Police Department of New York. The faithful and honest officer who does his duty shudders at the thought of being punished for doing the same; practical and beneficial reforms are at once threatened with destruction. There is no earnest effort for the general police and public good, but instead a lot of small and petty conspiring and searching to cast discredit on their predecessors and to surround the Commissioner with partisans, personal friends, toadies, and corrupt tools. Is it any wonder under such conditions that the better element on the force is to be pitied, and that it should arouse hot indignation in the breasts of the honest men to see the otherwise faithful personnel of the police force degraded, humiliated, played with, and punished? Under these conditions there can be no continuity of policy, no settled and standard rule, and no good traditions to be preserved. Fluctuation, change, unrest, upheaval, destruction, and not construction, prevail, and conservatism and high ideals of justice and fairness are discredited. It is not to be argued that a Commissioner should blindly accept the rules and policies of his predecessor; quite the contrary. The law of progress should prevail in the Police Department as elsewhere, but sensational and gallery playing, changes without principle or conviction, must all be made at the expense of the police force itself.

When I went to the Department I found that my predecessor had in operation what was known as the two-platoon or six-section system regulating the patrol and the duty of the men. In the campaign which preceded the first election of the present Mayor, and in which he ran as a partisan pledged to the execution of the platform upon which he was elected, there was in that platform a clause in answer to what was believed to be a great public demand for the restoration of what was known as the three-platoon or nine-section system. The Mayor of the city was pledged to restore that system. Three months after I assumed office I adopted it. I do not deem it necessary to enter into a discussion in this book of the two systems.

Shortly after my entry into the office an eminent clergyman in a sermon preached by him prophesied that the lid of the lower regions would be taken off in New York, and the cry went throughout the country, "The lid is off!" New York was not a paradise on January 1, 1904, any more than it was on the first day of January, 1906, when I claimed for it that the police conditions, so far as concerned the repression of vice and the enforcement of law, were never better, and I still maintain that claim. But when in addition to the prevailing condition in 1904 this call to the vicious went out, gamblers, pool-room men, touts, thieves, confidence men, pick-pockets, and disorderly characters started for New York from all parts of the United States. It looked for a few days as if the Western three-card-monte men would begin business on the street corners and as if citizens would have an opportunity on the sidewalks of the principal thoroughfares of taking part in the old county-fair shell-game. The accounts in the press of prevailing crimes and vices were appallingly lurid. Long lists of gambling-houses, which it was said could be entered by any citizen, were given in the news columns side by side with the advertisements of the massage parlors; one flitting pool-room became five fixed ones, and guessing contests were inaugurated as to whether there were five thousand or ten thousand; their numbers and the names of the occupants and managers were as prominently set forth as those of the theatres; whole streets were photographed as having been invaded by newly organized disorderly houses; pages of robberies within and without; unoffending men and gentlewomen garroted on Fifth Avenue; unparalleled murder records, from the case of the tramp who died in a fit on the Bowery to the body of the unknown picked up on the river front, were exploited, not by columns but by pages; amateur sleuths were turned into the East Side to give a census of the red lights which had been rekindled;

a vast and newly organized army of "cadets" and general scoundrels were located in nearly every part of the city; waves of crime, oceans of crime, swept the community in their columns; gambling, prostitution, blackmail, and graft held like huge, defiant, sulphurous clouds over the city, obstructing the heavens and causing the innocent and honest men and women to shudder. No one was robbed of less than a thousand dollars; no Harlem apartment yielded less than five thousand dollars loot, and the richer houses yielded revenues to thieves that amounted up to five figures. All were agreed that the good old times had returned with tenfold virility and shamelessness. The new administration was on trial with a vengeance, and was struggling against an ocean of suspicion and false reports. The main thing and the only thing was to convince the public that the administration was essentially and aggressively honest, courageous, and fearless, as well as morally sound, and, above all, to demonstrate to the force itself that there was no weakening, and that none of the evil prophecies would come true; that discipline must be preserved, and the laws enforced with vigor and earnestness; that the "lid" was on and would stay on; that the town was not open, and that the invading host must be driven out at once and the resident evil-doer repressed. It was no time for dealing with small and comparatively minor matters. A man fighting for his life is not apt to spend much time adjusting his necktie or considering whether his hair is mussed or his boots polished. There were many things in the mechanism of the department which time and experience would show needed changing, but the one and only thing at that time was to restore the reign of law, to reassure the people and get back its confidence, paying no heed to the hysteria of the press or mendacious critics, but to keep the machine moving steadily forward and in the middle of the road. It is needless to say it was a very trying time. The only criterion by which to judge a Police Commissioner is: Are the laws enforced? Is crime repressed? Are criminals apprehended and promptly brought to trial? Are the vicious elements divorced from any connection with the police? Does vice flourish or otherwise? Are life, limb, and property safe? Are the citizens free from annoyance on the streets by ruffians, disorderly women and men? In short, are they getting the benefit of a good police force? Is the city orderly, law-abiding, clean and decent within and without? Or is vice brazenly asserting itself without fear of punishment, and in collusion with the police?

Later on, for instance, I revolutionized during my administration, for the benefit of the city, the whole machinery in the matter of the purchase of supplies and the making of repairs in the department. Before that time the method of making purchases and repairs was open to great abuse and favoritism. The new system has saved New York thousands of dollars. It begot honest competition; it did away with favorites; it drove out fraudulent bidders, and gave the city the honest value of its money. This reform and others of that nature dealing with the internal affairs of the department had to wait during the first year's hard fighting for the supremacy of the law and the cleansing of the police themselves from collusion with criminal law-breakers and their allied interests.

The Police Commissioner ought to be divorced entirely from the financial end of the department. Pensions and salaries should be entirely under the Comptroller and managed by a bureau in his office. They should be paid directly from that office and through its agents. The Commissioner is on the fighting-line, is in command, and ought not to have his time taken up quarrelling over the price of rat-traps, coal-scuttles, drinking-water, soap, gasolene, scrubbing-brushes, towels, and curry-combs. If the qualifications for the office are solely those of a house-keeper, book-keeper, or foreman, it can be easily filled. The law wrongfully places him in the midst of a jungle of red tape and detail, from which, to get at the real police business, he must cut his way, until, under a sensible form of government, the purchasing, repairing, supplying and auditing of this great department will be a branch entirely separate from the police business proper. Why should the Police Commissioner have to spend five or six hours a day for nearly a week hearing arguments of interested cloth manufacturers on a case which, on the face of it, was plain from the start, or have to give up the direction of police affairs for nearly a week to look into the law and the facts, the equities and the other things in, say, the contract for police helmets, the shoeing of horses, or the merits of rival window-curtains? Very important matters, of course, but all this ought not to be laid on the Police Commissioner. Every unsuccessful competitor immediately assails the new Commissioner; tells him he is the victim of injustice; loads him down with innuendoes or insinuations that he has been cheated. I quite agree with Comptroller Metz that his department ought to have stronger auditing powers, and they ought to be provided with machinery to pass upon department accounts promptly and thoroughly. It is so in the army and navy. The secretaries of these two big departments have under them bureau chiefs and other officers who do all this business; and then, in addition, there is a special auditing bureau in the Treasury for each of these other departments, so that the war and navy accounts are overlooked and scrutinized by a power outside of themselves, and this every day in the year. I believe the Comptroller's office, in dealing with the city departments, ought to be modelled on that of the United States Treasury Department. The system there I know works well, and all the secretaries are left free to formulate their policies and to carry out the main object of their existence, and do not fritter away their time paring wash-women's wages, looking after the cost of flower-beds in Farragut Square, or scrubbing stains off the Peace Monument at the head of Pennsylvania Avenue.

Imagine the captain of a steamer in mid-ocean on the bridge, his vessel struggling with a hurricane, fierce and cruel winds, mountainous seas, blasts of thunder, shafts of lightning; the bulwarks have gone, the anchors torn from their fastenings; the boats and the deck-houses are being splintered; the engines are plunging and racing; the whole fabric is rending and groaning. Just at this time the little "knocker" among the passengers comes up on the bridge and tells the captain that as he represents the public opinion of the cabin he demands that he lay everything else aside and come down below and settle the important question as to the morals of the third mate, and whether or not it is true that he has one wife in Hoboken and another in Southampton; or that the passengers are unanimously agreed that he should appoint a commission to see to it that more raisins are put in the pudding. It is no doubt true that there are some passengers on the ship who would rather revel in scandal affecting the morals of the third mate than have the ship saved, but happily there are few captains who would agree with them.

Within a few days after going to Mulberry Street I ordered all the inspectors to Headquarters, and laid down the rule as to their responsibility, and demanded that the laws, especially those against vices which can only thrive by collusion with the police, be strictly enforced; that the streets should be kept free from disorderly and vicious persons; that all the laws should be enforced; that this attempt to fire the city with crime should have the hose vigorously turned on it at once; that improved conditions should be begotten looking to decency and good order in the streets, and that additional security to person and property both within and without the homes of our citizens should be secured. Now it makes no difference with what emphasis a Commissioner may say this and reiterate it through the officers immediately under him, it is absolutely essential that he himself, as far as possible, and at first hand, or through those in whom he has unlimited confidence, should know the situation. To threaten or plead with these officers is wasting time, if the Commissioner does not know the situation himself or has no means to find out. The Police Commissioner has several ways by which he may know the police conditions in the town, and the questions with him must always be: Are the police conditions good? Are the laws being infracted or otherwise? Are the police in league with vice and crime? If he were asked that question on the witness-stand he would have to fall back on the following sources of information: (1) What he knows himself by actual investigation, acquaintance, and knowledge of New York, its ways and conditions; (2) what the captains' reports show under the forty-fourth rule, paragraph B, where they are to report all alleged disorderly and criminal resorts, which include all suspected places, gambling-houses, pool-rooms, disorderly houses, suspected Raines law hotels, and the general police conditions; (3) what may be brought to his attention through the newspapers. This source of information he must be prepared of his own knowledge to correct and judge so that he will not be misled. He must take it for just what it is worth, and he must know its value; (4) by his mail, the larger part of which will be anonymous complaints. I read every anonymous letter that professed to give information. They cannot be slighted, because many people, from even bad motives, such as spite, jealousy, anger, and self-interest, will want to see the law enforced against their enemies or rivals. Some of the most valuable information came in this way. My instructions to the police were: pay no attention to the identity of the informer, or his or her motive, but ascertain the facts. If he has no knowledge of his own, if the newspapers by more or less general understanding and through policy suppress accounts of crime or exaggerate them, if his captains are disloyal, and, for fear of responsibility, do not report all the places they suspect, or assert their non-existence, and if he does not give sufficient attention to his mail under his strict personal supervision, seeing to it that every letter, however insignificant, is put before him, he will be imposed upon and the public will suffer.

He cannot punish officers for allowing crimes and vices to exist when he himself does not know whether they exist or not, and if he has no means at first hand of knowing how they exist, where they exist, and under what conditions, the trial of the officer in question will end in the upper courts in a mere farce and waste of time. I am thoroughly convinced that the Commissioner must centralize this information in himself. He might as well take an army into the field without a thorough knowledge of the enemy, the physical conditions of the country, the geography, and all the facts and circumstances, as to rely solely upon those under him in the districts and precincts. He cannot keep up the daily and nightly fight for the enforcement of law in New York, with no knowledge of the actual conditions, and with no definite details at Headquarters as to what is really going on in every precinct. That knowledge must reside in the commander-in-chief, the Police Commissioner. The Police Commissioner is practically the clearing-house for all police business. He must never at any time be dependent upon any one man, whatever his rank. Given the facts that there is crime in all of the precincts in New York—and even under the best conditions there is more or less crime and vice in all parts of a great city—suppose, then, you put all of the inspectors on trial, and they in turn charge all the captains, and the captains charge all of the men with responsibility—and this would be entirely logical—and the Mayor charges the Commissioner with responsibility — which would be equally logical—you would then have the spectacle in one day of having the whole force, down to the remotest doorman in every station, on trial. Then assume that it would be perfectly legal to just prove that crime and vice, however great or small in amount, prevailed in each precinct, there would be no alternative under such logic but to convict every man, and if a policeman permits crime and vice to flourish when he has the power and means to suppress and apprehend it, he ought not to be fined a day's pay—he ought to be summarily dismissed. This policy, therefore, would result in the dismissal of the whole police force. If you took all the police force to-morrow down into the bay and drowned them, every man of them, and culled another force with ever so much care and circumspection, unless you changed human nature and reconstructed some obvious and glaring defects in the present laws through new legislation, and the attitude of the public towards the police in general were changed, and in addition to that had the hearty co-operation of all parts of the city government and the support of public opinion, press, pulpit, and courts, in a few weeks the new force would be just as the old, except possibly a little worse, as impressed with the uncertainty of their tenure of office, as shown by the fate of their predecessors, and they would hasten to enrich themselves at the public expense, believing in the profound truth stated in his Sunday discourses by the younger Rockefeller, that the road to fortune lies in grasping opportunity, and the old admonition, *tempus fugit.*

IV

REFORMS NEEDED

A COMMITTEE of nine representative citizens last year gave a great deal of their time to a careful and painstaking investigation of the weaknesses of the present system of organization in the police force. They examined a great many witnesses, took a large amount of testimony, and formulated a bill which they presented to the Legislature. With the principal features of the proposition, so far as they went, I was in accord, but it soon became evident that the bill in question had excited an opposition too strong to make it possible to enact it into law. The main feature of the bill was an attempt to reorganize the Detective Bureau. Speaking for myself, I believe that there should be three radical reforms affecting the Police Department inaugurated into law. First, to begin with the head of the department, the tenure of office of the Commissioner is at present the chief source of weakness. Here is a man in command of nearly nine thousand men who has no tenure of office whatever, being liable to be removed any minute by either the Mayor of the city or the Governor of the State, without any reason being assigned, and possibly to gratify the caprice of the moment or the politics of the day. The men under him, down to the doormen in the station-houses, have life tenures, with provision made for their retirement and pensioning, and they cannot, as heretofore outlined, be dismissed without a trial, governed by all the forms of law and the rules of evidence, and reviewable by all of the higher courts of the State, with the chances of reversal apparently in their favor. These men see long processions of Commissioners come and go; they look for a change in every political upheaval. It is a notorious fact that in the pool-rooms of this city, for the last few months before January 1, 1906, bets were made on the continuance in office of the Police Commissioner, as to how long he would remain, and odds on this event were quoted as freely as on the running of the horses. A Commissioner has no sooner entered on the performance of his duty than the department begins speculating as to how long he will remain, who are behind him, how does he stand with the political government of the day, who will be his successor. His official life is a plaything of the moment. He is a king on sufferance—a temporary head over a permanent body, a general in command of an army liable to be removed before the last order he has given is carried out, the most powerful officer in the city in what he may do for or against the public welfare, with a weaker hold on his office than the man who scrubs the steps of the station-house. If he inaugurates a new rule, those who do not like it will give it a faint obedience, with a knowledge that its author is likely to be removed before it has become effective. If he starts a reform which is antagonistic to some interest, he may expect that those who would suffer by the new policy will at once begin to work for his removal or forced resignation. The police force, therefore, look upon no new policy, or any innovation which conflicts with their own ideas as to what they should do, as a permanent or fixed thing. All reforms necessarily have their opponents, and any opposition endangers the tenure of the Commissioner. The more original, radical, honest, and earnest he is, the less likely he is to remain in office. The elements of opposition will gather force, beget unity and organization, and the pressure on the head of the city government will become too great. A Police Commissioner must not be allowed to interfere with party plans or personal ambitions, or to destroy personal comfort. If the Mayor is weak, vacillating, and an opportunist in politics, the persistent opposition of one or more daily newspapers (in alliance with a few scheming power seekers for personal and political ends), exaggerating one fact and suppressing the other, and coloring the whole tone of comment into something like unanimous disapproval, will be notice to the police that another Police Commissioner will soon take his last official walk in Mulberry Street.

A combination of interests which thrive on the non-enforcement of law or make large profits by allying themselves in a business way with criminal and vicious groups, can bring a more concentrated and personal pressure to bear for the removal of a Police Commissioner than an army of law-abiding, honest citizens, who may be even enthusiastically in favor of the policy he is pursuing. The best they can do for him is to pelt the editorial rooms with sporadic notes intended for publication, but more apt to be fed to the office cat, if the policy of the paper is antagonistic to the course pursued by the Commissioner. The constant drippings of scandal-mongers, the carping of interested critics, the concocted stories of the secret agents of confederated law-breakers and their business allies, will usually offset any claims to executive approval, the favoring many having no opportunity of entering the official presence at the City Hall, or making itself felt immediately at the polling-booths. From the little creatures who burrow under the presses in Park Row, to the hardened professional agents of criminal and selfish interests, from the day of his entrance until the day he leaves, an honest Police Commissioner must expect a perpetual conspiracy against his continuance in office or the success of his administration.

REFORMS NEEDED

The authors of the charter of Greater New York, with a sense of humor keener than that of Mark Twain, deliberately stated that the Police Commissioner holds his office for a term of five years. They even gave him one year longer than the present term for the Mayor, so that he might lap over and be found in office by a new administration at the City Hall. In the next line, however, with a sort of April-fool wink, it says he can be removed at a moment's notice by the Mayor or the Governor, without charges and without trial. The whole thing, therefore, is deliciously funny. In my judgment, there will be no lasting reform of the Police Department until the Police Commissioner is given a solid and substantial tenure of office. It ought to be either for life or a long term of years, and he should not be removable except upon specific charges and after a full, fair, and impartial trial before the Appellate Division of the Supreme Court, with the right to be represented by counsel. The objection to this will be made that if you get a bad Police Commissioner you are tied to him, as it were, for life. This objection sounds more serious than it will be found on closer examination. The police force, assured of a permanent head, will begin to yield at once its own opinions to those of the commanding officer, become tractable and acquiescent, instead of disobedient, evasive, and antagonistic. Of course, like the recipe for hare soup, you must first catch your hare; so here you must, to begin with, select with great care an all-around, honest, able man of good judgment and much commonsense. The community will settle down to adjust itself, as it were, to such a man with a long tenure in office assured. There will be no incentive, moreover, to nag the Police Commissioner, to gossip about him, to spy on him, to confederate against him. He will be a part of the permanent police establishment, and he and the whole organization must stand or fall together; and, in addition to this, he will have strong reasons not to make sensational and spasmodic changes, but to beget a lasting reformation and reorganization of police conditions. His lifework will be before him and he can enter upon it with a steady tread, not by slap-dash runs and irregular movements hither and thither and that end nowhere. The fact, too, that he will have a fair trial before he can be removed is just to the public as well as to himself. If he is an honest and able man, such a trial will only serve to vindicate him and to beget for him a large volume of public confidence; and if, on the other hand, he is a weak, incapable, unjust, or dishonest man, there will be no difficulty in proving it and having him removed. A Police Commissioner with such a tenure and security in his office, need pay no attention whatever to the little tittering talks of the scandalmongers and rumor-venders who now roost like a flock of jackdaws around the gloomy recesses of Police Headquarters. He can devote himself unreservedly to the great public business. He can, in a conservative and constructive way, go on with the work of perfecting the machinery and adding to the efficiency of the police force, and, above all, begetting among the officers and men themselves a sense of stability, a knowledge that their work is continuous and progressive, and that the establishment has at last, like the Ark, after many wanderings, found a resting-place on the Ararat of permanency and public confidence. There is no doubt whatever in my mind that with this reform a great mass of the present evil would disappear from the police force, and that it would be especially welcomed by the honest and faithful men of the force. As it is now, sometimes the best thing a Police Commissioner can do is to remove a suspected officer and put him in some obscure and unimportant precinct. The officer so removed simply bides his time. He sees the angry clouds portending a storm about to break over the head of the Police Commissioner. He can watch complacently from his suburban retreat the successful efforts to get a new man into Mulberry Street, and it is most amusing, after one of these fitful changes to which New York is so accustomed, to see these returning exiles treading their way into the shabby old palace, once more restored to official favor, coming to claim their birthright like lost heirs, assuming an air of conscious virtue and modestly acknowledging congratulations on the end of their period of martyrdom, just as if they had been the most innocent of victims and the most wronged of men. As they come in, out into the wilderness go those who had the confidence of the former Commissioner, without regard to the honesty of their actions, their faithfulness, their merit, or their service. It is painfully reminiscent of the revolutions in Central and South America—the flying president accompanied by his faithful friends, barely escaping with their lives under the folds of the American or some other foreign flag; while the successful bushwacker, the new *Presidente*, is getting one hand on the custom-house and the other on the treasury, preparatory to making it comfortable for the shabby-genteel gentlemen who have come to his aid from a long exile in New York or Paris. With him, too, the future is full of uncertainties and the time is short. The ship will come in some day that must take him away in turn; and the shabby-genteels, and even the barefooted bravos must not waste their opportunities, so that when they do leave it may be with a consolation that while they have lost power they are not as poor as when they assumed it.

A Police Commissioner with a life or long tenure would not be apt to dabble in politics; indeed, he would be thoroughly independent of political organizations. As a matter of fact, too, they would fare much better at his hands, because if he listened to any legitimate suggestion they might make he would be perfectly free, without suspicion, to consider the merit of their requests. If he should admit a district leader to a hearing, it would not be a subject of suspicion and rumor that he had surrendered any powers of his office to politicians, or that the appointing power had compelled him to take this course. He could meet a district leader or a clergyman and hear their views on the same subject, and feel entirely at liberty to agree with either as he saw fit, without being the subject of adverse criticism; and, above all other things, such a Police Commissioner would have always with him, as a stimulus and encouragement, the fact that he would have the time and opportunity to carefully think out and work into practical shape those measures and ideas which he was convinced were for the good of the public and beneficial to the police force as an organization. If he was worthy of the office, he would grow and learn by experience, and never hesitate to reverse himself when convinced of error.

The next step should be to make the office of chief inspector of the uniformed force more or less permanent, and to give to this chief the initiative in the making of assignments and transfers. No man should be assigned or transferred unless on the recommendation of the chief inspector, and with the approval of the Commissioner. This would apply to details over which the uniformed chief should have full supervision under the Commissioner.

After giving the Police Commissioner a real tenure of office and not a sham one, thus considering the question not as a joke but as something serious and affecting the welfare of the people of this city, the right arm of the Commissioner should be strengthened by a radical reformation of the Detective Bureau. This is the most important bureau in the Police Department, and it should be not only the most powerful but the most effective instrument in the hands of the Commissioner. This reformation of the Detective Bureau should begin by placing at its head the very best man in the uniformed force that the Police Commissioner can find. He should be given an adequate salary, somewhat higher than that of an inspector. The men should be divided into three grades, so that the incentive to promotion would always be before them, and in this way the best could be gotten out of them. They should not come through the Civil Service Commission, but should be selected by the Police Commissioner himself on the recommendation of the Chief of the Bureau of Detectives. Worthy men on the police force, who had shown by actual test detective ability and demonstrated integrity, should be those from whom this force should be recruited.

No other country in the world selects detective-sergeants on the lines now laid down for our Civil Service Commission under existing laws. The civil service examination is no criterion whatever of a man's ability to be a detective-sergeant. A man might be an honest, faithful patrolman, of fair intelligence, being capable of passing a civil service examination where he would show that he read, wrote, and expressed himself with more or less accuracy, answering questions about the laws of the State and the city, and some hypothetical ones regarding general police duties, and yet be totally wanting in the detective qualities. He might not be observant, acute, tactful, shrewd, and, shall we say it, more or less cunning and suspicious.

Had this reform been affected by law while I was in office, such squads as that which dealt with gambling, pool-selling, disorderly houses, and kindred vices, would not have been necessary. In such a Detective Bureau all the material for this work would have been at hand. Moreover, had I had such a bureau as that I would have abolished every plain-clothes man in New York at once. When a captain convinced me that he needed so many plain-clothes men, I simply would have given an order to the Detective Bureau to send so many detectives into the precinct to report to the captain, and also required them to make daily reports to Headquarters. The wardman would have been a thing of the past.

All the captain of a precinct had to do was to see that the men sent him performed their duty, and, if they did not, to hold them responsible and make proper complaints against them. An honest captain would thus have no confidential staff to betray him and sell him out behind his back, and every honest commanding officer would have welcomed the change; a dishonest captain would have no band of blackmailers and collectors at work in the precinct. Then, too, the whole responsibility for the prevention and detection of secret crime would be properly centralized and the movements of criminals would be known at Headquarters, which would thus become a clearing-house for all the precincts in the city. I say this because I am firmly convinced beyond any manner of doubt that, so far as preventing and detecting crime, the work at Headquarters should be centralized, not decentralized. The Commissioner himself must know and direct, and the thermometer and barometer of crime must be in his office, so that he can tell at a glance what is going on in any part of the city, and under this reorganization his chief executive officer would be at the head of the department that dealt with crime and criminals in all their phases. An able chief would readily divide his bureau into subdivisions to deal with special forms of law-breaking and crime. He could try out his men and shift them from one division to another until he found what they were best fitted for, and hold always before them the opportunity of promotion on merit.

This great bureau should be, as much as possible, separated from the uniformed force. That is the way in London. A Scotland Yard detective scarcely knows the uniformed force, and they have nothing to do with him unless he calls upon them. There is located the great secret arm of the law—the enginery of justice itself. They are not even known by name and cannot be located by the uniformed policeman, and their names are certainly not bandied about by crooks as common property, and crooked members of the uniformed force have no opportunity of working against them in the interests of criminals. The present situation is a very bad one. Many of the detective-sergeants are neither detectives nor sergeants, and they come through no preparatory school and bear no credentials as to ability. The title "sergeant" means nothing; it is merely relative rank in keeping with the salary. I want to be distinctly understood in saying this, however, that I am not arraigning the detective-sergeants as a body. There are some very excellent men among them to-day, faithful and able, men who should be promoted and encouraged, and who would show their best ability under such a system as is here proposed. As it is now, they are covered over and laden down with incompetent associates—men lacking in the degree of intelligence for this work, and some few under a cloud of suspicion as to whether or not they are above temptation, and not a few unduly conceited in their estimation of themselves, so that there is no hope of progress.

I would not imperil the reform of this great bureau by attempting to legislate out of office those who are now in it. The law-making power seems decidedly averse to this provision of the proposed law, and this ought not to be disregarded so as to delay something that the Police Department needs so much. Many of these men, moreover, are nearing the age limit; some of them are possibly physically unfit, and under a new chief, with the powers which would be granted by this law, and acting directly under a Commissioner with a permanent hold on his office, the weak and the bad could be weeded out fairly and legally. No one should be appointed or assigned to this office or taken away from it except upon the recommendation of the chief of the detectives. Having given him this great power, he would also have to assume a full responsibility to the Commissioner for the results, for, after all, the police machine must be judged by what it produces in actual results. The number now in the bureau should be largely increased. There should be a systematic night as well as day service.

I am convinced that the Legislature will not give to a single Commissioner the powers which courts-martial have in the army and navy. If any change is to be made, therefore, it seems to me it would be best to have a judge something akin to a judge-advocate in the army appointed by the Appellate Division of the Supreme Court, who should be a lawyer of good standing and a man of the highest integrity, who should be given a salary somewhat near to that of the Commissioner himself. Before him all the trials should be held in all parts of Greater New York, and before him the Third Deputy-Commissioner could act as prosecutor. He should preside solely at the trials, and his decisions should be subject to approval or disapproval by the Commissioner, and in case of disapproval the Commissioner should state his grounds in writing, in which case the defendant should have the privilege of having the case reviewed in the higher courts, but otherwise, where the trial judge and the Commissioner agree, the findings in the case should be final; or, in lieu of this, the trial should take place before two Deputy-Commissioners and a member of the uniformed force one rank in advance of the defendant. These uniformed members of the court could be changed from time to time, a majority finding to be effective; the defendant to have the right to appeal to the Commissioner himself, who would review the case, and whose conclusions, stated in writing, would be final.

A permanent age-limit ought to be fixed for compulsory retirement, without regard to physical disability. This is so in the army and navy, and there is no reason why it should not apply to the police force. A man may be able to pass a physical examination and yet be superannuated, inefficient, and worse than useless—just so much dead-wood, carried in an establishment which is always on active duty. The only honest incentive a policeman can have is promotion, and that ought to be held out to him. It is so in all military and quasi-military establishments, but on the police force the men are allowed to go into a sort of dry rot, barnacled over with old laws, customs, and traditions, utterly incapable of progress, obstacles in the way of any reform, and bitterly opposed to innovations however beneficial. Moreover, these men, as they advance in years, grow naturally conservative, and having lived in an establishment where changes are the order of the day, become timid about expressing an opinion on any subject, and will stand aghast at the very thought of promulgating an original idea or any change in police methods of half a century ago. Nothing could illustrate this better than the old-style caps, dating back to the days of the Civil War, which I found the higher officers wearing when I first went to the department. These had not the insignia of the wearer's rank, but their grades spelled out like that of ash-collectors and hall-boys in the cheap class of hotels. It required peremptory orders to bring about the present change in that respect, a change which I am satisfied every one now is pleased with, it being noticed that the Fire Department has adopted the same design of cap for its members. It was so with the uniforms of the mounted men. A footman simply put straps on his trousers, put them over his shoes, and became a mounted man. The thing was laughable, and yet if the reform had not been forced upon the service it would have gone on for a hundred years without change. I am constrained to believe that some of these men probably would tell you that the uniform made no difference whatever — that any old rough-and-ready clothes would do, and that the older and more antique, the closer it was in touch with the ancient traditions, and therefore so much the better. As a matter of fact, the uniform has almost everything to do with it. There is nothing so unsightly, there is nothing so objectionable, as a slouchy, slovenly looking policeman who seems totally wanting in the soldier-like quality. His uniform should be carefully designed, made of the best material, fit him snugly, and should be kept in good order at all times. He should never be allowed to depart from the military proprieties, and the inspection of his clothing and accoutrements should be most carefully and exactingly made at frequent intervals, so that the men would be proud of their uniform and give the attention to it which it deserves. A well set-up, well-uniformed policeman, carries with him an air of authority and command which is essential to his position. This is recognized in all great world-capitals.

V

DISCIPLINE AND DEPORTMENT

I WAS constantly enjoining the men that they should at all times be courteous to citizens and in their intercourse with one another, respectful and deferential to their superiors; that they should never, on any occasion, use loud, boisterous, or vulgar language; and, on the other hand, it was the duty of those over them to set them a good example in this respect, and treat them as officers and policemen. There are constantly coming before the Commissioner complaints from citizens that officers use vulgar, brusque, sometimes indecent and profane language. Profanity on the part of officers towards their men is most strictly enjoined against in both the army and navy. For an officer to swear at an enlisted man or an officer under him is a most reprehensible offence in the navy, and I am glad to say I never knew but one instance of the kind during my four years' connection with that establishment, and the officer guilty of such conduct was a junior at that, and in bad standing with his brother officers.

I have never hesitated to punish a man severely, even if it was the first offence, where he indulged in profanity in dealing with citizens, or was coarse, offensive, or discourteous to them in his manner and language. I consider it one of the most serious offences that a policeman can commit. The Deputy-Commissioners, inspectors, captains, and sergeants ought to be obliged to set the men a good example in this respect. Above all others, the sergeant at the desk, who sits both as judge and policeman, who is the proper official in charge of the station-house to which either the citizen is brought or goes to make a complaint, and where he defends himself against an unjust arrest, or where the citizen goes for information, should be compelled by severe pains and penalties to be courteous and polite at all times and under all circumstances. A rude, unmannerly person sitting as police sergeant and insulting citizens by his words or manners, or showing indifference or inattention to their complaints, has no place on the New York police force, and the sooner he is gotten rid of the better. It is the fault of the captain when such a man is not put on trial, and the fault of the Commissioner when he is convicted if he is not dismissed.

Many a citizen has gone to the station-house with a just complaint or for reasonable information and been maltreated and insulted, or driven away and repelled by the desk-sergeant, where the citizen, from timidity or horror of publicity, failed to make a complaint against him. Citizens should promptly complain of these things to both the captain and the Commissioner, and the latter should consider these among the most important class of cases which come before him.

There is probably no official in New York who has so much power as the desk-sergeant. He can lock up the innocent man, arrested by a drunken or prejudiced patrolman, on a false charge; he can use his administrative powers to degrade an otherwise respectable man arrested for some slight offence, such as the violation of a corporation ordinance; he can go into collusion with professional bondsmen for personal gain; and by thus shaping his conduct he will corrupt the whole station-house and every man in the precinct. Next to him is the lazy and shiftless sergeant who is simply timing himself to get away and has no interest in his business.

Lack of courtesy is among the most frequent charges by citizens against the police, and contrasts to their disadvantage in this respect with similar bodies in foreign cities is often made. There are many men, especially in the Traffic Squad, who are models in courtesy, kindness, and humanity, but the other element brings the whole force into disrepute. This blot on the police can be wiped out if the men at the top are in earnest and they themselves set the example. A brutal and profane policeman is an abomination. Putting down a murderous mob may require rough, hard treatment, but such occasions are rare, not common. The night-stick is, on occasions, a great lawyer for the prosecution, with or without hot language.

VI

VICE IN NEW YORK

Is New York an unusually vicious city? This is a question frequently asked, and answered variously. Reform organizations, which had their inspiration in the Lexow Committee investigation, would probably say "yes." Americans who have travelled a great deal abroad will tell you it is comparatively a virtuous city; that in London and Paris, for instance, sexual vice is, at any rate, less concealed and is treated by the police as something which must be tolerated; that there is no public opinion in either of those cities demanding the same restrictive measures that are asked for here; that street-walking in London is open and offensive, even in the more fashionable and attractive quarters of the city; that gambling, among the higher classes of people especially, is not interfered with to any extent; that the excise laws are more liberal, providing for Sunday opening; and that, on the whole, there is more individual freedom in these respects in both of those great capitals than in New York. I am not prepared to either assert or deny these premises, but I think a careful investigation would show that gambling, prostitution, and evasion of the existing excise laws are more wide-spread and cover a larger territory in New York than in those European capitals where the vices are either regulated openly by law or confined by a sort of common consent to certain neighborhoods and places. In speaking of the excise law in this connection, it is to be remembered that disorderly houses have no licenses, and that therefore sales within those places are always violations of the excise law.

Religious people, especially, have always opposed the licensing or segregation of sexual vice, and we know in this State how bitterly they have antagonized the idea of permitting the opening of saloons by law on Sunday for a portion of the day. There is apparently no use to argue from any given facts, so far as this element is concerned. The thing is wrong, from their point of view, and there can be no compromise with it. That it exists, has existed, and will exist, is apparently a fact not to be recognized by them. It is foreign, however, to my purposes to argue on the practicability or ethics of license or prohibition with regard to either vice or the sale of liquors. This can be said: that where there is neither license nor segregation by common consent, nor permission to sell within certain hours and on prohibited days, there is very apt to be collusion between the police and those who break the law.

In the city of Washington, for instance, the disorderly houses have for many years been confined to one quarter of the city. This is not law, but custom. This locality is known to every one, and is carefully avoided by those who want to escape even suspicion. It is so located as not to interfere with the citizens in general; the neighborhood is isolated; instead of offering temptations to young people, it rather repels them, for to be seen there at all is apt to put one on the defensive. Any attempt to break up this quarter and scatter the vice throughout the city would be at once bitterly opposed by even the religious and moral elements in the community. All that the police do is to see that peace and order prevail, that larcenies and robberies are prevented, and that the inhabitants are kept under careful espionage. A neighborhood like this is often most useful to the police, because it is there that they hunt first for those dissolute and desperate men who are trying to evade contact with the law, and where much can be learned about the movements of criminals, either those who make their headquarters in the city or come from other parts. I never heard a whisper, during a long residence in Washington, of any attempt by the police to blackmail the women in this quarter. The neighborhood is specially policed. Street-walking in Washington is practically unknown, and professionally bad women rarely if ever are found in hotels, boarding, or apartment houses. The confining of the disorderly elements into one quarter takes a great deal, too, from the labors of the police.

It is a well-known fact to every one cognizant of matters in this city that the breaking up of vice in quarters where it is congested—in some instances from houses where it has prevailed for over thirty-five years—has only resulted in its invasion of tenement and apartment houses and the cheap class of hotels. There can be no question whatever but that the vicious woman is more to be feared in a tenement or apartment house than in a house notoriously used for immoral purposes. The mechanic's daughter across the hall, who works hard all day in a feather or tobacco factory, is apt to become curious about the woman who does no work and who wears fine clothes and jewels, to become dissatisfied with her lot and envious of the easy life of the other, and finally, after an acquaintance, to join the vast army of unfortunate women who seem to increase rather than decrease with the march of civilization; worse than that, this invader captivates the young clerk, mechanic, or student, who in turn becomes a drunkard and profligate, and finally a criminal. The inmates of the higher-grade houses soon find their way into the otherwise respectable second-class hotels and apartment-houses, where they lay in wait to prey on the unsuspecting, very often imposing upon decent and virtuous women who live in the same house with them. They are the advance-guard of domestic scandals and business failures, the providers of grist for divorce mills, the harpies who live, feed, and prey on the money which is so lavishly spent on them by their victims, who in turn rob their families and cheat their business associates, and resort to shady and criminal practices to keep up a double life. It is to be admitted, of course, on the other hand, that in a block given up more or less to disorderly houses, it shocks one's sense of right to think of the respectable and virtuous minority of hard-working and decent people who are compelled to live in the neighborhood and have this vice flaunted in the face of their children, sometimes pushing its ugly presence into the neighborhood of public schools, and openly soliciting from the windows and halls and doorways. This offensive exhibition, however, if the police are at all vigilant, can be suppressed — that is, if the police magistrates will do their duty.

The main thing, from the police point of view, with regard to gambling in all its forms, and the prevalence of prostitution and soliciting in the streets by depraved and professionally bad women, is that where these things exist there is a *prima facie* case that the police are paid for non-interference. If there are a considerable number of pool-rooms in a police precinct, the suspicion rests on the police captain that he, or those under him, are receiving money for allowing them to operate. It is the same with gambling-houses and houses of prostitution, and hotels or other places used for assignation purposes; and where this is wide-spread in a city like New York, so that these vices are found more or less in a large number of precincts in Manhattan, some in the Bronx, and not a few in Brooklyn, one is face to face with the alarming situation that the toleration of these vices is corrupting and demoralizing the whole police force. If the men in a precinct know or believe that the captain is receiving money for permitting a disorderly house, pool-room, or gambling-house to run, they will, of course, not only have no faith in him, but they will evade their duty in all respects, because they will have constantly before their eyes the fact that a policeman can be successfully corrupt and that the officers who command them are not only not doing their duty, but making money by failing to do so. The chances are, therefore, that some of the men who have this example before them will in turn become grafters and blackmailers. If the captain can collect a large sum of money every week or month from a disorderly house, the chances are that the man on post will insist on robbing the unfortunate street-walker and making her pay for the privilege of carrying on her infamous trade on his post, and, indeed, become a partner in her infamy, her quondam protector. The police lover and protector of these wretched women is the lowest form of degradation, and nowhere are these people so despised as among the decent and manly majority of the force itself. The corrupt captain will be in no position to bring them to justice; they could wither him with a breath, and in the inner circles of the police the corrupt men are as well known as the names of the streets. These men, when they attempt to reform, or make spasmodic attempts to perform their duty, are in turn blackmailed. Those who know of their crimes or who have paid them tribute will be quick to resent this change on their part, particularly if it interferes with their business. They will say to such a policeman, "You are a nice one to enforce the law; you are a nice one to talk about public morals; you know that I not only paid you myself, but you know I am aware of others who have done so, and if you don't reverse your policy and go back to the old ways, exposure is going to come." Once a man has put himself to the plough of graft and blackmail it seems almost necessary that he run the furrow to its end. The moral courage has oozed out of him entirely; he must henceforth pass his life in the threatening shadow, a slave to those who know his secrets, a weak tool in the face of opposition or threats.

I was never deluded into the belief that there was any great moral indignation on the part of the community as a whole against betting on horse-races, and I am quite sure that in the so-called respectable quarters the other vices have warm, if concealed, defenders. Large numbers of people are indifferent so long as these vices do not annoy or obtrude themselves offensively on them; others, honestly conscious of moral weakness, are charitably disposed, and quite a number believe it is a necessary condition to a great city; and then, of course, there is a large army of defenders among those who patronize or profit by their existence. I have yet to hear of a police officer being lauded by the general run of people for suppressing gambling or trying to stamp out the sexual vices, with the exception of policy-playing; there public sentiment was practically unanimous. Have you ever heard of any candidate for public office running on that platform? The mother whose children are removed from temptation by his action is pleased with him; a father whose son spent his earnings to fatten the spider in the pool-room will openly express his friendship. But one only has to go down on any good day to a great race-track in the vicinity of the city to see the well-dressed and orderly people from all conditions of life, the good and the bad, the respectable and the shady, the sport and the banker, and, indeed, all classes so well represented, to understand that in this speculative age and money-crazed country gambling has a strong and almost universal hold on the people. I wonder if the elements of chance and opportunity in a rich young country like this do not add to the gambling spirit? Are we worse or better than our fathers? I have before me as I write a seventy years' old scheme providing a public lottery to raise funds to build a church within sixty miles of New York, and a liquor bill for many gallons of "Wine of Portugal" and "Spirits," provided against a meeting of the church authorities.

With the decrease of religious belief and the growth, too, of a complex civilization, there is no doubt a greater toleration of all vices, and the sophistication of youth concerning those social and sexual problems that mark the darker side of life is now openly urged by many parents, with results far from good, I should say. Against advice and knowledge that leads to health and moral well-being no one can wisely say aught, but to familiarize a boy or girl with the chambers of horror and dark sewerways that underlie at points the social structure, will either beget discouragement and disgust, or bitter cynicism and a morbid attraction for the savage and brute freedom of the world of darkness and unbridled license.

With a shifting marriage-tie dissolved by the breath of the divorce court; with a lack of home life in big cities; with the increased number of the unmarried in both sexes, who flit here and there, from this boarding-house to that hotel, and back; with the close intermingling of the sexes in business and work; with the recognition of common-law marriages and temporary partnerships between the sexes, and with the growth in our big cities of Old-World class distinction, we are far removed from the age of the *Scarlet Letter*. Yet it must be admitted that the vast majority of the citizens of this great metropolis are virtuous men and women, devoted to their families and their homes, and even where the religious and ethical argument for virtue is not held as strongly as in former days, a sophisticated generation cannot fail to recognize that the virtuous family is the true unit upon which all that is good in our present civilization rests, and that, indeed, in more senses than one, virtue is its own reward. These people, therefore, can be relied upon to either be actively or passively friendly to a police administration which seeks rigorously to repress vice, so that at least it shall not intrude itself upon the notice of decent people or invade respectable and orderly neighborhoods. To allow people to break the law presumes that the police are paid, that high officers grow rich on the blood and tear-stained money of this army of wretched unfortunates, degenerates, and criminals; and, worst of all, these vices in New York are, as it were, syndicated, marshalled, drilled, and employed in the service of men who have grown rich on the weakness and wickedness of their fellows. The owners of property who reap large profits from the base and criminal uses to which it is put; the various business interests which thrive on the very profligacy and prodigality of vice, and who, when it is repressed, complain that with them trade is dull; and, lastly, and more potent than all, those men who have grown rich on crime and vice, to whom it is a legitimate industry, whose millions are stained with the blood and tears of wretched women and outcast men, who own the large Raines law hotels, where the woman is first robbed of the price of her infamy, and, when she is arrested, is compelled to pay them for the bond that releases her—rich and influential, swaggering and blustering, these captains of the industry of vice and crime reach out their influence into most unexpected quarters. They threaten the destruction of honest police captains and demand the transfer of inspectors who do their duty; they hound and persecute an officer who interferes with their schemes or lessens their profits; they drive good and honest policemen into being bad ones; they have a price for every man on the force; they have their agents at the bar, in the courts, and in the newspaper offices; they have friends in every political organization; they have votes to give and money to swell the campaign fund, and open pocket-books for those who can protect them from the law. With them professional bonding is often a great source of revenue. One of the most notorious bondsmen is supposed to have deeded over property to two or three lieutenants, who really are only his agents. These men go on thousands of bonds, and a recent opinion of the Corporation Counsel was to the effect that they are the best men from whom to take bonds, because they know whom they bond better than others and are almost sure to produce them in court. The law seems to be in favor of their having a right to brazenly come into the station-houses and openly, for a consideration, bail out the poor fish caught in the police net. The sergeant at the desk is often only their tool; and the captain and his plain-clothes men and the other officers have in many cases made arrests only to furnish victims and money for these unspeakable scoundrels. There should be a law against the professional bondsmen. There is no difficulty, constitutional or otherwise, against a carefully worded enactment that would curb this criminal industry. Is there anybody really in earnest to kill this business? Is it possible that it has friends at Albany as well as in New York?

Some time ago, to show how profitable this bonding business is, especially in dealing with disorderly houses, I may instance that one of the high-class disorderly apartment-houses was raided in the afternoon under unusual circumstances. The house was situated on one of the fashionable streets in this city, and in a neighborhood where it was surrounded by some of the richest and best-known people and not a few churches. When the mistress was taken to the station-house she became hysterical. She was a woman of good appearance, and had evidently been brought up under refining influences. It was the first time she had ever been arrested. The arrest itself was questionably legal, and the circumstances seemed to point to the fact that it was premeditated for purposes other than the enforcement of the law. The woman had considerable means and many rich friends, and was willing to pay liberally to be released at once. She was immediately provided with a bondsman and a lawyer, and my recollection now is that she paid three hundred and fifty dollars between the two of them. The lawyer she had never seen or heard of before, and, of course, she knew nothing of the bondsman.

I received an anonymous letter at this time, which bore the ear-marks of being written by an inmate of the house, complaining of this extortion and robbery, and I had all the parties brought before me. The woman came accompanied by a lawyer of good standing. She, the other women, and her servant, were loud in their declaration of how justly, legally, and honorably they had been treated by the police. The lawyer said he had examined the case and that the unknown lawyer who had been called in had earned his fee, which I think was three hundred dollars; his labors consisted in joining this later lawyer at the police court in the morning. I said to all the parties at the time, and repeat it now, that my belief was that the place had been "pulled" for the purpose of extorting money from this woman; that she was not telling the truth because she was afraid the police would drive her out of business, and would begin to really and honestly prosecute her if she did so; that the letter was written under the first feeling of indignation, but as soon as it was ascertained that the Police Commissioner was to investigate the case they all had agreed to a defence of the police. Of course, in this case, there was no positive evidence that the policemen got a part of this comparatively large sum of money, or that the friendly lawyer who appeared so suddenly at the station-house ever gave up a dollar of his large fee, or that the professional bondsman even ventured to offer a cigar to any of the innocent policemen concerned in the matter. The woman is still in business in the very shadow of a church-spire. I do not mention this case as an isolated one, but simply as an example of the way this thing is done.

Of course, when it comes down to low-grade people, the methods are more brutal and open and the revenues realized from each case are not so large. I never heard of a case where the police blackmailed the otherwise respectable men found in these places, but of course the escapades which many men well-known in the community have had, are a matter of gossip among those concerned in police affairs. A shrewd, able, clever, and plausible police officer of the higher grades, in possession of the secrets of the police confessional, can make unto himself many and very wealthy friends of the "mammon of unrighteousness," and I became convinced, after experience, that, as a general rule, the making of special posts of these gambling and disorderly houses and poolrooms is at once an unfair draft on the police force, a withdrawal of a number of men from the proper patrol, and entirely useless as a preventive. It seemed to be commonly conceded on every hand that the majority of the men so placed received so much each night from the keepers of the houses. In the case of a gambling-house, the stationing of a plain-clothes man at its door was something worse than useless. Five or ten dollars, or maybe more, would be given him in a night, and generally, in addition, a nice warm supper would be covertly conveyed to him, so that he actually became a protector and guardian of the place and was looked upon with a more than friendly eye. Before the passage of the Dowling act there was a time, for a short period, when the uniformed man at the door really interfered with the business. A strict watch was put on the men themselves, and they knew that they were shadowed. It was about the holiday season and the town was filled with visitors with plenty of spending-money.

The gamblers at that time made a very strong and united effort to have the uniformed men removed from the door. They said they were really preventing rich men of social standing, from other cities and towns, entering their places. It was idle to assure one of these men that the policeman was entirely friendly. Even out-of-town "best citizens" were timid; there was an air of station-house and publicity about it, and they kept away. It would sometimes happen that after the policemen had repeated his formula, such as "This is a gambling-house and may be pulled to-night," the old-timers shook hands with the "cop" and gave him a cigar.

There is one feature about toleration of vice in New York by the police which possibly makes it different from other cities. It cannot be denied that for many years corrupt police administrations and dishonest police officers have made systematic collections from this source. Of course the actual figures are not known, but they are undoubtedly large. The result of this long-continued custom of paying the police has made the keepers of disorderly and gambling houses not only willing but eager to pay the money. As a matter of fact, the manager of a disorderly house, whether man or woman, does not feel any sense of security unless some one representing the police authorities has received money. These men and women will withhold their money from the landlord and pay their "protection rent." Sometimes a certain class of real-estate agents whose business is in infected localities, will act as the go-betweens, and will collect the money under guise of rent. He will say to the woman: "You can have this house for two hundred dollars, with police protection, or one hundred dollars if you take care of yourself." Of course I do not attempt to state the figures accurately; it may be any sum of money.

A corrupt police captain, in precincts like the nineteenth and twenty-second, or a number of other precincts both in Manhattan and Brooklyn, doesn't have to force payments. They will thrust money upon him or on those under him. These men and women feel that when they pay their money they are going to be protected. That was the reason they were so bitter against the so-called Vice Squad at Headquarters. So long as that was in honest hands the interests of the people and the law could not be sold out by a captain; he was unable to make good. The victims who paid the precinct authorities found themselves raided and arrested and haled to court by the Central Office men, and when these raids came thick and fast it staggered the corrupt elements in the precincts. In the language of the sporting fraternity, the precinct people "could not deliver the goods." Of course, this shifted the temptation from the precinct to the Headquarters men. The latter had to be frequently changed, and kept under closest surveillance; but among them I must say there were examples of firmness and marked integrity, and a resistance to manifold temptations, greater than any I have known in the business world. Of over three hundred men tried-out, there remained only twenty-five of the squad proper on January 1st of this year. This did not include seven men in Chinatown or the squad really designated as the Vice Squad, which numbered just four men. The rule was to weed out, as with infectious diseases, on the first sign of illness. I made one mistake with these men. I ought to have had them up before me personally nearly every day, and to have encouraged them to state freely any complaints they wished to make. The squad, however, did great service against vice and crime. Here is the best evidence: All crookdom, in and out of the police, hated it, fought it, and helped to abolish it. Either you must give the Commissioner a real detective bureau, or he will have to organize an office staff on these lines. Ignorance may be bliss, but it won't do for a Police Commissioner.

It is actually, among certain classes, a badge of honor to pay this tribute-money to those who represent the law, or to the politicians who really do, or affect to, control the actions of the police. There is no disguising the fact that the district leader, especially of the majority party, is a power which the police must recognize. In the very nature of things, he probably knows more than the police themselves as to what vices are flourishing in the district. In the good old days he issued the licenses to break the law; he drove this man or that woman out of his district, and allowed that man or this woman to come in and do business. In return they paid liberally; and at election time, especially during bitter contests for supremacy, they were bled to the last drop, compelled to harbor illegal voters and floaters, and to exercise the rights of citizenship as far as they could go without detection. They asked no questions and obeyed orders. They were the regular and veteran troops who were put forward where the fighting was fiercest and the risks greatest.

In these times, the district leader selected the plain-clothes men for the captain. He secured the latter his appointment and promotion, and generally owned him body and soul. The world is certainly growing better, for in those delightful days, before a captain could be promoted, he would have to pay the leader from ten to twenty thousand dollars. An honorable and just-minded leader would immediately see to it that the worthy and generous captain got a busy and important precinct, where he could get back his money from the vicious criminal or other interests that broke the law, and as almost everybody in New York breaks some law with more or less frequency, the chances of recovery were good.

In this connection, and to illustrate how relentlessly the dishonest elements on the force pursue an honest man who gets in the way, there is a story of how, at one time, when the blackmailing and collecting system was in full swing, and men higher up were reaping vast fortunes of this money wrung from degradation, vice, and crime, a captain who had cleaned out his precinct and who stood like a stone-wall against its invasion by gamblers, prostitutes, and thieves, was sent into a far-away precinct on the very confines of Greater New York. As his precinct covered an immense amount of territory, he thought he would apply for a horse and buggy. He did this very timidly, expecting disapproval from his enemies at Headquarters, who, at best, he thought, would send him some broken-down vehicle with a spavined animal to draw it. What was his astonishment one day, when a very stylish-looking animal pranced up in front of the station-house door drawing rather a fair buggy. The horse had an arched neck and stepped with the vigor and spirit of a colt. The captain was an old policeman and it excited his suspicion; the thing looked too good. The horse was put away in the stable for a couple of days, and then the captain cautiously told a subordinate, who was a careful driver, that he might take the horse out and exercise him. The man harnessed him up, opened the stable door, sprang into the buggy, and they were off.

So far as that station-house and stable are concerned the horse and buggy never returned. The runaway is still a tradition in the neighborhood. The driver luckily escaped. The horse took the buggy over fences and through back yards and kitchens, and what little was left of it was finally captured miles away. That horse was an irreclaimably vicious animal. He had run away dozens of times. The man who first trained him had broken his jaw and taken a splinter of bone five inches long out of it in his efforts to make him tractable. They might as well have sent the captain a man-eating tiger in disguise, or put poison in his food. I will never forget the look of astonishment on the captain's face when the details were at last furnished him. If the thing had panned-out right, from their point of view, imagine the good cheer of the grafters at the captain's funeral. Probably they would have agreed that he was a good-fellow, but knew little about police affairs. As it is, he is still living, and an honor to the police force.

But again I must remind the reader that it will not do to bunch the bad and the good on the force. There are good men and true men, whose ideas of honesty are above that of politics or business, and some of them have made very great sacrifices, and continue to do so to this day, and the whole force, in my judgment, if freed from the shackles of its evil customs and bad examples until it had the moral courage to rise up itself and drive out the evil ones, would be as good if not a better police force than could be found anywhere else. The reader must not, therefore, every time he meets a policeman, think from the stories told about them that this particular policeman is necessarily a dishonest man or unfaithful to his duty, and that he does not truly represent the majesty and power of the law.

The resorts of vice in New York have shifted very much with the changes in the city. As every one knows, the city is being rebuilt, and vice moves ahead of business. South of Fourteenth Street, on the West Side, there are but few disorderly houses, and those are old landmarks in the neighborhood south of Washington Square. The New Tenderloin, which begins at Forty-second Street and runs up to Sixty-second Street, is rapidly depleting the ranks of the sporting vicious element in the Old Tenderloin. There is a steady effort to invade Harlem on the upper east and west sides, and here it comes in contact with the great middle-class population, the very cream of our citizenship, and here it should be resisted most strenuously. It is beginning to show its head in Brooklyn, and will grow there unless checked at once, and vigorously. It is a business, in a way, and changes its forms and modes like other businesses. The old-style disorderly houses are getting infrequent: flat-houses and apartment-houses, given over wholly to the residence of single women, and a certain class of Raines law hotels, have taken their place. Certain newspapers, which claim to be respectable, teem with thinly veiled advertisements of assignation apartments.

The most despicable form of vice of late has been the massage parlor, which advertises openly and flagrantly, and with very little reservation in the wording, in alleged respectable newspapers, column after column. It seems almost incredible that a newspaper claiming any degree of respectability would allow this infamy to appear on its pages. This class of advertising must be immensely profitable. Some of these advertisements are so suggestive as to be flagrantly indecent. I would not soil the pages of this book by reproducing them, although I have seen them come into respectable homes with the family newspaper. I investigated a number of these advertised places, and in one instance I called the attention of the newspaper proprietor to the effect of these advertisements and the character of the places. Some of them were the scenes of unspeakable orgies, and in many of them the victims were elderly men, where they were subjected to vile and unprintable treatment and robbed of their money. Wherever the police begin to clean up a precinct and drive the ordinary and well-known places out of business, these massage parlors at once begin to flourish. Of course there are legitimate massage places which have a right to advertise, and are patronized by decent people. It is foreign to my purpose to discuss, from the moral and sociological point of view, the origin of vice in the city, or the causes which fill its ranks. The clergy, my esteemed contemporary, Bernard Shaw, and those very rich young socialists had better debate that between them, for, in my poor judgment, it is much too deep for even "Mrs. Warren."

One of the most troublesome and dangerous characters with which the police have to deal is the Tenderloin type of negro. In the male species this is the over-dressed, flashy-bejewelled loafer, gambler, and, in many instances, general criminal. These fellows are a thorough disgrace to their race and have a very bad effect on decent colored people who come here from the South and other parts of the country. They never work, and they go heavily armed, generally carrying, in addition to the indispensable revolver, a razor. When in pursuit of plunder, or out for revenge, or actuated by jealousy, they use both weapons with deadly effect. In one case, one of these desperadoes almost literally cut a man in two with a razor, and in several instances they have inflicted fearful wounds on policemen.

If they sleep at all, it is in the daytime, for they are out at all hours of the night. In the afternoon they can be seen sunning themselves in front of their favorite saloons and gambling-houses, like snakes coming out of their holes. They pride themselves on being mashers, and generally have one or more unfortunate women in their train, whose earnings from a life of shame they appropriate. They swindle by all forms of gaming and every other way, those honest members of their own race who work hard and honestly. One of these fellows will get hold of an honest negro coachman or waiter, as soon as he gets to New York, and not only will he rob him, but before he is through with him he will probably make him as bad as himself. They are impudent and arrogant in their manner, and will block the sidewalks until white women have to go around to get past them, running the risk at the same time of being insulted. Some of them develop into thieves and dangerous criminals.

In the nineteenth and twentieth precincts there are two or three leading resorts where many of these fellows can be found at all hours of the night and day. The largest of these places was known as a sort of colored Haymarket. It occupied the whole house, and there was dancing on both the lower and upper floors. On the first floor there was a bar, back of that a large room with small booths covered with artificial orange-trees, and in the centre the couples danced. These places were sometimes run as clubs. They were resorts for both races. In all of these places were found quite a sprinkling of a low class of white women. Occasionally a white woman would be seen there who looked to be entirely out of place, being well-dressed and not especially dissipated-looking. These women drank and fraternized with the negro men. I took particular pains to have one of the largest of these places closed, and I made it known to them personally that I did not favor the mixing of races, because the mixture produced violent quarrels, ending sometimes in murder, and ran counter to ineradicable prejudice.

All of these mixed-race places in the nineteenth, twentieth, twenty-second, and twenty-sixth precincts have no redeeming quality, are breeding-places for crime, and present disgusting exhibitions of the degradation of one race and the worst vices of the other.

Last year I was called upon by a delegation of colored saloon-keepers, headed by a lawyer of their own race. They expressed themselves as very indignant because of my opposition to these mixed-race places. They accused me of being prejudiced against the colored race, which is quite untrue, I being a much better friend of the honest, decent, respectable colored people, both men and women, than the owners of these brothels. Through their legal champion they asserted with great emphasis their legal right to entertain white as well as colored women, and they took the position that the white woman had as much right to drink in their places as a colored woman, and that there was no legal bar to the social admixture of the two races, and that to differentiate between them and saloons exclusively patronized by either white or colored was an injustice, and without warrant of law. They asserted their intention to continue to allow white women to go in these places and mix with colored men and women. They also asserted with a good deal of pride that over twenty-five hundred white women were married to colored men here in New York, and threatened their political opposition to any administration which interfered with these well-known resorts. I consider them far more dangerous for a certain class of young white women than Chinatown, and there is every evidence that they are patronized at times by degenerate whites, both men and women, of a class far above the usual habitués. Indeed, these are the most profitable patrons and encourage the places, and, if they had the courage, would defend them openly.

The negro loafer is a more dangerous character than the white cadet, as he is subject to violent fits of jealousy, and, when filled up with the raw alcohol which is dispensed in the neighborhood, murder comes naturally and easily to him. The well-to-do negroes who run these places make quite a show in politics, generally belonging to the political organizations in the district and promising many votes on Election Day. They will shamelessly make bargains to sell votes of their own race to white politicians, and they are both grafters and givers of graft. The first people who should undertake to drive these fellows out of the city and into the workhouse are the respectable, educated, and well-to-do negroes themselves. I had no hesitation in saying this to a delegation of well-to-do colored men headed by a well-known negro divine. The race prejudices and brutality of white ruffians is no excuse for a failure of the better educated and progressive members of the negro race repudiating openly and emphatically these men and women who bring disgrace upon them as a whole. If one of these negro ruffians gets in trouble, either with the police or a white citizen, he is apt to appeal to the better class of negro, on the ground that he is being made the object of race hatred and prejudice in order to excite their sympathies; and it is in this wise that some of the riots and fierce outbreaks which have disgraced the city have been brought about in recent years.

The first thing that should be done with these people is to disarm them. The honest, respectable, and peace-loving colored people should join the movement to make these fellows outcasts and take away their revolvers and razors, and, next, to get a few hundred of them sent up to the workhouse for long terms as disorderly persons with no visible means of support. The police are often charged with dealing brutally with these people, but the average policeman is afraid to take any chances when making an arrest. He can take it for granted that the man to be arrested has a revolver in one pocket and a razor in the other, and possibly a black-jack, and that he will use them at once with murderous intent.

The vicious and drunken colored woman differs somewhat from her white sister, in that she, too, in a paroxysm of passion, and under the influence of liquor, is likely to use a weapon very freely, and not a few of them carry revolvers and razors. It is a crying shame that this disorderly and criminal element should handicap the decent and respectable colored people here in New York, and to be at all times a menace to the people and welfare of both whites and blacks.

There is also, in the Tenderloin especially, a very dangerous band of colored women who prey on white men. There was at one time quite a number of "creep joints" there. A white victim was robbed and the robber escaped through the cellar or the back yard. A great number of these women were arrested, convicted, and sent to prison, but, unless carefully watched, new ones will take up the work. These women rob white men with impunity, especially those who look respectable and well-dressed, because they know the chances are that the man will not care to disgrace himself by appearing in court against them. The men and women who conduct this game are constantly on the move. They will rent a couple of rooms to-day, rob a few victims to-night, and move to-morrow to another place. The men act as scouts for these women, and afterwards do the robbing.

Among the colored population of New York are very many deserving people, and one of the cruellest things about conditions here is that they find it impossible to live in neighborhoods where this element gets a footing. There ought to be in New York some locality given over to the residence of respectable, honest, and hard-working colored people, and I believe as an investment it would pay. A friend of mine had a colored coachman who was in his employ for many years. He was a model man, with a decent and well-conditioned family. He lived over the private stable of his employer. When the former disposed of this stable and told him he would have to find other quarters to live in, he gave up the place with tears in his eyes, because, he said, he did not know, in New York, a decent neighborhood where he could find a home.

In the better class of white apartment-houses he was not wanted, and he would not take his family into any place where this obnoxious negro element lived.

The true friends of the negro among the whites, and the real leaders like Booker Washington, cannot, in my judgment, impress too strongly the necessity of the colored people themselves repudiating these men and women and aiding the law officers in bringing them to justice.

The mixed-race resort, besides running counter to violent racial prejudices and traditions, is an unmitigated and disgusting evil, and the technical arguments as to the legal rights of a licensed resort should not prevent the police in placing it under constant surveillance and in enforcing the law with the greatest vigor. Hattie Ross, the colored missionary, herself was a depraved woman. I at first mistrusted her, but recent developments show that her worst charges are true. A negro beast holding a white woman—even a depraved one—in captivity, arouses the fierce spirit of lynch law.

If instead of being prejudiced against the negro race I was not really its friend, I would not have spoken as warmly as I did to various delegations of colored people who called upon me as Police Commissioner. Beyond all this, the subject is one of interest to all of the people of New York because, unfortunately, in the past it has been shown that race riots are likely to break out when most unlooked for and to rage with savage violence.

If the recent occurrences in the Tenderloin precinct will arouse public opinion, not only white but colored, against these infamous mixed-race resorts, it will be one of the best things that has happened in many a day. The police are certainly remiss where they fail to investigate at once any of these places where white women, especially young women, are seen to go, and I was constantly enjoining them to make frequent inspections.

The recent discovery by the District Attorney's office shows that there must be some centralized power outside of the precinct on the constant lookout for such places. The chances are that if the Commissioner had a force of his own the same information would have been given him as was given to the District Attorney in this case; and I have not the slightest doubt that in this instance, as in many others, the informants had no faith in the precinct people, whoever they might be, but preferred to deal with Headquarters. This happens in police administration every day. A man or a woman living in the neighborhood, or going there in the capacity of missionary or philanthropist, will rarely go to the station-house with this information; they prefer to deal with the District Attorney or the Police Commissioner.

VII

APPOINTMENTS AND PROMOTIONS

If appointments to the police force and promotions therein are bought and sold, or obtained by personal influence and "pull," without regard to merit, then the whole establishment is absolutely hopeless. There will be no incentive for any policeman to do his duty. If, in addition to this, transfers and assignments are solely matters of influence or money, then the demoralization is complete. The department will become a quagmire of corruption, a putrifying pest-hole, poisoning the life of the city. The policemen will buy the places, and then plunder and recoup themselves for the outlay; the law will be brought into contempt, and its enforcement be simply a matter of favor; to break it would be a privilege to be paid for, and immunity from its provisions would be a mercantile commodity hawked about and sold by everybody connected with the police, from the doorman to the Commissioner.

Revolutions at the polls, begetting new methods in the administration of the city government, would have no effect at all upon such an organization. It might, for a little while, check it, like the progress of some chronic disease, but it would break out again with renewed virulence and strength. If the police force of New York is really to be anything worthy of the name, it must be made sure, beyond any question, that men are appointed to it after honest examinations, impartially and fairly conducted, and based on reasonable and practical ratings, and that they are taken from their place on the eligible list by the Commissioner without regard to any outside influence whatever. My own rule was to take the men for appointment as patrolmen from the eligible list in the order in which they were presented to me by the Civil Service Commission, unless in the interval there was some charge made against any one which demanded investigation; otherwise I never skipped a name out of the hundreds appointed during my administration.

The responsibility, therefore, rests with the Civil Service Commission. If the Commissioners themselves are lax or dishonest, or if, however honest they may be, their subordinates are not above temptation, the fountain will be poisoned at its source. I have no charge to make against the present Civil Service Commissioners, and I have no facts which would warrant me in taking them to be other than honest and intelligent men; but, on the other hand, for years past the air has been laden with rumors and suspicions about these examinations. A large number of the police believe that the questions are often sold, manipulated, papers changed and "doctored." Even now suits are pending in the courts, brought by policemen to question the fairness of the ratings given them by the examiners, charging that changes were made in the percentages not warranted by the facts; that favoritism was shown. If you doubt my word, go and ask the first policeman, especially if it is one of the older men, whom you meet on the street, and if he has never been before the Commission for promotion he will tell you that he never had the money to buy the questions or get his ratings fixed, and was afraid to go down there, and that it cost so much to be made a roundsman; or if he is a roundsman he will tell you, if he gives you his confidence, that he would have to pay so much to be made a sergeant, and so on up. I do not indorse these beliefs. I simply state that they exist, and I deplore their existence.

That such stories and beliefs prevail is bad for the police. I tried always to root out these expressed suspicions in the absence of proof. I have heard stories, which of course I cannot authenticate, that men have been impersonated before the examiners. One of these funny little stories was to the effect that a man with one eye was represented by a man with two good eyes, who passed for him. The man who was short on eyes was promptly notified of his appointment on the force, but the examination by the police surgeons disclosed an obviously physical defect, other than the eye, which necessitated his rejection. As the glass eye looked just as good as the other eye, they could not find out anything about that by merely looking at it. And there are legends extant that men several inches below the standard height are to-day on the force, they having passed by the aid of taller men.

If there is an abuse of this kind, the Civil Service Commissioners, or their subordinates, could readily stop it by either photographing the applicant or by taking a thumb-print under the new method, so that no man could impersonate before the police surgeons the man who passed the civil service examination.

It would be a great thing for the police force if all this suspicion could be taken out of their minds. It is the plain truth, however, to say that it does exist. I have had it insisted to me that certain men on the list for high office have paid five thousand dollars for the rating which they received. You inquire as to whom was this money paid. You assert your belief in the absolute honesty and probity of the Civil Service Commissioners, and generally that is granted, but the rumor persists, goes along through all ranks of the force; it is the gossip of every station-house. All I can say, from personal observation, is this—and I disclaim again possessing any evidence whatever, because if I did

I would make it public — that the result of the examinations in many cases was a keen disappointment. Officers whom I valued most highly, honest men of intelligence and ability, with clean records, would get a rating far below a man in whom I had little or no confidence, who gave no evidence of anything more than ordinary intelligence, and who, in addition to that, had penalties attached to his record. Of course this may arise from the fact that these written examinations made by the Commission are an entirely different test from that to which a Commissioner, who had been some time with the force, would subject the man in order to judge of his capacity. But be that as it may, from the Commissioner's point of view I do not believe that the system provided the best men.

Of course the answer to all this is that the civil service law is rooted in the Constitution of the State and is backed up by public opinion, and in general by experience, and that no one wishes to disturb it; in all of which I concur, except as regards the detective-sergeants, of whom I shall speak later. If there should be the slightest reason for the expressed police suspicions with regard to the workings of the civil service examinations, then the whole thing ought to demand the most rigid investigation by both the city and State authorities. In fact, this Commission is so powerful for good or evil that I see no reason why it should not be, at all times, under the closest scrutiny. Eternal vigilance is the price of honest appointments and promotions. If a Civil Service Commission, either national, state, or city, is not square and above-board, it will be more than apt to coddle and do all sorts of favors for Congress and the Legislature and those in power in the city, instead of standing up manfully and fighting every adverse influence, whether legislative or executive. If it does favors for a weak Executive, or goes out of its way to unduly oblige the legislative branch of government, there will be little danger of honest investigation of its workings, and, indeed, it will then be in a position to defy the investigators.

I am clearly of the opinion, so far as the police are concerned, that the examinations should be both oral and written. Some men, whose papers before the Commission I have examined, answered the questions with a great deal of ability, and demonstrated at least a good use of the pen in the matter of handwriting; in fact, in some instances, the whole paper showed evidence of scholarship. Now the same man, who stood up before a committee of gentlemen in Police Headquarters, on being asked the same questions, would give halting, improper, and less intelligent answers, and would show no evidence of any such ability as the paper would indicate; and, *per contra*, the man with the paper rated much lower by the Commission would show a grasp of the subject at once, and be ready and quick with his answers and speak to the point. The whole trouble seems to be this: The power of appointment and promotion has been so seriously abused by the political heads of the police that the law has been swung to the other extreme, and the Commissioner is bound in iron rulings and enactments to be but an echo of the Civil Service Commission. In the matter of promotions, especially, the Police Commissioner ought to be given greater latitude. The rules should be enlarged as to the making of his selections, and he should be allowed to skip names more freely. Of course the stated answer to this will be that a politician at the head of the police will very naturally, in order to enhance himself with his party, abuse this trust. Well, the reply to that is simply this: There never will come a time again in the history of New York when any party will turn over the police to a thoroughly partisan administration.

The public, without regard to any party, will hereafter undoubtedly insist that appointments and promotions be made entirely on merit, and without the slightest suspicion of either a monetary, personal, or partisan consideration. I will not allow myself to believe that they will go back to the old order of things. Of course you can quibble about anything, and theorize against any reform, but the people will want to know and they will insist upon knowing, and not only knowing, but seeing, that men are selected from the eligible lists without paying a penny for the same, without falling back on any political organization, without being under obligation to any person in or out of politics. They will want to know, too, the processes by which the selections are made. They will not trust any Commissioner, however great he may be, or good, without having, as it were, witnesses of their own, from the general citizenship, who will be a jury to see fair-play.

I had puzzled for many days and weeks over some way of showing to the police, beyond any doubt, that promotions were being made fairly and by the open as well as the square deal, when it struck me like an inspiration that the only way to do this was to call in a jury of citizens of the highest character and reputation, disinterested, impartial, upright, and non-partisan; to lay before them everything—records, opinions, correspondence, open charges, or expressed suspicions—and, above all, to present each man, no matter how many hundreds there were up, and let them examine him, look him over, talk to him, question him, and make up their own judgment on him, so that, out of the whole list in any grade, they would, by a comparison of views and by relation to a standard to be fixed, select the very best men. It did not follow that the man rejected was not a fairly good man, but it must follow that the man selected was a better man. Given two men to promote, the best man for the police and for the public was selected—judged by practical and personal examination, by comparison of the records of the two men, their character, appearance, antecedents, experience, and, above all, by what they had done as policemen. Under this system a fair man was rejected for a good man, and a good man was set aside for a better man. Given a hundred men on the list, the principle was to get the very cream of the list and promote it, leaving the fair and passably good to stand aside, and, of course, utterly rejecting the bad and incompetent.

Accordingly, following out this idea, I invited a number of citizens, selected from all businesses and professions, aiming to get men whose verdict would carry the greatest possible confidence with the public and the police. If I had known a man to be one of my most severe critics, and yet believed he was honest and fair, he would have been the first man I would have asked to be a member of the committee. As far as possible, the object was to get a committee representative of the best public opinion of a great city, men who had won their way to the top of things and in doing so had enhanced their own characters and reputations. That I was most fortunate in this idea, and in the gentlemen who consented to serve, will be, I think, admitted by every one who took any interest whatever in this movement. The men selected were all men of independent character, far above suspicion of being influenced by anything other than a desire to do their full duty to the police and to the citizens at large. They were under no obligations to me, and they had no favors to ask and no ulterior motives to serve. They were entirely removed from personal or political influences.

In selecting this committee I did not abrogate my duties or rights as Commissioner. I simply asked the people of New York, through these gentlemen, to come in and view the processes and means by which promotions were to be made, and, in doing so, to get a more intimate knowledge of the police themselves. I am quite within the lines in saying that probably no other five eminent citizens know as much about the police to-day, in a really practical way, as the gentlemen who served on that committee. Other distinguished citizens have investigated the police by taking evidence, attending public meetings, and giving hearings, but, after all, they worked without the establishment. These gentlemen were admitted into the very innermost recesses of the police machinery; they saw it daily and hourly, if they wished to, in its actual operations; they did not have to theorize about it, or guess and speculate, nor did they have to listen to long-winded dissertations by volunteers about this or that feature of it; they met the men face to face, they saw the machinery in actual operation. They did not see it one day, but they saw it many days; they got to know the men, know their character; got to understand the officers; had ample opportunity of talking and cross-questioning the men themselves. So at least I have the consolation of knowing that five good and true men understand the New York police in a way that no other five citizens do, many of whom have talked much more about the subject than they have.

It is idle to say that the Commissioner does not need help of this kind—that a big-minded, strong man can find out for himself. Well, a big-headed man will think he can, and a man who is making a great bluff at knowing things he doesn't know will try to impose on the public an air of mystery, and to create the impression that he has infinite knowledge. This is bluffing, and nothing else; it is just a bit of political trickery, and no one need waste any time on it. No one man can find out as much in secret about a candidate for promotion as five men who are his peers in intellect and ability can in an open, square, and thorough examination, where everybody is invited to tell all he knows—indeed, encouraged to do so—where the man stands forth and the Commissioner challenges the public to say anything good or bad about him they wish to, and say it publicly; where the Commissioner invites public confidence, doesn't discourage it, tells the people all he knows, and wants to know if they know more. That is the fair, open-air, sunlight way of doing things. As against this, you have the old secretive process, the old mystery-room, the old assumption of infinite knowledge. The Commissioner makes the selections; he gives the names of the selected; he refuses to say anything about them; he looks wise and owl-like. At the same time almost everybody knows that the back-door has been opened by him; social influence, personal influence, political influence, lies, prejudices, misrepresentation, and maybe something worse, have been at work. They read the names and see good men turned down, crooks put to the front, indifferent men put over really efficient ones. The old way will not work any longer; the Commissioner has got to work in the open. He can do it by himself or he can do it by the committee. If he does it by himself, openly, in the trial-room, as I did, he will have to submit to public questioning as to his motives and his methods. The old method and the new are irreconcilable; the Commissioner must either disclose his methods and give his reasons publicly, or he must go back to the old way and let the police and public guess as to how he reached his conclusions. He cannot select men and claim some mysterious power of divination. People will look under his desk for the secret wire that makes the automaton work.

Dummy committees will not do. If the people

see old hacks on the committee, or unknown men, or if it is one-sided, personal and partisan, incompetent, or second rate, the public will jump to the conclusion that the jury is "packed" and that the thing is a farce. Above all, if the Commissioner calls in a committee he must give them full swing. No self-respecting citizen who is worthy of such a place will permit himself to be made a mere catspaw, or have his right to question checked or himself treated as a mere factotum or ornamental thing. He will insist on asking questions as freely as the Commissioner, and he ought to have the right to disagree with him. The Commissioner must submit to it or not call him in at all. The citizen called in to act on such a committee must be allowed full liberty of expression, have the right to call for persons and papers, and make his recommendation with entire independence, and then the Commissioner will have the supreme right, in the end, of agreeing or disagreeing with the committee, or any part of it, as he sees fit; that is his right under the law, and he must assume full responsibility for doing so. There is only one other course he can pursue: he can take the names, good, bad, and indifferent, just as he finds them on the list and promote them. This will leave the whole decision with the Civil Service Commission, and he will then have abrogated all the powers given him by law to that body. A clever crook, who can answer questions and write a good hand, can in that way get promoted at once, and a good man who misspells a word, but who wouldn't make a dollar or a million dollars illegally or wrongfully, will be turned down and go back to tramping the sidewalks.

There is one thing which the Police Commissioner, in dealing with this matter, must have in mind: the whole spirit of the age is for open dealing and investigation. It is an age of vast suspicion. Reputations in the world of finance and politics have crumbled and fallen so rapidly and astonishingly that the public are in no mood to take anything for granted. They want to know, and they must know in these matters, and it is perfectly right that they should know. There are proper police secrets, however, which of course no Police Commissioner ought to tell any one, and he must be allowed a large amount of discretion, and this will be readily granted him.

The committee began its labors first with the promotion of captains to the grade of inspector, and then later of sergeants to captain, and roundsmen to sergeant. The method of working was something like this: The gentlemen of the committee went up into the trial-room and sat on what might be called the "bench." The Commissioner, accompanied by his secretary and the chief inspector, occupied seats below them, acting more in the capacity of presenting the facts to a jury than being a part of the jury themselves. A sufficient number of officers from the eligible list to cover all the vacancies, with a considerable margin, were marshalled into the room and brought before the committee, in numbers large enough to fill the space within the bar, so that the Commissioner and the committee could get a good view of them personally and inspect the whole batch. Then all were sent out of the room and their names were called in the order in which they appeared on the list. The applicant then came forward and his paper record was examined. The public were invited to be present, the doors were open, and the press was always represented by whoever wished to be there. The whole proceeding was notoriously public and open.

The chairman of the committee generally examined the candidate on his record, questioned him about his duties, what he had done, what he would do under given circumstances. If there were any letters against him they were read, and he was asked to explain them. If the committee knew, or had heard anything against his character, he was examined and cross-examined at length about it. If any one wished to testify against him he was given full opportunity. The man's mental and physical qualifications were looked into. His rating on the civil service list was taken into consideration, but it was not paramount. If No. 55 proved better than No. 1, he was to be selected; No. 1 must step aside, because under no possible circumstances could that rating be the sole standard. It was entitled to consideration, but it was far from conclusive.

This winnowing process went laboriously, thoroughly, and painstakingly forward, covering a period of many weeks and months. There was no attempt to brow-beat any man. He was given a full chance to explain and answer; he was not hurried or coerced; he was treated firmly, but with all fairness and judicial impartiality. The examination was thorough, but where the matter was one of gossip or scandal which would unnecessarily humiliate or degrade him, he was given a chance to explain that in executive session, so that some enemy might not blacken his reputation or make him an object of suspicion among his fellows without his being allowed to defend himself. The main and dominating idea was to look after the interests of the force and the public, and to this the individual must subordinate himself, so that sometimes the questioning was quite personal and pointed, and very searching. I can only say that the decisions of the committee and the final support of the Commissioner had the unanimous approval of those who really understood and know the police, individually and collectively.

Those members of the press who spent many

years at Headquarters, who have a large acquaintance among the officers and men, were among the most hearty in approving the selections, and in agreeing that the very best possible men had been promoted; and in no instance, I am proud to say, was there one single criticism, from any impartial source, over these promotions. When it is considered that this was the largest number of promotions ever made in the history of New York at one time, the fact that there was so little criticism is, I think, really remarkable. For myself, I am inclined to believe that it was a thing of which I have most reason to be proud, because it goes to the root of the efficiency of the whole service.

Bad men will not give good results, and weak men will not prove strong in the day of trial. Men who pay and pull to be promoted are going to get their money back, and they are going to look more to those who pull for them than they are to any Police Commissioner; and, moreover, they are just the very men who would be cunning enough to keep within the letter of the law. The town can be going to the bad, crime rampant, vice brazen, and they can snap their finger at any Commissioner. They can do just enough to keep within the rules and escape punishment, and if the Commissioner punishes them, unless the evidence is conclusive, the courts will very soon relieve them. Under these conditions the best men are thoroughly disheartened and discouraged and some of them will retire or resign, or, if they remain, will perfunctorily do as little as possible. When a bad man gets promoted or honored by important place, and a good man gets punished for some technical infraction of the rules, the effect on the force is electrical from the top to the bottom. The watchword goes out: "Expect no justice; crookedness pays; don't do the full measure of your duty or you will make enemies; the Commissioner is trying to beat us, we will beat him; he is not fair to us, why should we be to him. If there is any way of overriding the rule we will do it." And beyond and above everything else, it drives the whole force, good, bad, and indifferent, into one solidified opposition. Under such circumstances no good man will tell on a bad one, and good and bad have only one object, to stand together as policemen against the Commissioner and all outside influences.

The police, too, are naturally cunning and shrewd: they were not born yesterday; they are quick to measure up things. When it comes to their own interests they are very alert. All they want to know about a Commissioner is: What is his standard? What is his theory? If they are opposed to him and it, they must find a way to beat it. Eight thousand heads and eight thousand minds at work, some with forty years' experience on the police; eight thousand men who know New York like a book; eight thousand men who have run through all the gamut of experience—life on the East Side, West Side, the North and the South sides; life in all parts of Greater New York; life in the courts; and, above all, thorough knowledge of laws, and the best of judges of public opinion as to just how much the public will stand; driven by the wretched system in force to all sorts of intrigue and back-door conspiracy; capable of immense self-control, and trained to an outward observation of proprieties. It is a hard combination for a Commissioner who is not himself in the open, fair and square, and the force against him. No, he must convince the policemen that he is just, that he will stand by them as well as against them, and that the game is open and that the dice are not loaded. It is useless to try to bluff an old policeman with mere talk. He has policed too many public meetings to be affected by eloquence or emphasis.

VIII

POLICE IMPOSTORS AND FAKIRS

EVERY profession has its impostors—medicine has its quacks, the law has its shysters, and the police departments, here and elsewhere, have their fakirs and gallery-players. There is nothing that sets the teeth of the average honest policeman on edge so much as to read about some of the alleged great detectives. These men always assume an air of mystery, like the long-haired quacks who diagnose the disease before they even hear the symptoms. If the case is one in which they have no official responsibility, they will shrug their shoulders, shake their heads and look important, and tell you confidently that the whole thing is being mismanaged. The air is, "If I were only there." Their one idea, when in office, is always to find a criminal to fit the crime. Given a crime to run down, you must get a criminal, no matter how or where. Think of it!—to actually confess that you couldn't find the person who perpetrated the given crime! It is preposterous; otherwise what would be the use of Sherlock Holmes? Imagine for a moment one of these men, after working at a case, admitting that he was baffled; that he had really no idea who was the criminal; that he was at his wit's end; that he couldn't solve the mystery. Why, even the friendly newspaper would cease to puff him. You hear a great deal, outside of police circles, about the tremendous successes these men have scored, whether as public or private detectives. I notice they never publish any books telling of their failures.

The founder, for instance, of the Pinkerton Detective Agency was really a great man in his way, and had a number of wonderful successes to his credit; and his successors are very able and intelligent men, for whom I have much respect; but they are no more successful than lawyers or doctors with the cases given them. Men die on the hands of the most eminent doctors, and all lawyers at some time lose a case; but if you let the great detectives connected with the Police Department tell it, especially if they have left the office, they never lost a case.

Why men and women were so foolish as to commit crime when these great personages were in office is something I often wondered at. There you were—a crime, the great detective, and, of course, detection, disgrace, and imprisonment. Probably those poor, misguided criminals broke the law only to add to the reputation of these wonderful sleuths, these deep students of human nature, these profound and mysterious thinkers. They could read your mind by looking at a pair of your old shoes. The truth is, that the whole idea of a police detective, so far as the public is concerned, is largely erroneous. The number of really good detectives is very few. There are more men at the bottom of that profession than in any other; and, like great lawyers and good doctors, the best men don't advertise themselves. Whenever you hear a detective detailing his methods and exploiting himself in print, you will know that he is really out of the business, or else he ought never to have been in it. To be a good detective requires, to begin with, natural capacity, keen powers of observation, analysis, and deduction, at least a fair education, and, in addition, a long experience with human nature in all its phases, a knowledge of the social and political conditions prevailing in the community, and a thorough acquaintance with all the undercurrents of life; a comprehensive knowledge of men and women lawbreakers, and, above all, a capacity for progressing with changes in the times and in the conditions, circumstances, and ideas of the day. A really able detective, with all this, you will generally find to be a modest, hard-working man, inclined, of course, to be reticent, but with no air of deep mystery, no taking you down into a dingy vault to tell you something of profound importance which really amounts to some trite commonplace of no practical value.

"Third-degreeing" prisoners is nothing more than cross-examining them with the use of police accessories. Some men, of course, are much better cross-examiners than others, and there is no doubt that with certain susceptible people a little dramatic touch as to place, time, circumstance, and manner is very potential; but when you meet a really clever and hardened criminal, who probably has been tried in court several times, knows the law, and is thoroughly acquainted with police methods, to start out with the bluff assumption that you know it all and only want him to confirm it, simply makes him smile. I have seen some of these old fellows look pityingly on when confronted with such methods. The scoundrel to whom I talked for over an hour, endeavoring to instil into him a fear of God and the law, and hoping he might say something which would aid justice, listened to me imperturbably and even pleasantly, and at the close gave me a profound and courteous bow, and wished me, with a marked Belgravian accent, "Good awfternoon," as he adjusted his silk hat preparatory to descending to the lower regions of Police Headquarters. A good word, in this respect, might be said as to the effects, for instance, on a first-arrest man or woman of being imprisoned for a few days in the awful dungeon at Police Headquarters. Some people would confess to anything rather than remain in that vile and fearsome den.

With first-offenders, especially weak-minded men and men stunned by the shock of being discovered for the first time, and some women, the process is at times very effective. In these interviews the conversational talents of the other sex are very much in evidence. A man, especially an old offender, can stand mute for two or three days, but a woman, unless she is thoroughly wicked, will naturally want to have something to say, and will not be willing to let the man do all the talking. If you will read the experiences of real detectives like the Pinkertons, or like those recently published by the Chief Detective of Canada, making allowance for the little literary embellishments, you will see that "the ladies, God bless them," have often furnished many a clew in unravelling a case.

A detective or police official who, in order to placate the public and to retain or add to his reputation, will push the prosecution of a man or woman without sufficient proof of their guilt, and only for ulterior motives, is worse than the real criminal. Such a one will sometimes reason like this: "This wretched devil is a bad fellow anyway; he is just as well off in prison as out of it—in fact, much better; he has no character, reputation, or future, and, if allowed to be at large, will be a menace to society. Why not put him away and please the public? Give them, too, a sense of security, restore their confidence in the police, and cease what probably will be a long and useless chase after the real criminal."

In a recent murder case there were several times when the police were so close on the trail that the man who afterwards killed himself, and who we all believed then, and are convinced now, was the murderer, might have been arrested and a case cooked up against him if those in charge of the Detective Bureau had been unconscionable fakirs and I had been willing to countenance it.

The average detective, strange as it may appear, is not a great reader of detective stories. They come from the ranks of the police themselves and work up, and few of them have any literary bent. They look rather pityingly on detective plays. I doubt very much if many of the professional detectives have ever read Sherlock Holmes, or, if they have, I am more than doubtful if they would think him really clever; they certainly would all vote him impossible. Their reading is generally confined to the newspapers, the actual facts transpiring in the lives of the men and women of the day. Here in New York, conditions with regard to crime and criminals, within the last forty years, have radically changed. A man who might have been a great detective twenty or thirty years ago in this city, if placed in charge of the Detective Bureau to-morrow would be utterly useless and inefficient. The whole conditions of life in New York are different. The personnel of the criminal classes is not the same. Certain crimes that were fashionable, as it were, thirty years ago, are now entirely out of fashion; certain methods in vogue by criminals in those days would be laughed at now. You might as well have talked to Hendrik Hudson about a steamboat as to explain that to the old men. Then, worse than all, the old men are conceited; they refuse to believe that things have so thoroughly changed. They delude themselves into the belief that things are just as they left them.

Around the police as well as firemen are a number of enthusiastic citizens who admire the organization as a whole, or have warm friendships for individual members. Men will run to fires to see their favorite firemen and policemen in action. Police enthusiasts of this type read and hear all the news and gossip concerning the department. Their ideas of the police and the administration are those of their interested police friends. Some of these people are very prominent citizens and they would frown on any contradiction of the statements of their police idols, who may be most unworthy men or clever schemers. Then, too, citizens at the very top of big affairs like to know intimately some prominent police official, just in the way many people like to know popular actors or public men, only in this case such acquaintance carries with it a sense of power and an assurance of possible extra protection. It is among these rich and influential believers in their assumed powers and knowledge that the police impostors are at their best and worst. Given a millionaire or some member of his family in trouble, and the police fakirs and mystery men have opportunities not to be neglected. Possibly you are cynical enough to think that maybe they help the trouble along in the first instance. I hope not.

New York was a comparative village thirty years ago to what it is to-day. Crime was then congested in spots; criminals' headquarters were as well known as the City Hall. The old-time sleuth would go down to certain places, mostly south of Fourteenth Street, and well known at least by reputation to all old New-Yorkers, and get some one to tell him who committed the last job, or probably have the thief himself give up the property. Start the old-timers talking about those dear old "joints" and you will give them a pleasant hour. Twenty years ago I stood on the steps of a down-town hotel with a celebrated detective, and in the course of an hour he pointed out twenty professional crooks, all specialists. They were as well known as the big men in the financial district, and it was considered a privilege to meet them. Those were the great days of old when the "raise your finger" idea originated —that famous saying that if a big police official but "raised his finger," crime and vice fled. You have to raise something more than a finger to get such results now.

Crime and criminals, at this moment, are widely scattered. They have few or no common and well-known meeting-places. Some of the most desperate criminals are very young—just beginners, their minds filled with bad literature and given over to vicious ways, degenerates associated with loafers, swindlers, and degraded women. The last series of burglaries and big crimes were all committed by boys and young men, up to that time absolutely unknown to the police, and who had no professional associates of the old type. Note the boy highwayman and burglar, "Sandrock" Smith, who terrorized the West Side, and the young fellow who secured the big bundle of collaterals from the City Bank. Vanity and the love of notoriety play a great part with these fellows. Some of them would almost commit murder if they were assured of much advertising and picturing in the sensational press, and a long detention awaiting trial, with plenty of "extras" and cigarettes, would be their idea of perfect bliss.

Down on the East Side they school and drill a little army of pick-pockets, beginning with boys at a very tender age. These boys practice new tricks every day. As the older men and women pass away they take their places; the ranks are being constantly filled. Under these circumstances a desperate burglar, who has committed his first crime, may be found in the Young Men's Christian Association or in decent employment during the day. The old veterans have all gone. They have had their day and passed their way, beyond prison-bars and police stations. Then the methods of securing valuables have changed; the modern storage-warehouse, deposit-vaults, fire and burglar proof, made of steel and well guarded, and protected by electric signals, make the financial district practically immune. On the other hand, the modern apartment-house, the tendency of rich people to live less and less of their time in town, closing up their city houses, the very size of the modern hotels, with their miles of hallways and numerous entrances, have all given a new field to the inside robber, in which he is reaping a rich harvest.

Not long ago two or three young men, who had deliberately started out on a career of crime, bought a doctor's rig and secured a hand-bag such as doctors carry with them. One drove and the other impersonated the doctor. The "doctor" drove up to the apartment-house, tried the bell of a special apartment thoroughly and got no response. He glanced up and saw that the shades were pulled down—a mistaken idea of the careful house-wife. This indicated that she was out. He then tried the bells of the adjoining apartments, and, with the bustling air of a busy doctor, went up, took out his bunch of keys, entered, and robbed at his leisure; brought down the plunder, walked out, and drove away. This was done over and over again.

In another case, two young fellows in overalls and with a ladder such as is used by the men who attend to the electric lights, entered a fashionable apartment-house on the corner of a street given over to the residence of rich people, and went boldly up past the hall-boys to a floor which was on a level with an adjoining row of brown-stone houses, all closed for the season, but filled with rich plunder. The ladder was carefully placed from the window-sill of the apartment-house to the roof of the adjoining building, and on this the two passed over. Once on the roof of the selected house it did not take long to remove the scuttle. These men spent some weeks in that house and in the adjoining houses—in fact, they found a very comfortable home while they carried off all the plunder possible; and there was no sign for the police on the outside, the shuttered windows, barricaded door, silent basement giving no indication of what was going on within.

The old veteran burglars, with a dark-lantern or half of a candle, a bottle of chloroform and a sponge, a bundle of keys, a big revolver and a knife, a kit of tools and a black-jack, belong to a school entirely different from those people. The old-time burglar survives now mostly in suburban places. He operates in New Jersey or Long Island, and attacks the isolated house; he has to make sure of the dog, and he goes armed as aforetime, prepared for a hard fight and a long chase if necessary. Then the army of confidence-men is constantly changing. The old fellows are either in jail or dead, and the new ones are not yet sufficiently known to the police; they have not built up their reputations, as it were. Strange to say, however, the old swindles still remain staple goods in the criminal market. Advertise it as you will, the deacon from the mountains of Tennessee or the peaceful villages of Indiana still comes on to get his bundle of counterfeit money, which he can't tell, of course, from the real money, and which he will religiously carry away to his neighbors in exchange for whatever good money they have.

A highly educated German gave five ten-thousand-dollar bills into the hands of the head of a clever gang of swindlers who had kindly tapped the racing-wires for him in a brokerage office at the Fifth Avenue Hotel. They received his money as a favor to him, as they were so busy taking orders from "Russell Sage," "George Gould," "John W. Gates," and "Senator Depew" to put their money on the same race. Most people, when they hear a story like this, laugh and say it cannot be true, but as I talked with the victim and the scoundrels themselves, and had indisputable evidence from the bank that the money, in bills of this unusual denomination, was passed over by it to the victim a few hours before he parted with it, there was left no room for doubt. In this connection the ways of the administration of justice are plainly shown, the leading men in this transaction, the big fellows at the top who got the fifty thousand dollars, were released on ten thousand dollars bail. It took just one of the bills to secure freedom in each case. Of course they will never come back to claim it, unless the police find them, which is very doubtful. The others in this case have just been convicted, but it has gone up on appeal and the issue is uncertain.

As a matter of fact, in this matter, the German gentleman who was allowed to mingle with "Mr. Gould" and "Mr. Sage" had never been, strange to say, in a pool-room in his life, and knew nothing whatever about betting on horse-races, having never made such a wager, and the whole thing to him was just as real and natural as if it had been true. The law in these cases is weak and uncertain, and encourages this prevailing and immensely profitable swindle. Anything that adds to the revenues of crime in any line encourages crime in general.

New York will never be free from this army of swindlers until the law is changed to resemble that of Massachusetts or New Jersey and is then fearlessly and sternly enforced by the magistrates. Running bands of these fellows daily into the courts and then running them out is a farce of the "Jack and Jill went up the hill" order.

IX

UNSANITARY STATION-HOUSES

The station-houses and the prisons connected therewith in a large number of the precincts in Greater New York are a positive disgrace to the city. This is notably so in the seventh (Madison Street), thirteenth (Delancey Street), seventeenth (West Twentieth Street), twenty-second (West Forty-seventh Street), thirty-fifth (Alexander Avenue), thirty-eighth (Westchester), fiftieth (Fulton Street, Brooklyn), sixty-third (Bushwick Avenue, Brooklyn), sixty-sixth (Canarsie), sixty-seventh (Grant Street, near Flatbush avenue), seventy-sixth (Flushing), seventy-seventh (Newtown), seventy-eighth (Jamaica), seventy-ninth (Far Rockaway), eightieth (Stapleton), eighty-first (West New Brighton), eighty-third (Richmond Hill). Many of the buildings used as station-houses and prisons are very old, have been allowed to run down, and are in bad condition. As a rule, the prisons are unsanitary, poorly ventilated, and without modern improvements. In some instances they are heated by stoves in winter which give out a poisonous coal-gas. They are damp, gloomy, forbidding, and incapable of being kept thoroughly clean, however industrious the doormen, who have too many other duties. In winter, when the windows are closed, the heat turned on, and the prison filled, some of the prisoners being drunk and incapable of taking care of themselves, the air is poisonous. Many of them are so situated that in summer it is impossible to get fresh air in any quantity into them. The cells in the present Police Headquarters have officially been adjudicated as the worst in this State. It is shocking to reflect that a great city like this has allowed such a place to exist for so long. In the administration of justice innocent persons are often arrested, and in more than one instance citizens otherwise respectable have been incarcerated for trivial offences which at the best will result in but a small fine. In the mean time, they have suffered the fearful degradation of being locked up in one of these black and filthy holes.

The prisons to be erected should be well ventilated, have modern plumbing facilities, and, above all, should be so constructed as to admit of being thoroughly washed and hosed, and lighted with electricity. In many of the station-houses the men sleep in overcrowded quarters, the beds being so close that in some instances they have to crawl over one another to reach them. In some of these buildings the dormitories are old and the walls have sunk, so that the windows are never thoroughly closed. They are freezingly cold in winter, and, being unprotected from the sun during the day, are heated like ovens in the summer. In the older station-houses there is no proper provision made for heating or ventilating them. The waiting-rooms, in which the men spend many hours while on reserve, are as a general rule dingy, dirty, uncomfortable, noisy, and in every way unattractive. In nearly all of the station-houses will be found an insufficient number of chairs for the men to sit on. The common sight is an old rickety table and a few old and worn-out chairs, dirty and soiled walls, blackened ceilings, and a rough board floor saturated and stained with years of use. The doormen, as a general rule, do their best with these houses, but they do not have sufficient assistance, and even if there were a large number of cleaners it would not materially affect the general bad conditions. There are no proper bathing facilities for the men. In the army and navy the shower-bath is universally used; tubs are dangerous and out of date. Well-tiled bath-rooms which would admit half a dozen or a dozen men at a time ought to be provided, with hot and cold showers. The bedsteads are some of them fifty years old, are uncomfortable and of a primitive type. Except that they are higher up, the dormitories are sometimes not much better than the prisons.

A wealthy lady offered to supply all of the station-houses with books, but there is no place to keep books, and the men have no provision made for using them. The reserve-room is generally on the way to the prison, and noisy processions of unfortunates are constantly clattering back and forth. The man with a book would find it difficult to get a decent chair to sit on. The offer had to be refused. In the army and navy the enlisted men are provided with the finest sort of libraries, and I know from my own experience with the navy that the men prize this. The books on shipboard are constantly in use, and good books at that. The policeman in New York spends his time at the station-house in the vilest of surroundings, in constant discomfort and at the risk of his health. Under such circumstances he has little inclination to read anything but sensational newspapers, and to swap stories and gossip about the department. The bad policeman gets a good chance here to contaminate the good one, and the whole arrangement makes for demoralization and hopelessness on the part of the rank and file.

The officers' quarters are thoroughly inferior. In the nineteenth precinct I seized upon the building next door and broke doors through. It was property owned by the city, and I furnished two nice floors there for dormitories. The captain of that precinct used to sleep in a room poisoned by sewer-gas, and subject to constant noises night and day. We managed to rig up a little place for him somewhat better.

The police surgeons as a body have condemned a great many of these houses in an elaborate report giving the details in full; the health authorities have inveighed against them; the Fire Department has protested against the danger to life; humanitarians, philanthropists, State investigators, and leading newspapers have implored the city to do something. My experience with the city authorities in this respect is not encouraging. Last year they cut down the appropriation for keeping these wretched and tumble-down barracks in somewhat decent order. Many of them need painting and cleaning; some of them have panes out of the windows, and it is difficult to get the money to replace them. In some cases the city has really no station-house at all for the men, but houses them in stables, as in the case of the sheepfold in Central Park. The best part of that building is given to the horses, and the part where the horses could not be put with safety to their health is turned over to the men. A great sewer opening is within three feet of where the men have to eat their meals. That the police in New York look so healthy, and are in the main a well-conditioned body of men, is owing to the fact that they spend so much of their time in the open air and are compelled to take exercise.

The mounted men, for instance, in Central Park, would probably all have been dead long ago from the sewer-gas which pours into the horse-barn, where they have to spend their time when not in the saddle, but for the fact that they get so much good fresh air and healthy exercise when on active duty. They thrive just as sailors do at sea, who stand the horrors of the fo'c's'le because they have to spend most of their time on the deck where the air is the best. Were it not for this the sick-list of the police would be appalling. The city authorities have either got to face the question squarely or let the whole thing go and get worse. You can get votes by building a school-house — a very proper thing to do—but there doesn't seem to be many votes in building a station-house; hence some of these people seem to be entirely indifferent. I appealed in writing and in person constantly while I was in the Police Department, but I never found any response.

It will cost probably two or three million dollars or much more to tear down and reconstruct a number of the station-houses and renovate and, in some instances, radically change the character of the others. The expenditure of this money could go on over a period of years, but the plan ought to be a systematic one. All of the station-houses should be constructed on the same general plan. It is a criminal waste of the city's money to have a lot of architects drawing different sets of plans, some of them grotesque and foolish. The station-house building should have a distinctive, individual character so that you would know it at once to be what it was intended for. This is the practice of governments in Europe with regard to public buildings of this kind. The station-house should be as distinctive as the green lamp in front of it.

The nineteenth, or Tenderloin, precinct, as every one knows, is the most important precinct in New York, if not in the United States, or probably in the world, from the amount of police business done there and from the character of the neighborhood. I found when I went to the department a set of plans for this building. Outwardly it looked like a second-class apartment-house. It gave no suggestion of its official character, and the internal arrangements were more fanciful than practical. The architect had followed the usual lines with regard to these structures. I selected a site for this building, having a southern exposure, with a small street or alley on one side, and sufficient space for another opening on the other side. The city authorities, however, overruled me, and selected another site near the present station-house, and, in my judgment, much too close to the public school there. However, that will not interfere with the character of the building. I sent for the architect in this case and had him make radical changes in the outward appearance of the house so as to cause it to look like a police station, and not a poor specimen of an apartment-house or cheap hotel. His improved plan I considered a very good one. I then appointed a committee consisting of old and experienced officers, inspectors, and men who had been on the police force thirty and forty years, and this committee was ordered to co-operate with the architect and to see that the plans were made practical and in keeping with the real wants of the police; that prisoners, for instance, would not be exposed in coming from the patrol wagons to the gaze of passers-by and young children in front of the station-house; that the present system of ushering all prisoners and complainants alike up to a desk surrounded by dozens of newspaper reporters was done away with; that the prison was thoroughly isolated from the rest of the station, and that it was as well ventilated and comfortable as any prison or detention place should be. In a word, that all those things which experience shows essential to be found in station-houses would be in the new building. These new plans were adopted, and the work is to progress on those lines unless changed by some authority. I feel sure that this new building will really be a model station-house; and if it is found in the practical operations that it meets all of the requirements of police work, then why should it not be made the standard for all other station-houses built on the same lines?

There should be a commission appointed at once, of which, of course, the Police Commissioner should be one, to consider this very important subject. A sanitary engineer, a doctor, an architect of the highest character and professional standing, and a practical builder should also be on the commission. There is no doubt whatever but that men are affected in their work by their surroundings, and it is degrading and demoralizing to the police to be housed as they now are. The city takes far better care of its horses than it does of these men. Men living amid such surroundings, and housed as policemen are, suffer a loss of self-respect, and they feel as if the community at large have no sympathy for nor interest in them, as otherwise they would not treat them like a lot of degraded outcasts.

We demand of the policeman that he appear clean and neat in his person and his uniform, and the wonder to me is, knowing what I do, that under all the circumstances he does so well in this respect. As the men are mostly married, it must be their wives who keep the majority of them looking so clean, wholesome, and well-groomed. They certainly owe nothing to the city of New York in this respect.

X

THE EAST SIDE

THE East Side, like every other side, has its virtues and its vices. On the credit side, in the main, it is hard-working and thrifty, diligent in business, mostly of the sewing, trading, selling, victuallizing, and drinking kind, and is, withal, more seriously religious after its own customs than other and richer neighborhoods. No one is really idle, for even vice is an industry there, and the men and women engaged in it work hard. A great army is at work on the little, but essential, things. There are no big machine-works or soap-factories, but there are thousands of little clothing-shops, restaurants, small stores, liquor dispensaries, and everywhere, in all tongues, trading, bargaining, buying, and selling. When there are no outside buyers the apple-cart man trades apples with the hat-cart man for a refurbished derby of the vintage of 1832. Down in the fish-market you learn facts about the fish-trade that are not generally known. You notice that the staple article of fish down there is carp—big carp, little carp, middle-sized carp, but everywhere carp. Now this fish is the coarsest and cheapest of all fish. It can live in any muddy pond; it wallows in mud like a hog, is a scavenger, and grows with remarkable rapidity. It was introduced into this country from Germany some years ago, and down there in the Ghetto fish-market it plays a most important part as a food product. It sells anywhere from three to four cents a pound, and, to do it justice as offered in the market, is the freshest of all fish, as there is always a plentiful supply.

As to the vices, they are mostly against property —pocket-picking, shop-robbing, ingenious swindling, cheating common carriers by substituting fraudulent packages for real ones, stealing cloth goods in bulk, and horse-and-wagon stealing. We generally associate horse-thieving with the far West, but, as a matter of fact, more horses are stolen in New York City in a year than in any State in the West. The careless grocer's boy leaves the horse and wagon standing alone while he goes in to deliver the package, and when he comes out it is gone, and rarely, if ever, is a trace found of it. If it had gone up into the air or down into the earth it could not have disappeared more completely. While the boy has been gossiping with the servant-maid the horse and wagon speed around the corner with a new driver, off to Hoboken, Long Island City, up into Westchester, down into Gravesend, into the depths of Brooklyn or Newark, Yonkers, or a dozen other places. Or maybe it has gone only a few blocks into a dingy stable; the wagon repainted as fast as brushes can get at it; the horse's mane clipped, his tail docked, if necessary his hair dyed until he and the whole outfit are placed beyond identification.

Gambling exists on a small scale in all parts of the Italian quarter and among the Jews, and there are not a few illicit distilleries; and over it all, sad to say, sexual immorality, far too wide-spread. The "cadet" and the open sale and barter of women have been practically abolished owing to police vigilance, but the quarter furnishes many recruits to the ranks of unfortunate women in all parts of the town. Fearful persecutions and poverty in the Old World, and bad environment, great temptations, and too much social freedom in the New World account for much of this. The horrors of the sweat-shop, the awful sordidness of life in the dismal tenement, the biting, grinding poverty, the fierce competition, the pitiful wages for long hours of toil under unwholesome conditions, physical depression, and mental hopelessness are all allied with the temptation to join that better-clad, better-fed, and apparently happier but awful army whose steps take hold on death.

The East Side is no less moral than the other sides, but the conditions are different, and, withal, in no one section of the city are there more devoted families, more affectionate and self-sacrificing fathers and mothers, more virtuous and religious households than right in the heart of the most congested portions of what are called the slums of New York.

Considering the fearful congestion of the population, the great number of families housed in each house, the closeness of the living quarters, the narrowness of the streets, and the mixture of races, the lower East Side presents undoubtedly the most complex and difficult police problem of any similar place on the earth. The density of the population in some parts of this quarter is wellnigh incredible. The police here are concerned not only with the peace, order, safety, and morals of the people, but in the interest of the city at large, and, indeed, if for nothing else than their own comfort, they have to be vigilant in the matter of infractions of the rules against the public health. In the worst tenement-houses the conditions are incredibly bad, and in the best they are nothing like as good as they should be. It is simply impossible to pack human beings into these hives opening on narrow cañons of streets and not have them suffer in health and morals. In cold days in winter when they are compelled to keep hermetically closed doors and windows, and in very hot days in summer when fires are burning in the stoves for cooking and washing purposes, the only place the inhabitants can get air a little purer than in their rooms is on the streets. The streets, therefore, are at all seasons crowded. The roadway becomes a foot-path, and wagons, automobiles, and trolley-cars thread their way through dense masses of men, women, and children, the latter being here much more plentiful than in the richer portions of the city. If the inhabitants were left to themselves they would make the street not only a pleasure-ground and promenade, but a market-place and refuse-heap. There are probably five thousand push-carts in this region, licensed and unlicensed, and selling everything from a pair of shoe-strings to a picture-hat, from a banana to a dressed goose, from a bunch of beets to a pair of shoes, from a stick of candy to an oil-stove. In some of the more densely populated and ill-conditioned streets the residents, too, have a pleasant way of throwing refuse from the windows into the roadway, giving to travel there a spice of adventure in dodging these missiles. In the Jew quarters the delights of the neighborhood are added to by the impounding of live chickens and geese awaiting butchery after the manner provided for in the Hebraic Code, so as to be made properly clean and acceptable to these people.

Much has been written about the Ghetto and Little Italy, and in addition to that you will find in this quarter also colonies of Greeks and various representatives of the Slavs. The police management is, on the whole, creditable, as up to this time there have been no very serious racial outbreaks, although there is an ill-concealed distrust of the Italians by the Jews. The Jewish population is not apt, unless under great pressure, to resort to force or to commit crimes of violence, and they have a natural horror of the baser sort of Italians who go armed with deadly weapons. At one time not long ago, when there was a great stir on the whole East Side about the Black Hand—the Mafia—in connection with some recent outrages, Jewish mothers would rush panic-stricken to the schoolhouses at the cry of the Black Hand to take their children home, and showed every sign of being panic-stricken.

When the two races first came in contact, and before relationship to each other was as well settled as now, the Jews used to peddle goods, especially jewelry, freely among the Italians, and this led to much trouble. The jewelry was sold on the installment plan, and if the Italian purchaser thought he was being unduly importuned for payments he was apt to get into a nasty temper, and in one or two instances appalling tragedies resulted. Italians, as is obvious, are very fond of showy jewelry, and the women especially were willing to assume obligations which the husbands failed to ratify so as to obtain the coveted articles. It soon became evident to both races that this trade was attended with danger, and it has fallen off greatly. The Italians also have their own push-cart people who cater to their peculiar tastes, which run largely to fresh vegetables. Indeed, it is one of the singular sights of Little Italy to see an array of most excellent-looking vegetables generally a week or two earlier than they appear in other parts of the city. I could never ascertain where these vegetables came from, but they looked very inviting. Their fresh look I rather suspected was increased by constant washing in hydrant water. The municipal bath decidedly improves the bunch of carrots, kale, and spinach, and the large and formidable-looking cauliflower. For staples you have odd and foreign-looking cheeses, and macaroni, of course, in all shapes and sizes, and gorgeous colored prints of the King and Queen of Italy and all the royal family. Bankers abound. The Italian quarter seems partial to banks, beer, cheese, and Chianti, the latter, in most instances, a very young and vigorous California wine which, acting in conjunction with what is known as the "finger" game, has probably added its quota to the number of deadly collisions which have unfortunately marred the history of the neighborhood. The "finger" game is as fine a prelude to homicide as has ever been invented. A bunch of Italians sit around a table in a dingy room and begin guessing at the number of fingers which each in turn releases suddenly from his closed fist. One man holds up a clinched fist before another man. Suddenly the man with the fist shoots out two, three, four, or five fingers. Simultaneously with the making of this motion the other tries to guess the number of fingers that will be released, shouting it out. His success depends on the accuracy of his guess. This game seems to furnish indefinite amusement, a large number of drinks, and even a free exchange of coin, and, unfortunately, many disputes which, under high-fevered excitement, has in a number of instances led to ghastly tragedies, more especially as too many of these people carry deadly weapons at all times of the day and night. I frequently appealed to the better class of Italians and the Italian newspapers to join with the law authorities for a stricter law and a more vigorous enforcement of its provisions against the carrying of these weapons. No one should be allowed, in my judgment, to sell any deadly weapon—revolver, knife, razor, or club—without entering the name of the purchaser on a book, and with a full description of him and stating his residence. These books should be open at all times to police inspection. The free sale and purchase of deadly weapons goes to the very root of the trouble.

The Italians are a hard-working, honest, and not undesirable people, and the great majority who are peaceable, law-abiding, and thrifty should not be held accountable for the bad acts of the criminal element among them. As the deadly affrays of the quarter rarely injure an outsider, there is a good deal of public indifference as to whether or not the man who has committed an atrocious assault or murder be pursued with proper vigor. This is all wrong. The community cannot hope that lawlessness thus encouraged and tolerated will always confine itself to this neighborhood and among these people. There are no people in New York who would welcome so much a vigorous enforcement of the law against the carrying of concealed weapons begetting crimes of violence as the large majority of the peaceable, law-abiding, industrious, eminently kind-hearted and friendly Italians. When they see the law authorities indifferent they naturally become terrorized themselves at the dangerous element among their own countrymen.

That there is such a thing as a thoroughly organized, widely separated secret society which directs its operations in all parts of the United States from some great head centre, such as the Mafia or Black Hand is pictured, I have never believed in the light of the facts presented to the police. That there are groups of criminals — desperate ones—whose blackmail if not acceded to is followed by violence, there can be no doubt.

Here is an Italian case—a true one: A Calabrian

peasant was standing not long ago at the corner of the Bowery and one of the cross streets. He had just come from the bank and had on his person something like one hundred and fifty dollars, a princely sum to him. He also had a watch of considerable value and some other trinkets not wholly invaluable. He was approached by a countryman from the same province, who called him by his correct name, and told him that he had known his people in the old country. They fraternized over memories of the old land, and talked about common acquaintances; and then the stranger said he had been looking for this man, because his brother was lying dangerously ill over in New Jersey; that he had been badly injured and was not expected to live, and he had deputized this countryman to go over to New York, find his brother, and bring him to him. He correctly named the brother, who really had been working in New Jersey. The unsuspecting Italian peasant, with profuse thanks for the kind offices of the stranger, and with impulsive Italian affection, agreed at once to start for New Jersey to see his brother and embrace and console him in his last hours. They started down towards one of the ferries on the North River, crossed the ferry to a railroad, and as the Italian with the money could not read English he was unable subsequently to identify the ferry. The only clew that could be gotten from him was that it had the letter "e" in it. As nearly all the ferries of the principal railroads on the Jersey side have this letter more of less prominently in their names, it was not an easy clew to follow, but it was thought possibly that the "e" stood for "Erie." At any rate, they crossed the ferry, got on a train, where he said he rode about an hour, and then got off, following his unknown guide, who took him off the highway and through a bare path, walking very slowly and telling him how anxious his brother was to see him, and how sick he was, and keeping up a rapid-fire conversation to distract him from any suspicions. When, however, the sun had set, and the late fall darkness came on quickly and found him alone in a wooded section with a stranger, he stopped short, showed alarm, and wanted to go back; but the stranger reassured him, and he followed his guide to one among a cluster of huts constituting a labor camp such as Italians put up when working on some public work or railroad. In this he was told his brother lay, and as he entered the door he was seized and bound, and found himself at the mercy of three or four ruffians, all his own countrymen. They robbed him of every cent he had, took his watch and chain, and then, drawing huge knives, they told him that if he ever mentioned the robbery to any one or put the police on them that they would kill him. They then bandaged his eyes, put him in an old wagon, and drove him over rough roads to an out-of-the-way railroad station, generously gave him two dollars of his own money with which to get home, and left him. The police trail—followed by one of the ablest Italian detectives in this country, who has handled thousands of these cases and brought a number of murderers to the electric chair, an able, conscientious, intelligent, and modest man, Detective-Sergeant Petrosini —led to a deserted laborers' camp in northern New Jersey, but of course the robbers had stopped there only temporarily, and left no trail behind them.

For the purpose of dealing with these Italian criminals I found it most effective to create a special squad under the charge of Detective-Sergeant Petrosini, and the results were most gratifying from the very beginning. These men were Italian-Americans who were regular policemen, and were at once put in plain clothes and intelligently directed by Petrosini, working in all parts of Greater New York. The very existence of this secret service among the Italians had a deterring effect on the professional criminals. If I had had the opportunity I would have been glad to follow this up by working in conjunction with the Commissioner of Immigration, Hon. Robert Watchhorn, who earnestly requested such co-operation in endeavoring to deport these criminals who bring such discredit on the Italian communities and colonies here in the United States. I am satisfied that an active participation by the Police Department with the Federal authorities in this respect would beget very important and satisfactory results from the beginning.

The East Side Jew rarely commits a crime of violence, such as assault or murder. Among themselves disputes are mostly confined to wordy arguments, some of which I have no doubt would be highly interesting to any one familiar with Yiddish. They are a logical and interesting people, and argue with great vigor and earnestness, but the argument ends as it begins. Those who have come here fresh from Europe, especially during the recent troublous times, have at once a great suspicion and fear of the police. The words "police," "law," "prison," conjure up dire possibilities in their minds, and for self-protection they naturally become evasive and secretive. The children prove themselves marvellously adaptable to the new surroundings. The first thing the new-comer generally does is to begin peddling. He either gets a pushcart of his own, hires one by the day, or peddles for some one else. The buzz of trade goes on at all hours of the day, and practically all hours of the night. They like good food, and no matter how saving and thrifty, they have their little pleasures. The Ghetto swarms with clubs—men's clubs, boys' clubs, women's clubs, associations. Their crimes in the main are against property. Of late it must be confessed this quarter has produced quite an army of pick-pockets, and altogether too many burglars, who confine their operations to robberies of silks, furs, and cloth from the neighboring shops and manufactories. A typical robbery of the quarter is to have a shop given over to the making of, say, shirt-waists, entered, and rolls of silk to the value of one, two, or more thousand dollars stolen in a night. Once stolen these goods disappear with the greatest rapidity. A system of "fences" is elaborately arranged, and two days after they are gone the chances are that the owner is probably rubbing elbows in a car with the girl whose shirt-waist is made of the stolen material. It is scattered all over Greater New York, Long Island, New Jersey, and up the river; cut up at once and manufactured into clothing. Everything is most ingeniously and cleverly arranged; nothing is left to chance; system, order, great shrewdness, and marked ability characterize the whole operation. The forced intercourse of the tenement-house gives the depraved and criminal, especially in the case of the young, a great opportunity to contaminate those who are compelled to associate with them. These children of misfortune and persecution are at once tossed into fearful promiscuity with manifold temptations and vices, and that so many fall, therefore, is not at all to be wondered at. It was here that the "cadet" flourished; and there are not a few Fagins who thrive on thieves' schools for boys —boys who are mere children. The children of the shop robber are very apt to follow their father's profession. These young boys are most skilful pick-pockets and pocket-book snatchers. A group of women in one of the Ghetto streets are marketing; along comes a boy about sixteen years of age apparently trying to ride a bicycle; he is stumbling and falling, mounting and dismounting. All at once he gets in the midst of the group of women, who have their satchels open, and down he goes, wheel and all, in the among them. He clutches awkwardly here and there at them. In the mean time, confederates have been busy picking pockets and snatching pocket-books right and left. The young thief is on his wheel in a jiffy; the plunder is slipped to him and he is off. This is only one of numerous tricks. As they get older they take to the car-lines, railroad stations, and public assemblages.

The population of the First Inspection District is 624,092, which is exceeded only by three cities in the United States—namely, New York, Chicago, and Philadelphia. There is an additional floating population of probably seventy-five thousand, chiefly strangers, sea-faring men along the river-front, lodgers in lodging-houses, and the flotsam and jetsam of a great city, who have no permanent abode, but go to swell the immense population on the East Side. There is in places a denser population to the square foot than there is in Bombay, India, which is supposed to have the most congested population of any place on the earth. Here, in a way nowhere else on the whole earth, goes on the assimilation of what might be called the crude, raw material of immigration into full-fledged citizens. The fires have hardly died out after the massacres in Kishineff before a steady stream of the wretched and unfortunate fugitives flying from persecution pour into these narrow streets and towering tenements. Every outrage, upheaval, or economic distress in almost any part of the earth is evidenced here by new-comers—pict-uresque in costume, utterly un-American in appearance, habits, tradition, and history. Jarring tongues, warring religions, and semi-barbarous customs are in evidence everywhere. I doubt if a police force anywhere in the world could handle these people as well, say, as they were under Inspector Max F. Schmittberger. Schmittberger, himself a man of administrative ability, speaking two or three languages, was well fitted for the task. A veteran policeman, possessed of adaptability and good judgment, he understood the district and the people thoroughly. He was a most striking figure in this environment. There was an air of paternal government about the neighborhood when Inspector Schmittberger in his official capacity would stroll along one of these streets—men and women running after him, telling him their troubles, asking advice, imploring protection, or begging mercy for some delinquent, and all speaking the various languages of their country and gesticulating violently. The Inspector gave his decisions like a Cadi. In one block he probably advised against a divorce and in favor of the taking back of a wayward girl, or he had announced the finding of a runaway husband, or compromised a case about allowing a vendor of many-hued ice-creams to push his stand two or three inches out on the sidewalk; arranged to look after the synagogue when the new Rabbi made his appearance next Saturday; warned the Greeks that there would be numerous battles of Marathon if the colony didn't leave some portion of the roadway free from the push-cart, or stop making striped candy in unsanitary cellars; refused pistol permits to Tony, personally rubbed his hands over several Italian gentlemen, detecting bundles of hardware that turned out to be guns and knives under their coats, and had them promptly arrested; warned several Neapolitan gentlemen that fire-crackers must not be fired off after 2 A.M. during the numerous celebrations in Little Italy; discoursed firmly with Hungarian subjects of the Austrian Empire on the habit of slipping Long Island brandy into the coffee in the numerous cafés; and was positive that weddings held in halls where beer kegs line the sides ought not to continue from early on Saturday evening until early on Monday morning, and that promiscuous sleeping on the floor of the hall itself was to be discouraged as a form of extreme sociability not warranted even by weddings; firmly refused to allow kegs of cider and frozen carcasses of geese, with geraniums planted in soap-boxes, old mattresses and feather-beds to remain any longer on the fire-escapes—and this every hour of the day and every day.

The intelligent foreigner, and if, indeed, the millions of Americans who know nothing about this place, want to study how under American laws and customs we assimilate and make over the raw foreigner, or even the semi-barbarous alien, let him go down here and learn. The educational process goes on steadily, and the police as a general rule are tolerant and show intelligence in handling these masses. Arrests are comparatively few, and many of these victims of oppression, persecution, and violence have to be assured first of all that the law there is fairly administered and that the police are for their protection, not to do them wrong.

A dishonest police administration of a district like this would affect the whole country. These people are going to stay here and they are going to become citizens, and their first impressions they will get mostly from what they see in the conduct of police affairs. The police are doing a far more important work, so far as the future citizens are concerned, than probably any other officials in this land. The subject must be handled intelligently. The police must study these people, their habits, customs, ideas, and somewhat of their history. And right here let me say a word for what is probably altogether the most remarkable institution in the United States. It is called the Educational Alliance, and is endowed by some of the richest and most influential Jewish citizens in New York. Men like Mr. Straus, Mr. Seligman, and Mr. Schiff have given great sums of money to it, and in doing so they have benefited the whole community.

This is the place where the children who come from Russia and other parts of Europe serve a short novitiate. Here they are put into shape as American citizens. Here is a little girl coming out of the school where they have been singing patriotic songs, American songs, waving our flag. She has a big bundle of books under her arm, and is about fifteen years of age. "What are those books?" you ask. "Well, history of the United States, geography, chemistry, grammar, algebra." "How old are you?" "Fifteen." "How long have you been in this country?" "Ten months." "Where did you come from?" She names an obscure village in Russia, one of those provinces where the Jews are most numerous. "Do your father and mother speak English?" "Yes, a very little." She has no accent; speaks English fluently and grammatically.

Her teacher says she never fails in any lesson. She is a hard student; has a good head; shows marked intellectuality. She is only a sample of thousands. Some of the girls are much younger, and have been less time in this country, but all are eager, bright-eyed, and studious. It is the same with the boys. We go up in the library of this building, which has in it a gymnasium, a school of dramatic art, school for sculpture, school for cooking, school for painting, headquarters for a military company, a savings-bank for children, with a large army of depositors of from two cents to a dollar; rooms for the teachers to live in, executive offices—it would take an entire book to tell all about this wonderful place.

The stone steps have been literally worn away by the millions of young feet that have gone up and down them. From time to time they have to be replaced. The building is practically never closed; something is going on in every hall and every room, on the roof; indeed, the roof is the most active place of all, for that is the great playground. But to the library. Here these Jewish children, many of them but a few months in the country, are lined up to take out books and return others. The officers of the library are very busy; the pressure is urgent, immediate. Each child wants a book, and generally knows exactly what book it wants. Out here are a number of boys ranging from eight to twelve, looking over the card catalogue. I put my hand on the head of a boy who might have passed for one of Raphael's cherubs—a handsome boy, with big eyes, clear skin, and good features, a manly looking little fellow too. "Well, my boy, I suppose you want a nice Indian story?" The boy looks up at me half-wonderingly and smiles rather pityingly. "No," he says, "I want Herbert Spencer's *Social Statics.*" The boy next to him wants fiction—*Uncle Tom's Cabin.* This book, I found, was printed in both Yiddish and English, and was in great demand. One could understand why these Jewish children, who had been driven out of Russian towns, felt sympathy for Uncle Tom and Little Eva. Of course they had no understanding whatever about a color-line, such as we understand it here in this country. Many of the boys are taking standard histories; not a few want books on social and economic subjects.

Although the politicians do not seem to fully realize it, there is a great army of socialists being recruited in this part of the city. It is an intellectual movement, and has many lecturers and readers and able defenders. The political leaders seem to think if they get these people bailed out of police-stations, or vote them the privilege of doing business with the push-carts on every day in the week, that the whole field of statesmanship has been covered. Dilettante club-men, who give dogmatic opinions on socialism, had better keep away from these trained, experienced, hard-studying, intellectual athletes.

These people, especially the young, are very inquisitive, bright, and progressive. The intellectually hungry multitude are being fed. Little girls take away books nearly as large as themselves. I would have liked to see the children taking a few books which would tell the boys how to be pioneers and fight Indians, and the girls how to behave when they were cast away on lone islands in mid-ocean; and, above all, fairy stories and good sea tales, with a dash of salt spray in them. I am quite sure they would not appreciate *Little Lord Fauntleroy*. These children meet real sorrow early, and run up against hardship too young to appreciate the less serious troubles of one whom they could only envy.

Back in the reading-rooms, old and young are busily engaged in reading works on sociology, political economy, history, biography, and, in a great many instances, scientific books and books of travel; some standard novels, Shakespeare, and American poets, the latter for patriotic sentiment, for patriotism is proclaimed here. One studious-looking boy, about fifteen years of age, is, like the others, making notes from a large book. I look at it and find that it is the history and critical study of the effects of the battle of Saratoga on the Revolution. I ask him why he is reading this book, and he tells me he is making an analysis of the character of Benedict

Arnold, and in doing so he wants to study the battle in which he took such a conspicuous part. I glance at the notes and I am dumfounded; they might have been made by the professor of history up in Columbia University.

I go back to the centre of the big room and look at all the activity of these children—inquisitive, active, and yet wondrously patient. Here is a race that can wait and wait until they win. There is food for reflection for any statesman, deep thinker, or any one who is making a study of the future of the United States who will go down to the Educational Alliance. It will give him thoughts to keep him busy for many a day, and he will know a great deal more than when he went there. It isn't just to know that Mr. Schiff, Mr. Straus, or Mr. Seligman, and other excellent citizens gave so much money last year to support it, or so many thousands of boys and girls go in and out, or that this is such a room and that is such a room, and that it does good. This is merely a surface look, interesting, of course; but here is a great factory where you are turning out the men and women of the future, thousands, hundreds of thousands of them. Here is the West Point where the Jewish battalions of industry and commerce, in the professions and in politics, are being drilled; here are the very children going down to the roots of things. Think of it! Herbert Spencer preferred to a fairy story by boys and girls!

In an honorable and fair competition the American boys and girls out in the little red school-house in the country, and up in the big public schools on the West Side, have got to meet these regiments. They will certainly not win by idling or slip-shodding their work, or spending their time chewing gum and reading *Bowery Dan, the Sleuth of Hester Street*, or pilfering money to go to cheap theatres to be fed on "Tracy the Outlaw," "Wedded, but no Wife," "The Shadow of Crime," or to see the antics of the "Buckingham Brothers." As the game is a fair one, if these East-Side boys and girls win out who can deny them the prize? Yes, you will learn a great deal more here than in books, newspapers, or magazines.

You can go down to one of the police precincts in this district and find more people in it than in whole lists of American cities. You could go down and find, in one block, more population than in some places that have three railroads running into them. A small precinct down here will show more population than a whole section of the map of New York State north of Yonkers. Just think of it! You could put Boston and all its culture down here and it would not have as many people as this one police district, and the same for Baltimore, Cincinnati, San Francisco, and my old Congress district over in Jersey City. And, by-the-way, there you are. Wouldn't you think that these people would run over these narrow boundaries—that this pitcher is so full that the water would run out—and spread out into New Jersey and Staten Island? No, they are very gregarious and social. Then, too, they are, after all, a bit timid and of course foreign. They feel much safer here, where they are in masses, than if they were scattered; and many of them don't take kindly to farm-life or the country, so that you could not get them off into farming districts.

The fifteenth precinct has a population of 156,375; the fourteenth, 127,493; twelfth, 115,705; seventh, 104,116; thirteenth, 89,035; fifth, 27,023.

Here are the nationalities: American, 25,677; Ireland, 20,833; Germany, 93,052; Sweden, 153; Italy, 30,612; Scotland, 11; Russia, 405,507; Greece, 390; England, 77; France, 6; China, 63; Hungary, 40,728; Spain, 209; Denmark, 6; Canada, 6; Austria and Slavonia, 6636; Japan, 60; West Indies, 9; Switzerland, 1; Finland, 29; Norway, 19; Belgium, 1; Cuba, 2; Poland 15.

Under the head of American are many children and young people whose parents have not been long in this country. Of the 25,677 I should doubt very much if it represented twenty-five per cent. of native stock; in fact, I think that is a very liberal estimate. Therefore, under the head of American, you are really dealing with the children of foreigners lately arrived from the countries which follow in the table. Under the head of Russians the race is almost altogether Jewish, and a large portion of Jews will be found under the head of Hungarians. How lonely that one Swiss, eleven Scotchmen, and six Frenchmen must feel! The police force assigned to govern this district comprises 1 inspector, 8 captains, 34 sergeants, 16 detective-sergeants, 38 roundsmen, 732 patrolmen, 18 doormen, 6 matrons; a total force of 853—or one patrolman to every 852 citizens.

The synagogues number one hundred and two. These buildings range from small halls to large and pretentious edifices. The reader will note the number of public and private schools—eighty-five. The public-school buildings are, as a general rule, good, modern, up-to-date, and well officered. The city has been very liberal in this matter. Indeed, some of these schools are most imposing buildings, covering a whole block, and the children who attend them are a vast army; and yet the overcrowding goes on. The city is building and enlarging, but the population grows. Of public parks and playgrounds there are five. There are free gymnasiums. Take it all in all, New York does well in this part of the city in the way of institutions, and spends millions of dollars in the work, which is of vital interest to every portion of the United States. There are many Christian missions here, dispensaries and libraries. The population reads a great many newspapers. The Jewish papers have an immense circulation. They are mostly printed in Yiddish. I hope they are fair and honest and American. I have heard them denounced by Jews and Americans.

All of the new-comers take kindly to politics. Politicians here are very active. Each party is after the new citizen, and they are willing to go a long way to get him. The politicians have no prejudices and few scruples, and what they want is the vote, so they don't trouble themselves much about theories. Little favors, big favors, must be dispensed every day and night; constant little acts of kindness, prominence at social and religious functions, championing the victims of outrages in Europe, burning words for despots, thick gloves in winter and picnics in summer are more effective weapons than learned discussions in reform clubs or scholarly and ponderous editorials in conservative journals that are devoted to literary style and to an affectation of philosophic calm far removed from the "madding crowd" of this Babel-tongued East Side.

XI

CHINATOWN

NEARLY everybody who comes to New York wants to see Chinatown; and all along upper Broadway, from morning until midnight, one can see huge touring-cars with signs telling one that for two dollars, or thereabouts, one will be taken to Chinatown and back, and shown all the sights of this Oriental quarter. Chinatown, so called, is a constant source of trouble and anxiety to the police. It is an ulcer-spot on the face of the city, which would be much better off if the whole place could be levelled and rebuilt. An ocean of business surges all around it; old tenement-houses give place to warehouses; but, like a little island in the midst of an angry ocean, Chinatown lives and thrives. One reason for this is that into old rookeries, dilapidated, ill-smelling, unventilated, and unsanitary, are thrown a great army of Chinese tenants. Every inch of the property, from the sidewalk to the back yard, if there is any, brings in rents out of all proportion to that of property in other parts of the city. Ten Chinamen will live in a little room ten by twenty, and, possibly, pay in rent what they could hire a flat for in Harlem.

Chinatown is inhabited largely by a lot of Chinese parasites who thrive and fatten on their unfortunate countrymen, a few degraded white women and degenerate white men, and some whites who trade on its vices. There is also a credulous army of tourists that throng in and out through narrow streets, buy joss-sticks at a dollar apiece in alleged joss-houses, and eat weird dishes and inhale strange smells. As the Chinese exclusion act is a bar to the importation of Chinese women, the so-called Chinese wives are probably, taken altogether, the most wretched, degraded, and utterly vile lot of white women and girls that could be found anywhere. Here and there among them are a few who show remnants of former decency. These latter are the victims who were first attracted by morbid curiosity to the mysteries of Chinatown, then, losing caste with even their own class in other parts of the city, they became slaves to the most degrading habits of Oriental civilization. Opium and alcohol are a fearful combination, and, when joined by nicotine, become, not the three graces, but the three queens of the bottomless pit. They soon leave dreadful and revolting marks on the human body and stifle the last signs of life in the human soul.

Everybody in Chinatown smokes "dope" or tobacco, and generally both. The Chinaman takes kindly to beer, and his white outcast friends to "rectified" whiskey or wood alcohol, and the tourists are supposed to swell the coffers of the big saloons with a "pull" by "buying wine." Everybody gambles. They bet on everything in Chinatown—on the news of the day, on the weather, on cards, dice, buttons, number of seeds in an orange—anything and everything in which the laws of chance play a part.

Out in any of the suburban towns around New York you will see the Chinese laundry sign. The laundryman is always busy, no one ever saw him idle, and the shop is always open; he is scrubbing, rinsing, and squirting water from his mouth like a douche over shirt-breasts, counting up change with the use of little black and white balls on a wire, looking wise, serene, and innocent. Chopsticking his English as he does his rice, unnoticed, and apparently noting nothing, John goes the even tenor of his way. His food costs him little, his lodging practically nothing, and when he deducts the rent of his little shop and charges up the starch and soap, the rest is all clear profit. He is his own banker, and only he and the rats know where the vault is.

John has one thing to look forward to: the New York visit. He must temper this austere and virtuous mode of living with a calm and carefully measured degree of Chinese deviltry. When John starts for his New York spree he looks just as placid and virtuous as he does in the midst of his labors. He has carefully made up his mind how much he is going to spend and what he is going to do. He is headed for Chinatown—wine, women, and song, or their equivalents, with, of course, the inevitable run-in with the gambling tiger. In fact, the gambling comes first and last; and when John gets back to Yonkers or Newark, East Orange, Montclair, or Little Neck, he looks just as innocent, honest, and contented as ever, but the money he took with him is down in Chinatown. The only sign of real deviltry about John when he returns is that he often smokes a big, black cigar, sold at about five for ten cents.

When John got to Chinatown his countrymen were waiting for him; in fact, he was overdue, and there was a volley of Chinese explosives in the way of language, and John goes into the fan-tan game at once, like a hungry cow into a fat pasture, only with very different results. It is not necessary to go into the details of the game. The one thing certain is that John is going to lose. These shiny-faced, overfed, and carefully shaved friends of his from Canton feel that John owes them the money, and they are going to have it whether they play the game with buttons, cards, or dice, or any other mechanism or guess-work. John will guess wrong in the end, and will be lucky if he has enough left for a big pipe of "dope" and is able to pay for a place on a narrow shelf in a living tomb, in which the air has apparently not been disturbed for the last century—I think this air, which is totally devoid of oxygen, is imported from China with the sharks' fins and is carefully safeguarded from escaping—and there he lies as dead, to all appearances, as the mummies up in the Metropolitan Museum, dreaming of far-away Cantonese enjoyments, and undoubtedly happy. As he is bred to this business, he can get up in the cold of the morning, stick his hands away down into his blouse, and cross over the Jersey ferry in the gray dawn back to East Orange or Piscataway, asking no questions and answering none.

The Chinaman who lives in Chinatown does no work, as a rule. These are the fellows you see idling there all day in and out of the alleys and shops. All these other Chinamen who work in the laundries, or even the servants in the big houses and on the ships, are all laboring for these bosses. These fellows are really a fine lot of scoundrels. They are very cunning withal. They are divided into various societies, "tongs," as they are called. They have alliances with white politicians and shady lawyers, and are exploited by all sorts of societies; are useful to guides, touring-cars, and white saloon-keepers, and good for a story for the newspaper men, and their acquaintance is sought by a certain type of men about town who want to appear as knowing a lot about the mysterious and unknown; but in reality there is nothing romantic or mysterious about these fellows, and the town is not a good specimen of the Chinese way of living. It is dirty, sordid, and mean, vicious and criminal, and, grafted on Western civilization, is abnormal and not even picturesque. If John, from Yonkers or Sag Harbor, does not lose all his money at the first encounter with the tiger, he has the delights of the Chinese theatre, the chop-suey, or may even be allowed to gossip, in a social way, with the élite among the womenkind to be found in the town. There are also Chinese delicacies and dreadful drinks, and everywhere bad cigars and worse cigarettes.

The head men of the "tongs" are clever fellows in their way. They have a sort of trust, so as to handle the profits of Chinatown, by which they grant permission to gamble, insure protection from the police, create the impression that they have a "pull" with the head "Melican" men, furnish lawyers for defendants in court, and give wise advice out of court. The profits are so very great that they have never been able to agree among themselves as to forming the whole thing into one trust, so there are two or three distinct factions, each of which claims the other is absolutely bad. There are a few Americanized Chinamen who, some of my friends who know them well insist, are really and honestly reformers, but I have always been doubtful if Chinamen are in any numbers ever converted to Western civilization, even when they assume our clothes and copy our manners. His own civilization and religion is so very much older than ours, and is so thoroughly satisfactory to him, that at heart I am quite convinced the Chinaman has a profound contempt for our ways. Heaven forbid that I should say a word against the good men and women, many of them my own friends, who are engaged in the work of converting the Chinese to Western ways and ideas. I wish them every success, and I sincerely trust that my own opinion is an erroneous one. From the police point of view, Chinatown is simply a robber's roost, thriving on gambling, swindling, and vice at the expense of the large army of honest and industrious Chinamen throughout this section of country.

The so-called Chinese theatre is a huge cavern of a place, suggesting an unventilated and uncleansed stable. I suspect that the whole acting there is fakery gotten up to impose on the Caucasian visitors. The playing consists largely of noise, and has been described over and over again, so that we need waste no time on it. Five minutes there would do man or woman, with a sensitive nose, for twice that number of years. It must, however, be a profitable venture, because it is always packed.

The leading citizens of Chinatown have their virtues, too. Outwardly, at least, they keep themselves very neat, and shave their faces, heads, and ears until they fairly shine, like billiard-balls. Narrow little razors are even inserted in the nostrils, and the growth of hair is concentrated entirely in the cue. The Chinaman buys and eats good food, having a weakness for chicken. Chinatown would scorn the food sold in the Ghetto or Little Italy. Chop-suey is getting a hold on New York. The chop-suey restaurant springs up in all parts of the city. The Chinaman is a good cook, and, with pork and onions, and two or three dozen other ingredients, this stew is becoming as standard as somebody's coffee or somebody else's breakfast-food. Then, too, the chop-suey joints are attractive to some people because they are entirely unconventional, and a great degree of freedom is allowed the patrons. The lone man who dines frequently in a chop-suey restaurant is apt to make friends, and there is generally a certain Bohemian atmosphere in the neighborhood of these shops. Many of the big "tong" leaders in Chinatown are financially interested in these places in other parts of the city.

If John is married to an American wife she will tell you that he is the best of husbands, and points to her clothes and her jewels and to the mingled Western and Eastern luxuriousness in which she lives. The half-breed children are not attractive, as a rule, most of them being unhealthy-looking.

A crooked police captain, given sole charge of Chinatown, could retire at the end of a year comparatively rich. Chinatown has its own government, for which two parties at least are generally contending. To this government all Chinamen in the town pay tribute—rent, blackmail, or whatever you may call it. In turn, the top man, if permitted, will deal with the police and the politicians, paying for protection and immunity. Fan-tan, the sale of lottery-tickets, opium-smoking, disorderly houses, and gambling in all its forms, if not strictly repressed, are to be found night and day. For this the ordinary Chinaman pays gladly and liberally, and if the police will not harry him, or, as it is called, "police him hard" and often, he has no reasonable fear of the courts. The conviction of a Chinaman is the rarest thing. Few magistrates and juries believe Chinese witnesses, and on cross-examination, through interpreters, they sit there moon-eyed and smiling, and contradict themselves a thousand times in half an hour. When the case is closed, if the witnesses on both sides are Chinamen, the best thing to do is to flip a coin in the air and guess head or tail as to which side ought to win. If the police and the magistrates are not eager to convict, all they have to do is to throw up both hands at this medley of testimony and bundle the defendants out of court. When the police themselves have made out a case, with their own witnesses, there are so many Chinamen to be sworn for the defence, and so many adjournments and lawyers' arguments, that the case may drag along for months and then be lost in some new excitement.

A crooked policeman runs very little risk in taking graft from Chinatown. Gin Sang keeps a little gambling-place in the basement, hands up his protection rent to another Chinaman, and he in turn to another, until it reaches the top man, who hands it over to the white collector, possibly an outsider, and there it disappears as completely as if it were dropped in mid-ocean. It has been handed up like a bucket of water at a village fire, but no one as yet has succeeded in tracing the chain. In this connection let it be said that in the world of graft there is a slang name for the Commissioner, and in the "olden days" the "collectee" would ask the collector if a certain nicknamed one was interested. A nod and a smile were reassuring.

Chinatown would not exist long if there was any really honest public opinion that wanted it driven out; but it has white friends, influential ones—the real-estate owner, the men in politics, members of rich societies, mistaken philanthropists, a little regiment of lawyers who make money out of it, newspaper men and magazine writers who exploit it, sight-seers who think it represents life in China, and some people who distinctly think that it is a decidedly picturesque addition to the town and a good place to take a country friend once in a while and let him see something old and Oriental. If an honest police captain, therefore, attempts to put a heavy hand on the place, there is at once an outbreak of sympathy for these innocent and honest-looking Chinamen, long articles in the newspapers about warring "tongs," and about good Chinamen, bad Chinamen, Christian Chinamen, and police brutality. The big, heavy-handed Celt on the police force is not supposed to understand the finesse of Oriental civilization; he is thought to be too brutal in treating this "yellow peril." Then, too, there is the suspicion, unfortunately founded on too many facts, that in times past corrupt police officials have derived large revenues from this rank and ill-smelling little town. A Chinaman in the shadow of the law would give up everything to a policeman, including his cue and his hopes of heaven, for the law in China means dreadful things if it gets hold of you, and the Chinese are well experienced in the ramifications of graft in their native land.

Not long ago I had, in the office of the Commissioner, Tom Lee, the mayor of Chinatown, so called, and Colonel Mock Duck, as the newspapers nickname him, with their respective counsel. What I am saying here is something in line with the talk I gave Mr. Duck and Mr. Lee, and they were good enough to acknowledge that I was not, even from their point of vew, far from the truth. Mock Duck represents what might be called the fighting element; and here again the carrying of deadly weapons plays its part among our polyglot population. If it were not for unceasing police vigilance, every Chinaman in this town would be found carrying a large-sized Colt's revolver. The Chinaman seems to have a great respect for the size of the weapon and wants the very largest caliber. This is easier for a Chinaman than for a white man, because he does not depend on the hip-pocket, but conceals this huge gun in the loose folds of his clothes. I told their representatives they ought to practise in the shooting-galleries, if they must shoot, as they are wretched marksmen.

On the occasion of their numerous murderous outbreaks they generally kill innocent by-standers. Not long since they killed an Italian woman, and I begged Duck to see that his fellows took to target-practice before beginning again. The Chinese feudist, when he steps out of the alley to fire at his rival, apparently closes both eyes, turns his head, and then works the trigger until the ammunition is exhausted. This accounts for the fact that hundreds of shots are sometimes fired with little or no effect, except possibly to people who are in no wise concerned in the fight. On the other hand, their mode of murder is very cunning. They will start an open row in one street of the town to attract the police, while a section of the clan around the corner are pouring storms of lead into the alleyways, basements, and across the street at their enemies. The best marksmen in Chinatown usually aim for the back. A broad, bloused back is a good target; and as the Chinaman doesn't take any chances, but presses the muzzle against his victim, there is usually some work for the Coroner. They entrap their enemy more skilfully than a hunter would stalk a deer, and the big American revolver, as I have said, is their favorite weapon. From the police point of view, this is an advantage, being more noisy than the knife.

The Chinaman is a good patient in the hospital, generally quiet and uncomplaining; and, while tuberculosis seems more or less prevalent in the town, I have noticed but very few Chinese funerals. They would be noticeable because they are gala affairs. I am not, however, an authority on the health statistics of Chinatown.

The most noticeable murderous outbreak in Chinatown was recently when they invaded the theatre, crowded to its doors, and, having fired off several giant fire-crackers among the audience, began pistol-practice on a number of selected victims. This was one of the most sanguinary battles in the annals of the town, and, so far as convicting any one, the police and law authorities are helpless. There is, moreover, a dangerous tendency on both the part of the police and the other law officers to regard racial outbreaks and murderous affrays, when confined to certain desperate characters, as matters calling for little or no action. If one Chinaman kills another in a feud, public opinion does not seem to demand any extraordinary effort to punish the murderer, and the same is frequently seen when one professional gambler or bad man murders another in one of the up-town resorts.

Italian murderers are proverbially difficult to convict where the witnesses are all Italians; and then, too, the unwritten law seems to be that the dead are well out of the way and that the rest of the community are not much concerned about the affair. I think this is a very dangerous state of affairs. It is sowing fearful seed here in New York to let the idea get abroad that one man can kill another in an affray and the police and law officers show themselves entirely indifferent. Murder, under certain conditions, therefore, becomes a crime of less offence than failing to shovel snow off the sidewalk in winter, and people yet wonder at the spirit of lawlessness in this and like communities.

If the top Chinamen, their white confederates, and the landlords were not making a great deal of money out of it, Chinatown would not last a week. Detective-Sergeant Costigan gave Chinatown the hardest blows it ever received. He had it on the run, and in another six months or a year there would have been no Chinatown. They were being slowly starved out of it. The white man with a "pull," the rich yellow man at the top, and the other interests that make money out of it, including the tourists' guides, were desperately bitter in their opposition to this new condition of police affairs. It was an opposition that ran deep and strong and carried powerful influences with it. Costigan had under him only seven plain-clothes men, but they were tried, true, and experienced; when it was necessary, outside agents were used.

Whether the operations against the town are directly from Headquarters or the precinct, it has to be made a special post. Of course, if the police policy is to let it run along in its own way, it will go right back to former conditions, and wherever it comes in touch with the police body it will corrupt it, and, moreover, be a trap for foolish women and degenerate men. It will spread and grow like a poisonous ulcer, developing lesser towns in other parts of the city, and then, in addition to all the other social and police problems, we will have a real Chinese question, too, in New York.

XII

HONORS FOR PHYSICAL COURAGE

THE worst critics of the New York police force are willing to admit that personal bravery and physical courage are marked characteristics of the force —stopping runaways at the risk of life, jumping off docks at midnight to rescue the drowning, ascending and descending again and again into smoke-choked and flame-begirt tenements to rescue helpless men, women, and children, standing between mad dogs and panic-stricken crowds, pursuing burglars to the death, wrestling with robbers at midnight on the roofs of houses, facing and putting down murderous mobs, however great in numbers, even better than veteran soldiers armed with rifles—all these and a hundred other exhibitions of devotion to duty and lack of fear go to make up the almost daily record of the New York police force. The men are stimulated to these heroic acts in no small degree by the fact that it entitles them to commendation, honorable mention, or honorable mention and the police medal, the highest form of honor that the department can give to a man or officer. These honors are very important to a policeman, because in making up his record before the Civil Service Commission they count for so many points. Under the rules of that body these honors can only be considered when given for exhibitions of physical courage. I have contended that it ought to be given for especially intelligent service, such as the capture and conviction of criminals, or moral courage in resisting temptation, as in refusing large bribes and convicting those who offer them, and in many other instances, and, as Commissioner, I have given commendations and honors for such work; but the Civil Service Commissioners insist that under the law they can only recognize those which come from acts of personal bravery. This I consider very unfortunate.

There is a tradition throughout the force and among the newspaper men who write exclusively about police affairs that many honors and commendations have been given to policemen for acts of alleged physical bravery which were entirely undeserved; that cases have been deliberately faked up on testimony which would not stand a cross-examination and Commissioners deceived into granting these honors. They will tell you of how a drunken tramp under nice conditions of summer weather will be disturbed in his sleep on the string-piece of some dock and rolled over into the water so that a couple of policemen could fish him out with a rope and then make their application for commendations or a medal; or of how the victim himself consented to a little sousing so as to help his friends on the force. They will even say that some of the runaways were not running at all; and there is one story, more or less authenticated, of a certain policeman who got a medal for stopping the flight of a mad steer, and who was made a hero in spite of himself. It seems that when this maddened animal was tearing down the street the officer joined the other citizens in getting out of the way, but the steer gained on him to such an extent that he had to dodge behind a lamp-post. The steer rushed to the post, struck it square with its head, and, one horn projecting on each side, the policeman was compelled to seize the animal by both horns. Round and round the post they went, the officer literally hanging on to the horns for his life and putting up prayers for the strength of the post. It would have been a sight to charm a Spanish bull-fighter. He held on until help came and the animal's attention was distracted in another direction and a few ounces of lead put in its brain. He was not the first man who found himself a hero without knowing why.

The number of applications for honors is very great. The foundation for the honor is generally laid by some citizen who writes the Commissioner, captain, or inspector, and tells him of the heroic action of the policeman in question, and possibly he is disinterested and thinks the man's case should be looked after. Investigation shows that the majority of these letters are genuine, but there is a suspicion over a number. Is the writer a particular friend of the policeman? Has the latter urged him to do the writing? Is the case being worked up in cold blood instead of one of spontaneous enthusiasm on the part of the citizen for the valor of the policeman, and are the facts as alleged? So many duties devolve on the Police Commissioner, and this matter of the giving of honors I considered so important, that I appointed a board of honor, so that the case had to sift through the captain of the precinct, the inspector of the district, and then to this board, composed of the First and Third Deputy-Commissioners and my own secretary. The idea worked well from the start. Under this careful sifting a large percentage of the claims were at once rejected, and a healthy division of opinion was shown by those who reviewed the case, the reasons being given pro and con, in writing, so that when the Commissioner finally came to act he had the result of a careful and impartial investigation by different reviewers all along the line until it reached him. This was done to rescue these honors from really becoming dishonors. When a man got a medal under this system his case was so thoroughly tried out that the rest of the force knew that he had earned it, for under this system objections were invited and evidence contravening that offered by the friends of the officer was solicited; and, indeed, the orders were that the board should, if necessary, sit as a trial court and examine witnesses. This impressed the force as fair and just, but of course it was not in all cases pleasing to those whose claims were rejected.

The medal is the highest honor the department can give. It ought not to be given lightly or inconsiderately, and certainly "pull," influence, and personal friendship should be entirely eliminated. The claimants for these honors, in many instances, use every personal influence on the Commissioner, and deluge him with letters from those who cannot in the nature of things know the real facts in the case. Under the above system the medal came to have a real meaning. Everybody in and out of the force knew that the man had earned it, and the policemen looked up to the wearer and respected him; whereas, in many instances, formerly they looked upon him as a fakir and impostor, and had no respect for his courage, either morally or physically. In a number of cases the board would divide as to whether the man should have commendation or honorable mention, or honorable mention with or without the medal, and in a large number of cases they found he had only done good police duty. Physical courage does not always imply moral courage, and in some cases men without any physical fear have been found otherwise utterly unworthy.

There was one man who came before the board about whose courage there could be no question. This man jumped into the East River at midnight, on one of the coldest and most tempestuous nights of winter, to save a man's life. The current of the East River, as every one knows, is very swift, but on this night in question it was laden with ice-floes. The unfortunate man who had fallen into the stream and the policeman who jumped to save him were carried by the swift current half-way across the river in the ice-cold water, before the policeman could reach him and bring him ashore. Every incident connected with the affair was dramatic and thrilling, and there was no hesitation about awarding a medal. Between the decision to give him this medal and its actual deliverance it came to my knowledge, to my great pain and disappointment, that this man was of very weak fibre. His unfortunate weakness did not take the form of grafting or shirking his work. He was afterwards tried for a number of small offences. I never will forget my painful interview with him when I laid before him the charges that had been made against him. The poor fellow was just as morally weak on certain sides of his character as he was physically brave. As I talked to him he could do nothing but stand there, while the perspiration and tears ran down his face.

Some of the very bravest men, physically, have, in the ordinary line of duty, where it required ability to resist temptation or called for an exhibition of civic virtue and manliness, proved lamentably weak and unreliable. On the other hand, a big, brave, manly fellow is apt to have good stuff in him all the way through. Sometimes a policeman who wouldn't hesitate to rush out in the street and stop a maddened team of horses, and probably be dragged by them and have nearly every bone in his body broken, would be a man you would hesitate to trust with any duty that required integrity and uprightness. However, this is not confined to the police, for every one who remembers the period after the Civil War will recall how often the criminal courts were called upon to pass sentence on men who had been the very bravest of soldiers. Personally, I always want to believe that a brave policeman or soldier is a good man every way and under all conditions. Where two or three officers are concerned in a brave deed, it is sometimes difficult to adjust the individual merits, and little jealousies will creep in. There is one thing certain, there ought to be a reviewing tribunal apart from the inspector and captain. This was found necessary in the army after the Spanish War. The board there passed upon all the cases resulting from that war, including that of the President himself.

I can only answer for these honors given during

my administration, and I am sure that, under the system then adopted, those who received them were worthy of them. I regret that the law does not allow the Civil Service Commission to take a wider range in allowing for these honors in marking percentages. Before this commission, honors only count as for one grade or rank. If a patrolman received either commendation, honorable mention, or honorable mention and a medal, it would only count on his promotion to roundsman. Thereafter the honor would be of no use to him in any examination he might enter for promotion to other ranks.

Honor to whom honor is due, but be sure it goes only to him who has earned it. Unworthily bestowed, it reflects no credit on him who receives or on him who gives.

XIII

THE POOL-ROOM EVIL

THERE is no form of gambling so popular and altogether so prevalent in Greater New York as the selling of pools on horse-races. This is really a great industry, and employs quite an army of men. It has a strong hold on the populace in general, and among all classes of people. It is generally favored by the politicians, not because they are more immoral than other men or more addicted to gambling itself, but the district leaders of all parties, especially those belonging to the party that happens to be in power, are allowed to name most of the employés for the pool-room. For instance, a man would not, as a rule, open a pool-room in any assembly district unless he had some sort of assurance of friendship and protection from the political leader, or knew, at least, that he was not an enemy, and in return the leader is allowed to name the employés, the number, and the salary, which, on the average, is about five dollars per day per man. Sometimes a thriving pool-room will carry a pay-roll of ten of these men. The men literally do nothing to earn the money; it is simply a way of allowing the leader to take care of his constituents and lieutenants.

I do not mean to say that every leader could drive the pool-rooms out of his district, but I do say, from experience, that where the leader is unalterably opposed to them they will rarely be found in his district, and if they do try to do business he will be the first man to complain. I know of one assembly district where the leader drove every one of them out, notwithstanding the fact that they tried to bribe and bully him. He was a thoroughly honest man, and when a pool-room invaded his district he came to me directly, giving me all the facts he knew, and served notice on them that they must get out. This resulted in driving all pool-rooms out of his district.

A political leader will often know more than the police about all forms of vice in his district, and he can be a great aid or a powerful and dangerous opponent. When it is considered that immense sums of money are spent at places like New Orleans, so that horses may race before a scattered handful of people all through the winter, and that all this machinery of men and horses is working simply for the pool-rooms in New York and a few other large cities, one may get a faint idea of the profits of this business. If pool-selling were thoroughly extirpated in New York, including the making of hand-books, it is doubtful if any of the great winter tracks would keep open and pay expenses; there would not be sufficient people at these tracks to make bets, and without betting horse-racing would stop, except, possibly, as the sport of a few disinterested gentlemen who might run horses for the delectation of themselves and their friends, and, of course, at an entire loss so far as any money returns were concerned. The morally sterilized, betless race-track is just as reasonable and as probable as roulette-wheels at church prayer-meetings. In summer the race-tracks near New York draw many from the pool-rooms. It is a question simply of physical proportions and money: the track will not accommodate as many at one time as all the rooms, and many who go to the latter to bet two dollars could not afford to go to the track and pay for an admission. The difference in morals I leave to others; no "mere cop" could deal with the question.

Pool-selling is heavily capitalized, and is interlaced with big enterprises, and adds to the revenues of the telegraph and telephone companies. It was demonstrated beyond question that the Western Union Telegraph Company did receive very great revenues from selling information with reference to horse-racing. Before they were driven out of this alliance by public opinion the racing bureau was an open feature of their headquarters in New York, managed and carried on by an experienced corps of men, themselves in close touch with the sporting world. A man who opened a pool-room contracted with the company for a wire service and an operator. The operator had to be paid for every day in advance; the company did a strictly cash business; the operator brought the money to the office every morning before he started for his afternoon work at the pool-room. The race-tracks under special contracts with the company gave it a monopoly of the racing news, and it in turn sold this at an immense profit to itself.

The Western Union directors did in good faith take the company out of this intimate relation with pool-selling, but the profits were so great that the temptation was too strong not to patch up a new method of doing the business. There is now a new and independent concern to furnish pool-room news, and is backed by a syndicate of leading sporting men and politicians.

Of course this new company for selling news to pool-rooms has to get its own information from the track over the wires of the telegraph company, and very naturally it must pay for its prompt deliverance so that in turn it can furnish its patrons in the pool-rooms with the results on the track. If the law was enforced strictly, and there was a really strong public opinion behind the effort to suppress pool-selling, no telegraph or telephone company would be allowed for a day to aid and abet these so-called news-distributing agencies, when it would be proved beyond question that they were simply agents for the pool-rooms, and if there was any doubt about the law new legislation would be had. Suppose the Police Commissioner had the power to John Doe all concerned, and was clothed with magisterial powers for that purpose? He can issue a warrant now, but that does not reach the point aimed at.

I asked the telephone company—practically there is only one company, and of course they look at this matter largely from a business stand-point—to give me their co-operation. Their legitimate business is so very great that I am willing to believe the statements made to me repeatedly by its officers that they did not want any alliance between themselves and the pool-rooms. They had no pool-room department, and in many instances they showed a laudable desire to aid the police up to a certain point. They also manifested — something rather unusual in modern corporations—a desire to look at the question from the moral as well as the business side, and exhibited a praiseworthy sensitiveness about having their company connected in the public mind with this vice. Both they and the telegraph company, however, were entirely unwilling to go into an alliance with me by means of which they would delegate to me some of their corporate rights to inspect their own property—that is, to allow their men to co-operate with those of the department in demanding inspection of suspected telephones and telegraph instruments by going in at racing hours on the premises and insisting on the company's rights to see that its instruments were not used for the purpose of breaking the plainly expressed provisions of the penal code. They took the general ground that it would not be proper to subject any customer to police espionage as to what he was doing with the instrument hired. Such action, however, would only have been taken in obviously suspicious cases, and where both the company and police authorities were agreed that no danger would come to an innocent holder of a telegraph or telephone instrument.

Subsequently the telephone company did co-operate with the police in detecting customers who supplied pool-rooms in the vicinity by allowing the latter to connect their instrument by a private wire, so that an innocent-looking telephone in a drug store or liquor saloon would really be dead to the place where it was located during the racing hours and connected by wire with a pool-room in the neighborhood, the latter place furnishing its own telephone transmitter and receiver. These instruments can be purchased in the open market, so that if a man wanted to start a pool-room, say, a block away from a friendly liquor saloon, all he would have to do would be to buy a telephone instrument, run a wire to the liquor saloon, have the liquor man allow a connection to be made, and the latter's instrument, especially during the racing-hours, would then become a mere dummy. There are many expert telephone and telegraph men in the employ of the pool-rooms.

If a telegraph or telephone instrument was taken out to-day from a pool-room, confiscated, and sent back to the company, the chances are that the same concern, under a different name, would go down in a few days and get a reinstatement of this service; or possibly the very same party, under an assumed name, would get the service next door to the raided premises, or, failing this, apply to the courts for an injunction against the company. These cases were numerous, and were contested by the telephone company.

The pool-selling industry was not permanently injured by the police attacks so long as a complete and absolute divorce could not be established between the telegraph and telephone companies and the pool-rooms. It must be admitted that the temptation, from a financial point of view, to both companies is very great. They can stand, as it were, on their rights, which is to furnish service to any customer who is willing to pay for it; close their eyes, make no investigation, and see to it that the payments are promptly made. I have no evidence whatever that the companies charge different rates to the pool-rooms from other customers, and I am willing to believe such is not the case.

After all, we hark back to the main point, which is that there is no united, insistent, and earnest public opinion demanding the suppression of pool-rooms. It is true a Police Commissioner who winks at them or closes his eyes to them is an object, and very justly so, of public suspicion, and every police official in district or precinct where pool-rooms may exist is on the defensive. The general public, in my judgment, is not so much concerned about the pool-rooms themselves as they are as to whether or not the police are getting paid for letting them run. It is, of course, equally true that every once in a while some organization — civic, social, religious, political, or philanthropic—will jump into the arena and begin a violent agitation against these places, and the same can be said of the newspapers. A newspaper will go along for months, maybe a year, ignoring the pool-room evil; then all at once, if it wants to fight the Commissioner, or for some personal or political reason, or because its policy has changed with regard to the department, it will come out and give whole pages to the location of these places and the wide-spread character of this vice and its connection with the telegraph and telephone companies.

There is no uniform line of conduct in the newspapers with regard to this matter. Sometimes they will all ignore it, even when it is at its worst, and then again, when it has been reduced to a minimum, they will exaggerate it. The readers, therefore, of the daily papers are practically in ignorance of the true state of affairs. Once in a while they will shriek for a rally to the defence of the public morals, and then, when some object is achieved, apparently the thing is dropped. But the Police Commissioner is the sworn officer of the law; he ought to know whether pool-selling is going on or not; he cannot abate it unless he has knowledge at first hand. Captains and inspectors are certainly not going to place evidence before him on which they can be tried, and, as stated above, the newspapers cannot be relied upon. Now, in my judgment, he not only has a very grave legal responsibility, for which he ought to be held accountable, but the moral side of this question is far-reaching and ought to appeal to every just-thinking man and woman.

From the beginning of my administration until its close there was not one minute in which a ceaseless warfare was not kept up on these institutions, and for which I personally incurred the bitter enmity and hatred of influential men in and out of politics. I never deluded myself that I was earning any great public encomiums in doing this work; in fact, it was quite otherwise, and, indeed, then and now, men not in any wise interested in the business, and who claim to be my friends, thought my activity in this respect a great mistake. They said, and said truly, that the general public are absolutely indifferent to a hard and fast suppression of gambling; the open town has many friends. As against this my own views are given elsewhere herein. Honest citizens, misled by newspaper statements, were quick to upbraid the Commissioner for giving any attention to this work at all, and the men engaged in the industry, and their friends, were constantly pointing out the increase of other crimes and telling the public it was because the Commissioner had a large number of men engaged in the work of suppressing pool-selling. As a matter of fact, when I left the office, the number of men engaged as Headquarters men in enforcing the law against vice numbered just twenty-five—not sixty, or two hundred, as stated in the newspapers—and no body of men connected with the Police Department worked harder than these; and, by the culling process, there were no more honest men connected with the police force. They all had been through the fire of temptation and come out unscathed. The head of this force, Sergeant Costigan, was one of those rare men who are naturally, aggressively, and absolutely honest. He could have been made independently rich in a short time had he wished to do so. He was threatened and bullied and tempted in a thousand ways, and still remained an honest and, if anything, a better man than when he began the work. He was, withal, a most modest man, who never boasted, and talked little of himself. Men like that should be encouraged in every possible way; they are the very salt of the police force.

If the community really understood the pool-room evil I am sure it would not be tolerated. It is all very well for respectable and well-to-do men to say that there is no reason why they should be deterred from making a bet on a horse-race if they wished to; that they are allowed to do so at the race-tracks in summer; and that in London and other great European capitals, even in the leading hotels, men freely make wagers among themselves as to the result of horse-races. I have no inclination to discuss the ethical question with reference to gambling in general. Possibly quite a number of people will come forward and say that this sort of betting is not as bad as the prevailing craze about "bridge," where bets are made in private houses; and it may be asked why a party of rich men and women should be allowed to bet on "bridge" contests on Fifth Avenue, and poor men and women should not be allowed to gamble on horse-races on Second Avenue or the Bowery.

Gentlemen who come back from Europe and indignantly tell how they were allowed to make a bet at such a hotel in Paris or London, demand to know why they should not be allowed to do the same here in New York, ignoring the fact that there is not any wide-spread form of this vice in London, Paris, Berlin, or St. Petersburg as there is in New York; that in this case, and especially in this city, the great industry is backed by large sums of money, and is, indeed, in the end, feeding and fattening on the poor and the desperate, the weak and the criminal. It is far more insidious than the Louisiana lottery, and it goes home to the same people. Look what a hue and cry was raised about the Louisiana lottery; how the whole country arose to it; how the entire powers of the Federal government were used to suppress it; how it revolutionized the politics of a great State, until it was finally driven out of the country. There the poor and deluded ticket-buyer was kept in suspense for a considerable period before the drawings; but in the pool-room he can get results in a minute; and in some of the poorer districts the amount wagered is even less than the cost of a fractional part of a ticket in the lottery.

When, through the disinterested efforts of the late Captain Goddard, the policy evil was driven to the wall and its rich backers sent to prison, the pool-rooms immediately began to adapt themselves to the situation. The small bettor was encouraged. No book would be large enough to tell the amount of misery and crime which the pool-room, with its two, three, four, or five hundred clerks, mechanics, and laborers, small store-keepers, employers and employed for patrons, brings upon the whole community. My mail as Police Commissioner was stained with the tears of mothers begging the suppression of the place which was rapidly converting the son from an honest, industrious, and reputable young man into an idle degenerate, a swindler, and a criminal; or the wife was imploring me to close the place where the husband spent the money which was intended to clothe, feed, and support his dependent family; brothers and sisters begging police protection from this spider's nest in the neighborhood. Betting on horse-races, for the infatuated victim, is the most insidious and dangerous form of gambling. The wretched victim is constantly stimulated with the idea that he is betting on his judgment and knowledge; hence pages in the newspapers about the performances, form, and pedigree of horses, the honesty and ability of jockeys; and hordes of half-crazed men and women rushing after tipsters and touts like herds of poor, doomed cattle climbing the fatal gangway to the slaughter-beds at the big abattoirs.

If three sample raids could be made to-morrow on the East and West sides and in Brooklyn, where at least from two hundred to three hundred men would be found in each one of the pool-rooms, and their histories truthfully set down, there would be a shout of indignation go up from the whole community for the strict enforcement of the law against these places.

The pool-room business, like others, is mainly a trust; a few men reap the large profits. An independent operator in the pool-room business stands about the same show as the small fellow fighting the tobacco or beef trust. Here, for instance, we start a pool-room on the East Side in a rather poor neighborhood. An old and unsightly loft is rented by the man who is to be the manager. This manager is often simply an employé of the big syndicate that runs the whole business. The landlord asks no questions, makes no inquiries, and is only too glad to get a generous rent. The rent is generally larger than it would be from an honest tenant. Frequently the powers that be in the neighborhood let the landlord understand that his friendship in this matter will be reciprocated. The police must bring home to him a guilty knowledge, and in the district courts any attempt to evict the tenant, if submitted to a jury of the neighborhood, generally fails.

Successful prosecutions of landlords, even when the police are in earnest, are nothing like as numerous as they should be. If the case is started it wabbles along, finally is lost in the maze of other things and forgotten; or the landlord, after one or two legal victories, gets insolent and brazen, and defies the police, and the pool-room is as firmly established as a reputable business on the corner. The loft once rented, a partition is put up, dividing the room into two unequal parts. Often there is no door whatever in the partition, only a small hole that would trouble a fat pigeon to go through. Behind the partition are the human spiders themselves, principals or agents of the big octopus. About one o'clock in the day, or about the beginning of racing-hours, say, at New Orleans, the wretched army of unfortunate and desperate gamblers, after having passed through several outer guards and two or three doors stronger and thicker than those of some safes, gather in this dingy, illy ventilated, smoke-poisoned room; for in order not to make the thing too public the windows are generally blinded, and the average gambler pays little attention to what he is breathing, fevered as he is by the devil of chance, and possibly throwing dice as to whether he will go home after the day's session or go to the river and the morgue.

In many of the pool-rooms, to make sure that the victim cannot escape by any possible means with his money, there are various games, such as stuss and Klondike, played in the large outer room before opening time and between and after the races are over. The main thing that the victim wants to know is the names of the horses, the jockeys, and the betting-odds as established at the race-track. An attendant before the race pastes lightly on the wall a sheet called the "dope-sheet," which gives this news. The poor, foolish crowd cast their eyes on this, and the jabber and chatter about horses goes up; tips and pointers are exchanged, and the wretched assemblage is at fever heat. The crippled newsboy who sold papers until two o'clock this morning, and who slept last night in an alley, will search his tattered clothes for the dollar and a half earned by that slavish work, and hand it through the little hole in the partition, where the big, human hawk swallows it with the same ravenous zest as his brother in the natural world would gobble up a poor, newly born little field-mouse. No one sees the man behind the partition. In some cases it is so arranged that the hand which takes the money cannot be seen by the bettor; the police spy might seize the hand or note marks on it, or quickly ink it with indelible fluid, so our hawk has to be very cautious.

When the police are honestly and vigorously fighting the pool-rooms the latter become exceedingly cautious, cunning, and ingenious. The guards are doubled, barriers are strengthened, modes of escape are cleverly planned. Sometimes the "dope-sheet" is let down from the floor above by unknown hands, and the victim might go there for a year every day and never get a glimpse of the unknown manipulators, who have all planned to make their escape at the first stroke of the police axe, the first shout from the man below, or the first friendly warning of the electric buzz.

THE POOL-ROOM EVIL

When I went out of office on January 1, 1906, there were less than forty pool-rooms in the whole of Greater New York, and these places were protected by the highest writ known to the courts—that of injunction. The obtaining of these injunctions was a great imposition on the courts and an outrage on the community. Here is how a sample injunction was obtained: A place was rented in one of the up-town streets; on the outside door was painted a doctor's sign; in an outer room leading into the pool-room some few ear-marks of the doctor's business were installed—a tattered medical book, a skull that seemed to grin and laugh at the whole business, as if some new phase of life had opened up since it went under the sod or rolled off the dissecting-table. "To what base uses may we come at last!" The poor, outraged head of the dead used as a decoy and protection to these irreverent and greedy swindlers. The wretched degenerate who had once been a doctor is brought from one of the saloons on the East Side, and answers for his name on the door. Having long ceased to practise medicine, he is now simply a sot and the butt of the liquor den which he frequents. He is given a few dollars and a cheap suit of clothes, and is kept sufficiently sober to be exhibited at the place for an hour or so every day.

The next thing to do is to get the police to raid it as a pool-room. If the captain is dishonest he will make a bargain with the proprietors to run off a fake raid. The hour and time is fixed; the police batter in the doors, crack the windows, and find the doctor surrounded by his "patients," examining their tongues and feeling their pulses. He is shocked and outraged and indignant. He and the proprietor and the "patients" hasten to prepare their affidavits; a well-known firm of lawyers who make a specialty of this work are called in; a bundle of papers is taken over to Brooklyn; the judge instantly grants the writs, denounces the Police Commissioner, shrieks for personal liberty, talks about Russia, and threatens the Governor if the Commissioner is not removed at once. The writ now is really a license. If the captain is an honest man, it is flaunted in his face and he is dared to put his finger on the sacred place which it guards. If he is dishonest, and in on the game, he makes a few showy threats and informs Police Headquarters that the place is now protected by injunction and asks for further instructions. If the Police Commissioner should instruct him to raid it and invade it, the Commissioner would very probably be hauled into court, held for contempt, and sent to jail.

If one were sure it could be closed and stay closed he might be willing to stand even the unsanitary surroundings of Raymond Street jail, in Brooklyn, which, under any circumstances, might be equally as pleasant a place as Mulberry Street. But if the place were closed as a doctor's office, it would probably open in a few days as a rug emporium, and, when raided, men, and even women, found examining a choice collection of rugs. In one place, where the dummy business was selling what was called "boys' pants," a pair of little knickerbockers, about nine inches long, covered with the dust of years, and made up of wretched shoddy cloth, was marked twelve dollars. This legitimate industry was upheld in a Brooklyn court as one of the mainstays of trade in the metropolis, and the police were enjoined from even looking at it, or practically from passing by the house in which this "business" was carried on.

These injunctions, among other things, enjoin the police from making special posts of these places or warning the people against them, and the same, of course, applied to Raines law hotels and disorderly houses. From the first I insisted that this was not the law and that the courts could not enjoin the police from this proper surveillance and protection of the public, and from legitimate efforts to enforce the provisions of the penal code. A few weeks ago the Court of Appeals decided this matter, and the police have now their legal and proper powers restored to them, so that these writs will not have the value they did before.

The decision, of course, very properly says that if the police wantonly, unreasonably, and without evidence break into any place, claiming that there is a felony being committed there, that they do so, as it were, at their own risk, and may be held, individually, in damages for their illegal act. This decision, in my judgment, is altogether with the police. If they should break into an innocent and honest man's house, of course they ought to be made to suffer damages; but if they break into a place where reasonable and circumstantial evidence points to the commission of a felony, and when they know that the proprietor is an ex-convict, a notorious breaker of the law, a man of no character and of evil reputation, even when they make a technical mistake, a jury of decent men will not be apt to hand out large sums to the complainants. The injunction, therefore, need no longer be a scarecrow to prevent the police from honestly enforcing the law. In several cases, after attempts were made to convict these perjurers, letters from me to the District Attorney urged that if one or two of these people could be sent to State-prison for a long term, the whole fabric and swindlery upon which these injunctions rested would come down with a crash.

Now it is often said and believed by a great many people that an honest police captain can get the necessary legal evidence against a pool-room. I agree that if a captain is thoroughly aggressive, earnest, and absolutely honest, the pool-rooms in the main will avoid his precinct; but the police have not the powers of the District Attorney's office. The Commissioner has no John Doe proceedings at his hand; the powers of the Dowling act are not lodged in him; he cannot send for the men whom he has arrested in a pool-room or gambling-house and subject them to a severe examination so as to get their evidence; and after trying with police and outside agents to get into pool-rooms I can truthfully and impartially say that in many instances it is very difficult — that is, where the department is systematically and consistently trying to suppress them.

I flatter myself that the pool-room business was reduced to a minimum at the close of 1905; that a great moral purpose had been achieved—namely, the driving out of the poorer class of bettors and the almost absolute prohibition against new-comers. On the first day of 1906 the pool-rooms in New York had regular lists of customers and had a fixed number of patrons. Again and again, after unusually clever plans have been adopted, they have refused admittance to men whom they could not possibly suspect, saying that after the 1st of January, 1906, they hoped the business would again be open so they could take in new people. They were all looking to January 1, 1906; lively betting going on inside as to how long I would continue in office. In one instance, a man actually obtained work on a new building, and, being a good mechanic, worked honestly at his trade, and then with money obtained from his fellow-workmen, and in his overalls, and with good credentials, tried to get in a pool-room in the vicinity. The proprietor was perfectly honest in telling him that they would not let in any new customer, but that if he would come around after January 1, 1906, he was sure that he could run the business a little more openly. The same was true of an agent who worked as a waiter in a restaurant that led to the pool-room. He handled the roasts and hash for six weeks, but they couldn't let him pass the threshold of the strong doors to make a bet; they would allow some one else to take his money up-stairs, but he never got inside of the pool-room.

One pool-room of prominence which was captured during that period was Wakely's, on Sixth Avenue and Forty-second Street; Wakely had long enjoyed such immunity that he became bold and careless, it being freely charged that he was a favorite in police circles and had powerful friends in other walks of life. Of the latter there is no doubt. He had one or two "scares," but he got overconfident, and it was freely boasted at the time that every police official in that raid would suffer; that the shores of Flushing, the woods of Staten Island, and the shady lanes of Wakefield were waiting for them, and that they had turned their faces towards Dismissalville, marked, possibly, by heavy fines on the way. I have not heard so far that any great good luck has followed the raiders. It required real courage for a policeman to raid that place, and he should have the encouragement, approval, and support of the Police Commissioner. It is not merely the question of stopping one or more pool-rooms in a case like this, but the moral effect on the police themselves and the community at large is very great. It is an advertisement that the police administration is not afraid of any power, and that it is in earnest. No dishonest administration ever really and earnestly strikes a blow at the great money interests behind vice; being dishonest, they are afraid of retaliation and exposure. In this connection, too, the plight of an honest policeman is sometimes pitiful. If the Police Commissioner is not behind him in supporting him he is thrown at once to the wolves and remorselessly sacrificed.

It is very unfortunate, but true, that a large number of the people, misled by the newspapers and agitators of one kind and another, and convinced, I regret to say, by the demonstrated dishonesty and inefficiency of some of the police themselves, come to the conclusion that the whole body is thoroughly corrupt; and therefore with them it is always more or less popular for the Commissioner to crack a head, find a policeman guilty, excoriate and dismiss him. No Police Commissioner will ever succeed in the office who is not as quick to commend and support as he is to punish and reprimand. Suppose, for instance, that every newspaper in New York, and every city official from the Mayor down, should raise one long shriek for vengeance against the police officials who made such a raid? Suppose that all the powerful interests that centre in and around such places as this, and all their friends in and out of office, should demand that these officers be humiliated, degraded, transferred, and punished by the Commissioner, and at the same time he knew that they were thoroughly honest men, zealous officers, intelligent, able, and, above all, courageous, both physically and morally. What would be his duty? There cannot be but one answer to that: He should stand by them to the last against the whole combination of newspapers, public officials, crooks, and their friends, so-called business men, and other interested people, and defy them so long as he was Police Commissioner to put an angry finger on such officers. When he has done this he can look the public in the face, and he can afford to express his contempt for the little manikins and accidents in office, and the subsidized and corrupt scribblers who bring disgrace on honest journalism, and who prostitute a high calling, a noble profession, to base designs and sinister and dishonest methods.

If all the victims of the pool-rooms in New York

could come back from the poor-house, the insane asylum, the prison, the river, the graveyard, the potter's field; if all the vast army of wretchedness that grovels in low groggeries and prowls in alleys, and lives God knows how and sleeps God knows where, could be marshalled up as part of the fearsome array of hopeless and helpless pool-room victims, the indifferent pulpit and the shamefaced press would beget a real public opinion which would aid and encourage those who are to enforce the law. There would be hearty co-operation between the police and the District Attorney; graft, "pull," and politics would be swept aside and this evil practically annihilated.

Policy and pool-selling are twins, and prey upon those who can never afford to enter the big gambling-houses. I wonder who was the wag who sent me an anonymous letter once asking me to raid Nos. 2–6 William Street, which is the Cotton Exchange. Come to think of it, was it really a joke? A few gentlemen, who, of course, are not gamblers, were at that time slaughtering the lambs in the cotton-fields down there and fixing prices without regard to commercial conditions, nature, or the laws of the Almighty.

However, what I am trying to say is that the gambling spirit is wide-spread in the community. With the Dowling law as a weapon, I do not believe that gambling on any general scale can be carried on in New York if the District Attorney exercises his powers, and there is an earnest co-operation between him and the police. The well-to-do man who patronizes the high places will not take the risk of being exposed through this law. Some time after the law was passed, and when Mr. Jerome put it in operation, I made up my mind that the gambling situation, to a large extent, was in his hands. Of course it does not absolve the police from every effort to repress it, or from at least ascertaining where it is located, getting all the evidence they can with regard to it, and in treating it the same as they would the pool-room. If the gamblers know the police administration is in deadly earnest for their suppression they become cautious and timid, and this, communicated to their patrons, drives off the latter. Rich patrons go to the houses when they think the powers that be are allowing these places to do business.

I have no reason to believe that the police get any considerable revenues from the large gambling-houses, especially since the passage of the Dowling law. Of course a gambling-house will "sweeten" the captain if he is willing to stand for it, just to get his good-will, and they will do the same for an inspector. A big, top man may be protector of some large and exclusive gambling-house—a sort of partner. Generally the better ones have an influential clientage and they don't like to be annoyed with police interference. They all contribute to political funds; they do so without any threatening, and it is really a part of the business. They stand, as it were, for a certain assessment, which may go wholly to politics or to the police, or to both; and they have agents in places where one would never suspect. They are naturally anxious that the press shall say nothing about their workings or start an agitation for their repression. When the press is silent, business thrives. A sensational story about large losings begets a deep silence around the gambling-houses. Generally, if the loser has a business reputation at stake, he will say nothing; if he is a sport, of course he is too game a man to talk about it.

The roulette-wheel is a most popular form of gambling in New York. A deacon in the church of a near-by city told me not long ago that the man who manufactured nearly all the wheels in use in the United States was his neighbor and fellow church officer, and that lately he had confessed to him that there was scarcely any such thing as an honest wheel, and that the fraudulent direction of the wheel was one which could not even be discovered by expert investigators. I presume, from what he said, that there is a nice adjustment and balancing of the wheel which makes it capable of answering the hand of the manipulator as he desires. To avoid controversy, I should say I have a lot to learn about roulette-wheels.

The combination gambling-house and pool-room is not infrequent. That was the case at Wakely's and in a house cleared out some time ago by the police on Thirteenth Street near Fifth Avenue, and it is so in many other places. These places are called double-deckers, the gambling being generally on the upper floor.

I have heard men say that a police inspector or captain can readily get the evidence against a gambling-house and pool-room such as will hold in a court of law. It is true that a pool-room or gambling-house cannot be long in a precinct without the captain knowing it; but if it is running with great caution and secretiveness, he or any outside agency, however sanguine they are, may find the getting of such evidence very difficult.

That brings us to this: What should a really and aggressively honest police captain do to get pool-rooms and gambling-houses out of his precinct? He must try by every possible means to get evidence in the usual way, but he must not stop at that; if he does, he won't succeed. Talk about it as you may, he has got to enter upon a war of extermination, and he has got to keep at it every day and every night. He must literally hammer them down, and he will have to take all the legal risks of raiding them. There should, of course, be no brutality or wanton assaults; but no captain will ever keep pool-rooms and gambling-houses out of his precinct, no matter how honest he is, if he is not willing to put the mailed-hand on them and harass them in every possible way the law allows. He can drive the disorderly persons off the sidewalk in front of the places; he can rigorously excise the saloons which permit the hand-book; he can call in the Health Department and inspect the premises, especially during the racing-hours, to see if they comply with the building laws or infract the health rules; he can pursue the landlords without cessation; he can arrest the professional bettors whenever he gets the opportunity, as disorderly persons living without visible means of support; and, in one word, he can serve notice, not by talk, but by actual work, that he and they are engaged in an irrepressible conflict, and that either he or they will be driven out of the precinct. If he begins to compromise and apologize, or goes at the work half-heartedly, of course they will win out easily. It is a game in which they match wits. When they get an injunction, he must get something more effective with which to meet it; he must fight the injunction in the courts by showing that it was obtained on perjured evidence.

When the proprietor or manager of a gambling-house, pool-room, or disorderly house knows that a captain is thoroughly and aggressively in earnest, knows also that the captain is watching his plain-clothes men and detectives, and cannot be fooled by them, he will, as a general rule, move at once out of the precinct. There is one thing certain, in such a precinct the evil will not increase and spread. If this is so, it will be asked why cannot the Commissioner, if he ever finds out the conditions in a precinct, try the captain and convict him solely on the ground that such places exist? The answer is that given before. The rule of law is well settled. At the trial the Commissioner must produce evidence beyond a reasonable doubt showing that the captain had a guilty knowledge of these places and made no effort to suppress them, and in this respect the captain will be protected by long lines of decisions showing that these efforts must be those strictly and clearly within his legal powers and not otherwise. If this is not done, the courts will overturn the decisions of the Commissioner as fast as they are made. No people know this so well as the police; in fact, I should say that the average policeman is a pretty fair lawyer when it comes to police trials. There is one thing every policeman reads, and that is the review of police trials in the upper courts. They can quote the decisions with the glibness of a professor in a law-school.

The reader must forever get out of his mind the idea that, in New York, pool-selling and gambling are sort of sporadic vices conducted here and there by shady characters, dangerous, disreputable, and criminal men. It is indeed true that the admitted agents who run some of the low order of these places are ex-convicts and men with bad or criminal records, and in a few instances they are desperate and dangerous men. But, taking the thing as a whole, it is simply a vast business run on business principles, backed by men of influence and power, capitalized liberally and on a strictly cash basis; there is no watered stock or over-issuing of bonds on the part of these syndicates; everything is down to actual money.

This great business has its alliance with other business interests. It helps the sale of luxuries, dress, jewels, wines; it asks no questions about rents, it pays the highest; it employs an army of shrewd men with "pulls" in politics, and has friends among the press men; it is a liberal contributor to campaign funds; and, to tell the truth about it, there is no more generous giver to charity. Indeed, some of them are most exemplary church-members, and when the police administration is honest and persistent, some of them are great agitators for reform of other abuses. They hire the best talent at the bar when it is needed. On the big cases, when they go up on appeal, they are represented by the most distinguished and able counsel. They control the pen of able writers. The Louisiana lottery, just before it was exiled, hired a clever and studious writer in Chicago, whom I knew personally, to write a book on gambling from the historical, philosophical, ethical, and moral point of view. It was an intensely interesting history of gambling from the earliest times, with ethical and philosophical deductions favorable to the business. The book was freely distributed to legislators and congressmen and wherever it was thought it would do the most good.

The gambling fraternity in New York have their clearing-houses and exchanges just as well known and just as prominent as those of the business institutions in the lower part of the town. The little fellows in this business, just as in the other big speculative concerns, hang on the words of the top man. A hint that there will be a change in the Police Commissioner's office, or that matters had better be kept quiet for a month or so, is just the same as a tip given by some master of finance in Wall Street.

There is always much talk about "the man higher up" in connection with gambling, and the public, at least by inference, are sometimes told that he is located in the Police Department, or that he is the dominating factor in some political organization which happens to be responsible for the government of the day. I do not know how it was in other administrations, but I can say, as far as the last one is concerned, that there was no man higher up connected with the police establishment officially. With operations carried on by the Commissioner himself, he could not assure immunity to his friends. By the general consensus of opinion, this great business of late has been conducted by a syndicate of men with both money and political influence. Of course, just as in the great trusts, here and there a small fellow will break in and begin to do a little business on his own account. If the police are dishonest, such a one will suffer at once, and the big interest's affairs will not be touched; but as the last administration operated directly from the Commissioner's office, no one could give a guarantee to the big men at the top that any place was secure, and the chances always were that the heaviest blows would fall on the big, strong places. If the police have only one arm, that of the precinct, these clever and ingenious men will immediately set about to devise schemes to paralyze it; if instead of one arm it has two arms out, and each one independent of the other, the situation is then troublesome to them, and they will fight desperately and wickedly. It does not take long for a syndicate like this to reap an immense harvest of money. Three hundred pool-rooms running in all parts of Greater New York, probably fifty or even one hundred gambling-houses, and then such a syndicate would reach out and begin to take hold of the houses of prostitution, assignation hotels, and in time, as it grew rich and strong, it would no doubt control the tremendous liquor interests. By this time it would be a power almost equal to government itself. If you will locate the syndicate and the names of those concerned, and pick out the ablest, boldest, and the most experienced, popular, and plausible man among the rich men who control it, you will undoubtedly put your hand on the so-called "man higher up."

When the people become as earnest against pool-selling, gambling, and other prohibited vices, with the almost unavoidable corruption of the police thereby, as they are just now against fraud and peculations in offices of trust, whether in government or insurance companies, and will resent their continuance just as hotly as they would an attempt by the big trusts to raise illegally the price of the necessaries of life, then, and not till then, will this shameless defiance of law cease. If the majority in New York want a wide-open town, as against reasonable restriction or strict enforcement of the law, they will get it even if they have to bribe the police to be allowed to obtain such freedom. The hope for better things lies in arousing them to a true knowledge of the situation and the facts; for their hearts are yet sound, and there are signs in the sky that health-giving winds, which may be a bit rude at first, will soon blow over the face of the land, and convince the managers of the big partisan machines that there are more votes in favor of an impartial and courageous enforcement of the law against prohibited vices than they have hitherto suspected.

XIV

USING OUTSIDE AGENTS AND RAIDS

THE difficulties of enforcing the law under existing conditions, especially in the matter of gambling and pool-selling, without the aid of outside agents, is well illustrated in what might be taken as a sample case. On one of the numbered streets near Fifth Avenue there was running brazenly and openly for years a combination pool-room and gambling-house—a three-story and basement house, in what was once a fashionable neighborhood—given over entirely to these purposes. It had a strong and influential outside backing and a big clientage. Every afternoon between one o'clock and six great numbers of men, young and old, clerks, book-keepers, salesmen, mechanics, laborers, store-keepers, saloon loafers, and men who live by their wits, would gather in this place to bet on the races or play other games of chance. It had been carried on the police books as a suspicious place for a long time. It had a heavily armored front-door, and all the accessible windows from the sidewalk were strongly barred. To send for the captain of the precinct and tell him he must close this place with the uniformed force would be about the same as telling him to stop the tide rising in the North River. Even if the captain were thoroughly in earnest and honest, a policeman in uniform would no more be admitted to this place than he would be allowed to invade the White House. When the proprietors got ready to admit a uniformed policeman they would be willing to send for the court and the jury and plead guilty. Stationing a policeman in front of the door would be entirely useless. If he would take it, they would offer him five or ten dollars every day he was there, just to "sweeten" him up a bit, and his perfunctory warning would be received by the old-timers as a good joke. The only hope the captain would have of getting evidence would be through his plain-clothes men. These are not long in a precinct before they become thoroughly well known. The crooked element in a precinct keeps close tabs on the plain-clothes men; they know every member of the captain's staff within an hour after they are assigned to the precinct. In some cases they have been known to photograph them when they appeared at court. Even if they are not known, the captain cannot be sure of them. A plausible, clever-talking, plain-clothes man will often fool an honest captain and be doing business on his own account. Then, if there are a number of them, and any one of them is dishonest, he will simply be a spy on his fellows, and tip off their movements to those interested. Sometimes one plain-clothes man will manage to get himself admitted to a pool-room; it may be on an understanding with the keeper. The captain will allow him to go there for maybe a week or so, betting on the races, so that he may get the confidence of those running the room and lay the foundation for admitting a comrade, as the police magistrates demand two witnesses, although under what law I could never understand, and even then the mill of justice will grind little grist unless the police are strongly corroborated by outsiders. After the first man has frequented the place and spent considerable money, he has then got to get the second man in. By-the-way, I have never heard of a policeman seeking evidence winning in a pool-room. I suppose they always bet on losers to make the case stronger. Now, if he is not honest he will make a great bluff or show at taking in the second man, but, notwithstanding all his protestations and seemingly shrewd lying, the astute proprietor, being of course tipped off, rejects him, and the effort fails. It is very rare, indeed, that two plain-clothes men of the captain's staff ever succeed in getting into any one of these houses at the same time.

The people who ran the house before alluded to just laughed at the precinct authorities, and it is quite possible that the precinct authorities, in turn, laughed at the Commissioner, and both would have been laughing at him yet if heroic measures had not been taken. Outside agents had to be employed here; but underground wires seemed to run from this house to various places, and it looked as if no move against it could be made, the managers being at once put on their guard. One agent only reported that he had obtained admittance.

What should the Commissioner do in a case like this? I know what some judges would say from the bench—that he should proceed in the old-fashioned way to get complete and convincing evidence beyond reasonable doubt. I would have paid a large sum of money out of that intrusted to my care in order to get further evidence against this house, and would have considered it a good investment. The best that we could do with this case, under my own personal supervision, was to get one outsider in, but when he undertook to bring in a police officer in plain clothes, an unknown man selected from another part of the city, some one undoubtedly tipped them off and they refused admittance to the officer.

There were just two things for the Commissioner, in my judgment, to do: to demand of the inspector and captain that they close the house, or to take charge of the case himself. Of course, a Commissioner can convict an inspector and captain on any evidence or no evidence, so far as he is concerned, but it will only be going through a farcical form. In this case, as was said before, the Commissioner would have to prove a guilty knowledge on the part of the inspector and captain, and that they had used all legal means in their power to suppress this place by getting evidence against it.

This place stood right in the heart of the city, within a few doors of one of its main thoroughfares. You could go down there in the afternoon and see the customers streaming in as openly as at a place of amusement or legitimate business. One afternoon I went down there in person, watched the crowds going in, while the proprietors smiled benignly at me from the windows of the upper floor. I think they actually felt, in a way, sorry for me. The whole thing seemed so hopeless and a bit comical. I am quite sure I amused them.

On the west side of this house a large warehouse with a blank wall towered several stories over the roof of the gambling-house. Next door, and part of a row of houses, was a disorderly Raines law hotel. The hotel and the pool-room had back yards, and there was a suspicion that there was an entrance from one house to the other on the inside, and also by way of the yard and roof from one to the other. The one witness who had been in stated he had seen a roulette-wheel in operation, as well as pool-selling. It was determined then and there to seize the place so quickly as to hermetically seal it, and to act under that rule of law that allows the police to break in where they have good reasons for believing that a felony is being committed.

The thing now was to make the movement so secret that no possible leak could occur. For many reasons I considered this one of the most important houses in the city. If we could successfully break it up we would strike terror into the hearts of the big outside backers and possibly bring the precinct and district authorities to shame and trial. No one outside of my own office knew when the movement would take place or what was on foot, and the police concerned did not know where they were going until almost directly in front of the premises in question. The first place seized was the Raines law hotel, at the same time the fronts of both houses and the back-yards being at once covered. The squad who entered through the hotel went up on the roof and over on to the roof of the gambling-house, and, just as was anticipated, they had hardly reached there when the scuttle of the latter place was heaved up and the gamblers, with the roulette-wheel and the other paraphernalia, appeared, intending to escape by the hotel. The efforts to get out of the back and front were equally useless.

The capture of the gambling machinery was of itself sufficient in law to vindicate the raid on the combination gambling-house and pool-room in question, but, in addition, over three hundred men were found in the house, and a bar in full operation.

The house had the usual protection of calling itself a "club," but there was evidence that they had been selling liquor without a license. All the usual telephone and telegraph apparatus, on a large scale, racing-sheets, cards, and other evidences were found.

At this place, for the first time, it being after the passage of the Dowling law, the names and addresses of every one present were taken, and where doubt was expressed as to the name being a true one, written evidence was secured. Where the man, young or old, is respectable and engaged in some decent business, there is nothing that he fears so much as to have his name published as an habitué of a gambling-house. His employers are apt to get rid of him very quickly, and if he is in business his credit is destroyed. Then, too, if he is found afterwards in different pool-rooms, he becomes known to the police as an habitual gambler. If the law allowed the arrest of these patrons, and their being locked up until they found bail, or allowed the Police Commissioner the same power as the District Attorney, to compel them to give evidence, he would have the pool-rooms at his mercy. A former Police Commissioner arrested the patrons and used to take them in wagon-loads to the station-houses, but the magistrates viewed with horror this outrage upon the liberty of the citizen, and ordered that these excellent gentlemen should not be interfered with in that way in the future.

This place proved to be a perfect fortress, and it required quite some hard physical work to get out all the exhibits that might prove of value as evidence. I am glad to say that it never again opened. The case, after dragging through the courts, ended with a small fine. These fines would never stop gambling in New York, and, of course, no one expects them to. They are generally imposed in an apologetic way, with a reprimand to the police, and everything goes on nicely and smoothly, just as before. In approaching places to be raided, we sometimes loaded the policemen into huge furniture vans, which did not disclose the occupants until just in front of the door of the premises. The first big effectual raid in Chinatown was made in carriages that rolled down the Bowery and into the narrow alleys and streets of the town, simulating a big Italian wedding-party. Even then the dens were barricaded so quickly that axe work that would have done credit to the late Mr. Gladstone had to follow. The axe supplements the Constitution.

Going to the police courts for warrants ends in many cases in failure. First, you have to have two witnesses before a warrant will be issued, and, besides, it sometimes happens that before the warrant is executed the place is tipped off. When so many people are concerned it is hard to keep this kind of secret. The magistrate and the Commissioner may be both deceived and betrayed. When the officers enter to execute it they find a number of well-dressed gentlemen lunching, or the place is entirely deserted and turned into an innocent shoe-store, or an exhibition of rugs, pictures, or boys' "pants," or a nice, gray-haired old "doctor" is dispensing medical advice.

The necessity for outside agents is to be regretted, but under present conditions they are at many times indispensable and I have met a few who were eminently faithful, able, and honest. It goes without saying that I encountered a number who were quite the opposite. The whole sum of a police administration resolves itself into this. Is the law enforced? Are the gambling and pool-rooms closed? Are the disorderly houses and disorderly women being properly repressed? Are burglars and robbers and footpads being sent to prison? Is life and property safe? It won't do for a Police Commissioner to turn around and say: "I have saved so much money; I haven't used any outside agents. Here is a great triumph in economy. Here's your money back." Of course, if nothing is done, no warfare is carried on against vice and crime, it will cost nothing. If a Commissioner does nothing to suppress vice or prevent crime he need spend no money. If you don't want evidence, why employ agents? If you don't want to know, why pay to know?

If pool-selling in New York is unmolested and

the police connive at allowing it to run and flourish, and the Commissioner tells them they can employ no outside agents, but must find legal evidence to convict, then the situation is simply one of entire surrender. The law has hoisted the white flag, the army has disbanded, economy is triumphant, vice and crime reign.

Every Police Commissioner who has buckled right down to the hard work of enforcing the law against crime and vice—and the same is equally true of the District Attorney—has, in times past, had to employ outside agents and adopt methods more or less expensive. In this way it costs money, just as in other wars. What would you think of a general who might withhold his fire until he had computed how many cartridges he could save in money by not firing at all; or wouldn't make a move against the enemy for fear of breaking down a few artillery carriages? Or take the case of an admiral commanding a battle-ship who should refrain from firing the last decisive shot because he had made a calculation that it would impair the life of a gun and cost the government so much for the shells. On the contrary, doesn't the government pay out hundreds of thousands of dollars on experimental work, in target-practice on land and sea, only to be prepared for war? Army manœuvres cost hundreds of thousands a year; naval manœuvres even more. And this fight for the supremacy of the law is just war, and a higher and better thing than either military glory or conquered territory.

Money should not be wasted, of course, but in the fight in this great big town to enforce the law the thing you must get is victory. Law must beat down lawlessness. The agents of vice and crime are ingenious, clever, and shrewd, and have large resources of money with which to thwart justice and to impede police effort; and in this perpetual warfare the police authorities must be equally prepared to fight to a finish, and to meet new tricks with clever strategy, to employ all sorts of tools on all sorts of occasions, and to enforce the law no matter how much money it costs. No Commissioner has the right to waste money, and he must exercise proper vigilance, and demand economy on the part of his subordinates; but the moment you begin to cramp a captain in a big precinct, or a police inspector in an important district, and fail to give him his legitimate expenses, and those of his agents, you are practically telling him not to enforce the law at all, and he will not be slow to take the hint. If he asks for agents and money and does not get them, he has a good defence in any court of law, and no one knows it better than he does. To hoist the white flag of surrender to any law-defying evil in the community is to invite the corruption of the whole body politic, let plausible sophists, devil's advocates, and the only "friends" of the Constitution and liberty say what they will. What New York City wants is to get the full worth of its money, but it wants the best police service in the world and is perfectly willing to pay liberally for it.

XV

TRAFFIC

THE traffic problem in New York involved two difficulties: first, the physical one as to the island of Manhattan; and second, the political and social conditions throughout the greater city. With the increase in the height of buildings, while, of course, the island itself grew no larger, the population has become more and more congested. The inhabitants and occupants of these towering structures, commercial and social, have to use the same outlets that were intended for a much smaller stream of pedestrian and vehicular traffic befitting the beginning in earlier days.

Of late years, as the country in general has grown richer and the leisure class has increased, New York has rapidly become to the Western Hemisphere what London and Paris are to the Old World. A mighty host of visitors pour into its streets and avenues by day and night, fill its hotels and shops, and crowd into its various places of amusement. On the streets themselves the motor-vehicles must also be taken into consideration, especially where they struggle for headway with swarms of trucks, light wagons, cabs, and carriages. To complicate the problem still further and make it a more intense one was the fact that, with very few exceptions, the leading avenues and streets are double-tracked and traversed by almost unbroken lines of more or less swiftly moving trolley-cars, this being the means of transit for thousands of our population both for business and pleasure.

The man or woman in a hurry to catch a train, or to keep an engagement of importance, riding on one of these cars, chafed indignantly at the almost incessant stoppages when some bull-headed truck-driver in front of the moving car stubbornly refused to budge an inch in its favor, ignoring its angry bell with outbursts of shocking profanity.

Here the social and political conditions come into play. We are still a comparatively young country, and the city is marvellously cosmopolitan, and all are intent in that push and drive for material betterment in which politeness and courtesy and the fine points of chivalric behavior have to give way to the ruder methods of physical development, so that the horrible struggle of the streets aroused no great demand for betterment, and existing horrors had come to be accepted as normal and proper. The jostle and struggle between the driver and pedestrian in the streets had been for many, many years a fixed condition, quietly accepted by the multitudes. The driver, on his part, believed that the street belonged exclusively to him, and, whip in hand, he sat on his throne as one beyond the law. As there were no systematic attempts to regulate his behavior, he pursued his brutal and savage way unchecked, with no respect for the law or its officers.

The citizen went daily, with more or less courage, through greater perils and dangers than an arctic explorer, a sailor, or a hunter of dangerous wild beasts would encounter, glad at times to gain the curb, frequently escaping a violent and cruel death by a hair's-breadth. It never occurred to him that the officers of the law had any authority in the premises, other than to occasionally help a crippled man or assist a helpless woman or child over some of the more dangerous street-crossings.

To place men at the more congested crossings was as far as the Police Department had gone in endeavoring to protect the population. Here, amid a sea of fearful turmoil, profanity, and shouting, the stalwart member of the Broadway Squad would bravely venture now and again to pilot a party of fear-stricken citizens of both sexes across the dangerous trail, and while the time of passing was shorter, the passage itself was much more perilous than when the long-haired and valorous scouts of the early sixties led parties of peaceful emigrants across the savage-infested plains to build up the now prosperous and thickly populated States of the West. Across this dangerous passage the blue-coated convoy occasionally had his attention arrested by the cries of the citizen who had ventured to follow in his wake, and whose rescue could not be made until the larger party had passed to the other side of the street. The whole conditions were those of a society without law, or respect for it, barbarous and appalling; a wonder and a horror to all visiting foreigners, the terror of the multitudes of metropolitan visitors, and the ever-present danger and discomfort of the permanent residents. Not only did this condition threaten the lives and limbs of the citizens, and cause them vast discomfort and inconvenience, but it was most demoralizing in general in begetting a spirit of rampant lawlessness. The old and young constantly saw the law disregarded. There was utter unconcern for the rights of others, and all were led to believe that life on the streets was a savage struggle for existence.

The first attempt to bring some sort of order out of this chaos was made by Deputy-Commissioner Captain Alexander Piper, under a former police administration. He began, with the co-operation of some public-spirited citizens, a systematic attempt to enforce what might be called the common law of the road. He introduced islands of safety, so-called, such as are at Twenty-third Street and Fifth Avenue. These are simply granite-coped standing-places, in the centre of which is an ornamental lighting structure. These islands diverted the traffic into separate lines, and in times of heavy congestion allowed the pedestrian a brief respite in the sea that surged around him before undertaking the other half of his journey.

The rules of the road, that heavily laden and slow-moving vehicles must keep to the right and left, and lighter and more quickly moving vehicles to the centre, and that turns should be made at proper angles instead of scraping the curb, to the great danger of the pedestrian, were distinct advances on the former absolutely lawless period; but these rules themselves could not be enforced by any amount of newspaper writing, or by a few men on the crossings here and there—something new and more radical was demanded. I went to the Police Department with the conviction that the regulation of the traffic in the streets in New York was a question superior to nearly all others with which the police had to deal, and I am, after two years of service, convinced beyond any doubt that my first impressions were more than correct. What has been done must not only be maintained, but there is still room for improvement and progress. I consider this question infinitely more immediate and pressing than a mass of small details and red tape which the law heaps upon the Commissioner. If one big thing of supreme importance could be brought about for the public good, the little things could wait for the little days and the leisure which comes after the huge struggles which produce great results. The first thing demonstrated was that the man at the crossing could not in himself solve the traffic problem; second, that the man on foot must be supplemented by the man on horseback. Looking back at it, I am sure that the question would have made no progress without the use of the mounted policeman and the iron standards and ropes. The first step was to create a departmental machinery to deal with this problem exclusively. To this end the Traffic Bureau was formed.

The first head of the bureau was Inspector Donald Grant, but he did not find the work to his taste, and preferred to be assigned to a district. It was at this time that I was most fortunate in securing the services of Captain Stephen O'Brien, a man of great natural talent and aptitude for the solution of the questions involved, and an honest and fearless public official.

For a time the innovation of the mounted man hung trembling dangerously on the verge of ridicule, but in the end the horseman won out. His very presence demanded respect from the lawless elements, and gave a new sense of security to the citizen. The mounted squad was increased in numbers, and much painstaking labor was spent upon the proper uniform, which involved more work than many women give to their dress; because, after all, the clothes count, and the former uniform was most objectionable, if not ridiculous.

Sir Howard Vincent, the creator of the modern London police, on his recent visit to this country, before the change was made, said that the men and horses were fine, the latter being especially good, but that the uniforms were beneath criticism.

The present uniform, we believe, pleases both the police and the public. The next step was to lay down rules to get order out of confusion and system out of the terrible turmoil which surged, swore, raced, and struggled at the most congested points. The first rule laid down with reference to congested spots was to create a large safety zone far beyond the idea of the little islands with their lamps. Take, for instance, the conditions on Madison Square on the first day of the year 1906. At any time between the hours of 8.30 A.M. and 6.30 P.M., when traffic rules are in force, a small child could walk unaccompanied and in safety, after crossing the railroad tracks on Twenty-third Street, all the way from the Flatiron Building to the Worth Monument. Here was a large space enclosed by iron standards, connected by ropes, with entrance spaces at intervals for pedestrians and cabs and carriages waiting for passengers who were temporarily in hotels or shops in the vicinity. In these big areas pedestrians stood or walked in perfect safety, while the tide of vehicular traffic, like a river confined in strong banks, flowed around them in all directions. On the west side one stream flowed south, on the east side the stream only flowed north, and on the south the traffic was diverted from west to east over Twenty-second Street into Broadway, crossing the latter and flowing north, or keeping to the right and going south. The mounted men were stationed at all places where the streams divided. These men also patrolled the zone, ready to clear the way for the fire-engines, to stop runaways, to hasten to danger-points, and to put an instant and heavy hand upon recalcitrant drivers or chauffeurs. The men had to see that the waiting carriages kept within the enclosures, and at all points that the rules and regulations were strictly enforced. This place may be taken as a sample. There are other points, as, for instance, at Herald Square, at the entrance of the Brooklyn Bridge, at the Circle on Fifty-ninth Street, at Times Square, at Union Square, and on West and South streets. At first the opposition to these rules was most violent. Drivers swore and raged, and rich owners of private equipages, who were compelled to go a short distance out of the way, protested emphatically against their enforcement; store-keepers thought that they only should be considered, and that only their rights and interests were paramount; other big business interests, which had a selfish monopoly of the streets in front of their establishments, had no good words for the new idea, and the politicians could only see confederated cab, carriage, and wagon drivers crying for vengeance at the polls. They shrunk timidly from any connection with the new order of things, and for some time the Police Commissioner and his aids stood alone, conscious that the great public could only articulate sighs of relief and impotent declarations of friendship, as against storms of threats and protest from the interested minority. When in course of time the system was introduced into Brooklyn, the great guardians of the Constitution and the rights of man rose in wild fury; and those powerful enjoining and commanding writs were trained upon it in the shadow of the court-house itself, and it suffered a defeat which, I trust, is temporary.

If the safety zone had not been created and mounted men not introduced, and the stream of traffic diverted and directed into channels, so that the public could see for themselves what could be done, the fierce struggle in the streets would have gone on indefinitely, to the loss of life and limb and the disgrace of the community.

That the citizens desired this system was shown by the demand for an increase of the Traffic Squad in all parts of the different boroughs, and mounted men patrolled on January 1, 1906, the leading thoroughfares of Brooklyn and Williamsburgh, to the greater comfort and safety of the citizens.

The Traffic Squad itself was at first an unpopular branch of the service with the force, but is now popular. It is immensely favored by the people, and it has been charged that I have shown it a great deal of favoritism. Such is not the case. That I am fond and proud of these men I admit. The work that they do is done in view of every one, and in all kinds of weather, and often under the most trying circumstances and with risk to health, life, and limb. The horses cannot stand too long a strain day in and day out, and hence the hours of the mounted men have to be shortened as much as possible. A horse carrying a heavy man and his equipments, even standing for seven or eight hours every day in the year, will soon show the strain. It is much harder than drawing a light wagon. These horses are really a fine lot of animals, costing the city a large price each, being a much better mount than in any army of the world, including that of the United States. Some of them show at once such high intelligence and prove so adaptable for the work that before they have been long in service their value far exceeds their purchase price. The men, as a rule, are very fond of them, and in some cases the attachment is pathetic, and an attempt to part man from horse painful.

From the beginning, the system has had more or

less opposition from certain lawyers and judges. They affect to believe that the government of the streets rests entirely with the Board of Aldermen, and can only be enforced by ordinance, and that even this board under constitutional limitations cannot itself divert traffic or reserve any spaces. I do not believe that this is a correct legal view, and in this respect I am joined by at least two of the leading judges in the Appellate Division of the Second Department. In the winter of 1905 I drew up myself, and had presented through Mr. Veiller, of the City Club, an amendment to the city charter increasing the powers of the Police Department in this matter. I am sorry to say that this attempt to get new legislation met with rather general indifference, both at New York and Albany, and hard work in the closing hours of the Legislature barely saved it from defeat. When the original draught was sent to Albany it contained the word "divert"; this word during the legislative processes was stricken out, and the word "direct" substituted, but even as it is the layman who cares to look at it will see at a glance that it appears to be very strong, and now that the courts have decided that the franchise-granting power of the aldermen can be taken away and given to the Board of Estimate and Apportionment, I can see no constitutional objections to giving the Commissioner of Police sole control of regulating vehicular traffic in all the streets and avenues of Greater New York. One thing is certain, and that is, the reform has not come to stay until this is done, and the legislation must be so clear and emphatic as not to imperil this great measure of relief by the whim or prejudice of any judge. It should not be placed in the hands of an elective body, subject to the caprice of an individual or the vagaries of a political organization under the pressure and expediency of elections. A united effort of the lesser personal and private interests against the greater public rights might, under the fearsome pressure of political expediency, destroy the new order. There is another thing equally certain: the whole system will die out and become inefficient under any Commissioner who is not earnestly and honestly its friend and supporter. The Traffic Squad will not give the public the best that is in them unless they work under a friendly Commissioner and are thus encouraged to do their best and put their hearts in the work.

The things that remain to be done, in my judgment, are these: First, that the Traffic Squad must be a selected corps of the very best men on the force, whose qualifications are known; they must be encouraged to do their very best.

The next thing to do must be to make the safety zones permanent, surrounded by granite or other indestructible copings, with exits and entrances at proper intervals, and ornamented with lamp-posts for use at night, the whole to be made attractive and pleasing to the eye, as well as useful. This will necessitate a much smaller number of policemen than at present, and will give still greater security to the pedestrian. It can be very readily accomplished by the city authorities. The work might well begin at the Circle, Madison and Union squares. Up to this time the work has been done so well that the drivers obey many of the new rules from habit, and require less policing. They turn certain corners of the safety zones now as a matter of course. This seems likely to lead to a dangerous conclusion —viz., that the number of men and horses now engaged on this work can be sweepingly reduced. Take every man off the work to-morrow and I admit that by their very momentum the rules would, as it were, enforce themselves for a short time. You might as well abolish the Fire Department because there are no great fires every day. Even after you take down the fence, custom and habit would restrain the trespasser for a time, but not long. Holland might as well take down or weaken her famous dikes, and then trust the treacherous and rebellious ocean not to invade her, as to sap and weaken and practically abolish this squad and then expect the rules to be respected.

A plan which I outlined last November in a letter to the head of the city government, must, in my judgment, be added so as to strengthen and buttress up the whole system. No permit for a carriage, cab, automobile, or other vehicle should be granted allowing it to stand in front of any building on any avenue or street where there are car-tracks, and where the space between the curb and the nearest rail is not over twenty-two feet. It was also pointed out that any driver of a cab or carriage who refuses to obey the new traffic rules should have his license revoked. The licensing power can be made the most powerful means of compelling them to obey the rules and regulations as laid down by the Police Commissioner. No opposition, however violent, on the part of these people could withstand such an attack as this on the part of the city authorities. Were this principle agreed upon, a law should be passed making the granting of these permits for stands and the licensing of cab and carriage drivers rest solely with the Police Commissioner. If the Police Commissioner had this power he could defy the most dangerous opposition of selfish interests, and the uplifted finger of the policeman in the midst of the traffic would be as powerful in New York as in any of the great European capitals. The cursing driver would no longer obstruct traffic and annoy the passer-by. No other great world capital would allow this dangerous nuisance. It would mean authority, power, law, and systematized order and respect for human life. Licensing and permission in the matter of street traffic should not be made the sport of politics.

The time must come when in New York, as in the big European capitals, every driver and chauffeur must have a license. Every other engine-driver but those who run automobiles has to be examined and licensed. A man, boy, or woman can run a one-hundred-horse-power engine capable of going seventy miles an hour on a crowded street without examination as to fitness, and without license, and before the same person could manage a heating-boiler in an apartment-house he would have to be examined and licensed. If the Police Commissioner had the licensing power, he could force the incompetent and ruthless small-boy driver out of New York, and the brutal and insolent driver who degrades his calling would have to seek some other occupation, and the chauffeur fined a stated number of times would not drive automobiles in this city. If the issuing of licenses and permits were given to the Police Commissioner, the rules could be enforced without friction, and a deference and respect for authority begotten which would be astonishing to the people of New York and the vast multitude of visitors. This new plan would be emulated by every city of importance in the United States. Every step made in advance here is immediately followed elsewhere.

All over the United States the public mind is bent upon two things—better roads and streets, and the enforcement of law thereon. Progress on the highways must not be made a deathly struggle for existence; crossings should not be death-traps. Men, women, and children should not fall on the streets and avenues in larger numbers than men do on sanguinary battle-fields. The new traffic rules and regulations in New York have at least accomplished these things:

First: The street-cars, to the great saving of the time of the people and the conserving of their comfort as against overcrowding, move on cleared tracks infinitely faster. The figures show astonishing improvement. The hard-worked motormen are benefited by making their trips on time.

Second: Although population and consequent street congestion are increasing, and despite the immense increase in the number of fast-moving motor-vehicles, the number of accidents has markedly decreased.

Third: Where the traffic rules are strictly enforced, the pedestrian can move about freely, without nervous apprehension, crossing and recrossing streets even in the busiest hours with more safety than similar places in smaller cities.

Fourth: The night traffic service in the theatre district between Forty-seventh Street and Thirty-ninth Street is of great advantage to the large number of people who come and go to the places of amusement, especially those who ride on cars. The old way allowed mobs of soliciting cab and carriage drivers to block the crossings and intervene between the citizen and the street-car. "Hire me, or walk," was the ultimatum. The system here is most bitterly opposed by private and personal interests and needs strengthening by public opinion. Recently certain interests tried to defeat it at the Metropolitan Opera-House, but it won out on its merits.

Give us good roads and the best-paved streets, and over them put the shadow of the law and the well-ordered decency of civilization. Beget order out of chaos and make the officer of the law respected.

The automobile in New York is of great importance in any traffic problem, and was put well under the control of the police in this city. There were ten or more auto-cycles connected with the Police Department, all of them capable of great speed, and able to overtake the most reckless automobile driver. They were well located at the places where the speed limit was most likely to be infracted. In addition, a more or less successful trial was made of signal-boxes located along speedways at proper intervals. The automobile was timed on entering this policed track, timed in the centre, and, if necessary, arrested at the end. Instructions to the police in dealing with automobilists were not to argue, but be firm and to keep their temper; to arrest or warn as the circumstances warrant.

Thorough trial and much experience convinced me that centralized effort was better than precinct work, and these men either had been or were being absorbed in the Traffic Bureau. The signal-boxes were manned only for a short time, but I contemplated putting them on the Coney Island and Staten Island boulevards, and some other long runs, where complaints against over-speeding were frequent, and giving them further trials. Experience beats theory, and this "Yankee notion" imported from Massachusetts was entitled to a trial.

I don't believe in trapping the automobile driver just to make a show as to the number of arrests. I believe it is a pernicious system for the policeman to hide himself at the foot of a hill and make so many arrests a week by pouncing out upon them at a given spot where they are most likely to exceed the speed limit, and where there may be a minimum danger to the public. When the white caps were put upon the automobile police in summer, several violent anti-automobilists declared that every automobile driver would see the caps, and, of course, not exceed the speed limit as long as they were within sight. If the men honestly patrolled, these caps would scarcely ever be out of view on the long, straight boulevards and avenues.

The whole object of the law and the police is to conserve the safety of the public on foot, and if this can be done with a minimum number of arrests, so much the better. The pedestrian has the first right on roadway as well as sidewalk. To this end, the automobile police, who are a very intelligent body of men, have, as a general rule, shown good judgment and tact in the matter of making arrests. These men must be carefully supervised by the central authority to keep them up to their work, and, above all, to see that they do not corruptly or arrogantly abuse their great powers. A dishonest bicycle policeman might levy tribute for a long time without being found out. The man who pays him to avoid arrest will no more tell than the man who pays the customs' officer to pass his baggage without examination. If these men are not directly controlled by the Central Office, and get slack or dishonest, the public must suffer in life, limb, and comfort. A machine speeding in the vicinity of a school-house, when the children are leaving the same, must be held to a strict accountability, and a machine in congested places like Fifth Avenue, or in the Park, should be kept well under control and held to the standard fixed by law. Numbers should be carried both forward and behind, and especially made plain at night. Those coarse and reckless owners who use machines to exhibit their arrogance and air their vanity, and often to advertise their newly begotten wealth, should be carefully watched for infractions of the law; the taking of a machine from a garage without the owner's permission should be severely punished by law as a crime; lights should be compelled to be carried from the time of the setting of the sun, especially in short winter days, when darkness comes on early; the speed, I believe, should be fixed on some such principle as is now being tried in New Jersey. Under no circumstances should the law officers of suburban places, any more than the police of New York, be allowed to share in the amounts of fines or costs imposed. Indeed, the automobile law, in the light of larger experience, needs intelligent, fair, but radical revision. Since I went out of office I have had presented to me cases where one-hundred-dollar bills and checks for considerable sums were rejected by a bicycle policeman.

The rule-making power must be fixed in the Commissioner. There must be no question as to his right to divert as well as direct traffic, and issue licenses and permits, which should run in his name and with his authority. When this is done he will be in a position to attack, in a systematic and effective way, the question along the river-fronts both east and west; to relieve the present congestion and disorder on streets like Greenwich and Washington, by throwing north-moving streams into one narrow street, and south-moving processions into the other; to facilitate trade and commerce on the river-fronts and ferries to the advantage of New York as a great port, now menaced by the serious opposition of other cities; to extend and strengthen the system into other congested streets and avenues; to protect the people who ride in public vehicles from extortion and abuse; and, as his powers grow for the public good, to license, regulate, and control all push-carts and street-venders.

If the people of New York want this reign of law, this sense of security on the streets and public places, this advance in civilization and social well-being, this improvement in morals and manners, they must not underrate the evil forces in ceaseless opposition, sometimes in open revolt, more often in secret intrigue for private, political, and personal interests against the rights and welfare of the overwhelming majority of the people. To hold what has been gained, and to advance along the lines indicated, there must be absolute unity of purpose between the departments of law and police and the heads of all other branches of the city government. Divided councils, cross-purposes, and an unfriendly attitude to this reform augur treason to the rights of the people.

XVI

THE SOLIDARITY AND PREJUDICES OF THE POLICE

You often hear it said on platforms and in pulpits, and read in the newspapers, that policemen will never tell on one another, of how impossible it is to get the police to be witnesses in a police case, and that if they do appear they will calmly perjure themselves in favor of the accused. Predicated on this is the charge that the police are all corrupt and criminal, and that therefore the policeman who fails to tell on another is a crook, or otherwise, as an honest man, he would take pleasure in coming forward and giving evidence against a brother policeman. This is not true. There are very many honest men on the force, honest in the sense that they would not take a bribe or evade their duty, but they will not volunteer information against another policeman, and on the stand, I am sorry to say, would make poor witnesses for the prosecution. They are in other respects honest men. In the first place, a man in a lower grade will not, as a general rule, testify against an officer in a higher grade. That is looked upon by them as a breach of discipline and has many hidden terrors behind it. If a patrolman were to testify against a roundsman, for instance, he would expect all the roundsmen to look out for him thereafter—the honest roundsman just as much as the crooked one—and he would tell you at once that he expected they would drive him off the force. The same feeling goes up through all the ranks. Then in the rank itself there is a brotherhood feeling and the bond begotten by organization; so that all the patrolmen feel they must stand together. The same is the case with the officers above them. This feeling is somewhat akin to the conditions among the classmen at Annapolis and West Point.

Then I believe there is another cause not so generally known. A majority of the police are either Irish born or of Irish descent, although the percentage is not as great as most people suppose, there being a very considerable native element, many Germans, some Italians, and not a few other nationalities. But the Irish were the earliest and the most pronounced policemen, as it were, and they have been associated with the force ever since its foundation. It has been largely officered by Irishmen, and Irish traditions and feelings have been incorporated into the very organization. You can see the influence of this on the other elements among the police. The Normans who went to Ireland, as is known in history, very soon fell into the Irish ways and speech, and, as the documents of the time tell us, became "more Irish than the Irish themselves"; and so the Irish spirit permeates all ranks of the police. It would ill-become me to praise the virtues of this spirit too highly, but still I must say, and I think every one, including President Roosevelt, will agree with me, that it is the finest sort of material out of which to make a policeman. President Roosevelt has said that if he wanted a really hard piece of dangerous or fighting work done he would call upon the Irishmen on the force. Besides courage of a high order and the soldierly instinct, the Irish policeman by birth or descent is also kindly, humane, patriotic, cheerful, and witty, and inured to hardship, and has a certain racial alertness and adaptability to circumstances which well fits him for this calling. He fits into a military or quasi-military service as if born to it. The individual prominence of a policeman also attracts the Celt, and at the same time he can understand and sympathize with the class or clan feeling of the organization. In Ireland for seven hundred years there has been one name, there has been one character, which excites not only horror but a certain superstitious awe, and that is an "informer." In an almost constant state of rebellion against alien rule, fighting in the open and conspiring in secret, wherever opportunity offered, the informer was developed. In a land where all law was alien law, as might be expected, more or less disrespect and hatred prevailed against the law and its officers. The latter had one ally, the informer. Neighborhoods, yes, whole counties, might set their face against the execution of law which especially touched religion and politics, fight it, strive and conspire against it, nullify it, handicap, hinder, obstruct, and even destroy its agents; but here and there out of some hidden corner, out of some cavernous recess, came the most obnoxious, despised, and hated of all people in Ireland, the informer. Nothing can better illustrate this than a short extract which I make from the latest production of that able living Irish novelist, the Very Rev. Canon P. A. Sheehan, D.D.

The old, blind, but yet bitter ex-Fenian is talking to Kathleen. He says:

"'Close that book, Katty, and listen to what I'm goin' to say to you this blessed night!'

"He had always something so important to divulge, and he always spoke in so oracular a manner that Kathleen was not too much surprised. But she closed her book and listened.

"'There was wan class of Irishmen that you never hard me spake of,' said Thade, 'partly because I wouldn't dirty my mouth wid them, and partly because no dacent writer iver mintions them; but I must spake of 'em now. Can you guess what I mane?'

"Kathleen guessed MacMorrogh, and O'Brien of the Burnings, and the clan that met the Munstermen returning from Clontarf, and would have annihilated them. She also guessed at the shadowy Danaan, and then came down to every barrister who took place and power from Ireland's enemies.

"'No!' said Thade. 'You have mintioned a bad lot enough. But you haven't sthruck on the worst a-yet.'

"'Apostates!' shouted Kathleen. 'They who have abandoned their country and their God!'

"'You're near it,' he said, "but you haven't hit it yet.'

"There was deep silence, Katty pondering over the fire and trying to conjecture what lower depth of infamy there could be.

"The old man rose up, and he was very tall on his feet, and stooping over to where the voice of the girl directed him, he said or rather hissed, in a tragic voice:

"'In-form-ers!'

"Then resuming his seat, he said, more calmly, but still oracularly:

"'There may be a hope for these misfortunate, misguided min, who have dirtied their hands with English gold; and I am not the wan to say that even a Souper may not have a chance. Some people are now getting so tindher-hearted that they'll sind Turk, Jew, and atheist to heaven. But no wan ever in his right sinses could forgive an informer. We have forgot Keogh, and Scorpion Sullivan, and the rest of their dirty tribe, but we haven't forgot, though we never mintion their names, a Corydon, a Nagle, or a Carey!'

"After this burst the old man, whose white, sightless eyes seemed starting from their sockets, subsided into momentary silence. But it was the pause between the thunderclaps. Standing up again, and leaning over towards the girl, who was drinking in his fierce spirit, he said:

"'To quote the words of a man who didn't know what he was talking about at the time: "Hell isn't hot enough nor eternity long enough" for thim!'

"Kathleen was almost frightened, but she shared these sentiments so fully that her indignation conquered her terror.

"After another long spell the old man said again:

"'Do you think that you understhand all that I mane by thim words, a girsha?'

"'I—I think I do,' said, or rather stammered, Kathleen.

"'Thin," said the old man, reaching the grand climax of his revelations, 'you must know that you have wan of thim reptiles benathe your own roof.'

"If he had told the girl that Satan was in her house, under the disguise of a wild-cat, or that there was a familiar ghost haunting the garret under the roof, she could not have been more surprised and shocked.

"'They left their counthry and wandhered like Cain, vagabones, over the face of the airth. But they left their spawn, the spawn of reptiles, behind them.'"

The hatred of the informer is ground into the very bones of the Irish race in all parts of the world. An Irish mother would far rather see her son dead than hear that he had gone on the witness-stand to be an informer in a political trial in Ireland.

Not long ago I was talking to an otherwise thoroughly honest and upright policeman, and I said to him: "Now, suppose you knew a man in your precinct was a crook and was taking bribes; yes, suppose you caught him at it. I know that you yourself would not take a bribe, not only from what I see of you, but what I hear from others; but under these circumstances would you tell on him?"

"Commissioner," he said, "I wasn't born in Ireland, but my father and mother were, and, thank God! none of my name were ever informers either in the old country or in this. I would be ashamed to look my children in the face if I turned informer."

"Well," I said, "what would you do to such a man?" He said: "I would never speak to him or have anything to do with him. If I met him I would only know him so far as the rules and regulations made me. Besides that, everybody in the precinct would know he was a crook. Every honest man who served with him would look down upon him and despise him, and he would go with his own kind. If there were five other crooked men in the precinct they would, when off duty, get together; but as to telling on him—well, informing is a bad business. My father was ninety years of age when he died, and he used to tell us children of the fate that followed informers in Ireland—the devil would sometimes claim their bodies before they even got to the graveyard, and to the tenth generation ill-luck, misfortune, and a curse went with them. And did you ever hear of any good happening to a policeman who informed? Show me a 'squealer' or a 'kike,' and if you will let me tell you, I will show you a fellow who at heart is a coward and a disgrace to the police."

"Well, how about an officer above you?"

"Well, I have served under men, and all signs

pointed to the fact that they were making money and were not straight; but that was none of my business. I had to obey orders. Other policemen did the same, and I was no better than they were."

At one time a certain committee of eminent and well-known citizens began to collect evidence against a certain official. They promised immunity to every policeman who would come forward and tell everything he knew. Everything was made most secretive; the names were carefully guarded; the witnesses were taken to a selected place far removed from the usual police environment and there made their statements, which were taken down in writing and the record secretly preserved. Yet I found the names of these witnesses were thoroughly well known to their comrades, and I must, to be perfectly frank and truthful, say that the few with whom I came in contact were impostors and liars, and when they were caught in a wrong and about to be punished would whimper and say they were being persecuted for turning informer. Now, the most absurd thing about all this is to say that it is something peculiar to the police force. Any one who has anything to do with the army and navy knows that is not true. Soldiers and sailors don't "peach" on one another any more than do the police, and sometimes they will shield a worthless scoundrel against proper punishment, and even lie for him, while they despise him. It seems, therefore, ridiculous for people to be constantly holding up the police as wonderful examples where a fraternal and organization spirit shields evil-doers and criminals. For some of the reasons given I think this is more accentuated among the police. However, the result of this solidarity and prejudice is much more against the general good and more dangerous to the public morals than similar conditions in the army and navy.

This solidarity of the police was well illustrated by a policeman to whom I said: "Why don't you policemen who are honest and clean and straight get together and run the crooks out? Come down and tell me all about them. Go to the courts; drive them off the force." He said: "We don't get any show in the courts, and the public make no difference between us. They think we are all crooked. Now," he said, "the other day there was a man tried for his life down in the Criminal Court. Every policeman in New York believes that man is innocent. He killed a ruffian in self-defence, but the court, prosecuting officer, and the whole machinery of justice seems to be engaged in driving him to the chair. Why, down in the court-house all they talk about is the bad policeman. They call us all loafers, thieves, crooks, and murderers. The newspapers do the same. Nobody speaks out for us. Now, what do we do? Why, just naturally we get together and stand behind that man. We take a part of our salary every month and give it to his wife, and help to pay for his lawyer, and we will be behind him to the last man, to the last minute of his life, and after that we will take care of the orphans. Why shouldn't we? He is as innocent as I am, and if I had been in his place I would have done just as he did, and you would have done the same. Now, go down to the court-house and look at it — thieves, ex-convicts, prostitutes, cadets, procurers, disorderly house keepers, all received with open arms, coddled and talked softly to and sympathized with while they give their evidence against an honest and innocent man; and, mark me, if they don't get him on one charge they will have him up on another, for the newspapers and all the well-known enemies of the police are on the trail. Now, Commissioner, you know it to be a fact yourself that if any man, no matter who he is, gets up and calls the police grafters, thieves, crooks, and murderers he gets applause; whereas, if he stands up for them, you yourself know better than anybody what he gets. No, I am not going down to the court-house unless I have to.

"Now, another thing; the average policeman looks up to the big men in the town, in business and in the large corporations, in the banks, insurance companies, and in politics; and, mark my word, he knows more about them than most other people, and he compares the policemen around him with these people, and the result of it is that he comes to the conclusion that the police as a body are far more honest with the temptations they have than most of the other people in town. I know numbers, of policemen who wouldn't take a dishonest dollar. I know some men connected with other businesses, in politics, on newspapers, and at the bar, who would take anything from five cents to a hot stove and no questions asked. And what's the difference between what they call a system for collecting graft on the police force and the systems in the insurance companies, at the City Hall, and at Albany? Go down to-morrow and tell the District Attorney that you have a charge against a policeman, and every assistant will be fighting to see which will get you to his room. Go down to the newspaper offices to-morrow and tell them you know something to the credit of the police, and watch the janitor getting you into the elevator as quick as he can and heading you for the door. In other countries a policeman is looked up to. Everybody has a good word for him. Big bankers speak kindly to him; the newspapers rarely have anything to say against him and a great many things to say for him; the pulpits praise him, and the honor of the police service is as carefully looked after as the honor of the army or navy.

"Well, if you want to get us into the reforming

business for good, let the public opinion swirl around. Discharge the policeman down in the court-house, arrest the ruffians, crooks, prostitutes, and dive-keepers who are witnesses against him, and send them to the work-house; let the papers come out and tell the truth about the affair; let the Commissioner commend him and give him a medal for upholding the law and ridding the town of a possible murderer; let his wife and little children, who sit now in gloom and disgrace, feel that they have public opinion with them, in church and court-house.

"Show us the time when we go into a court-house as a witness that the criminal won't get the best of it, and that our word will go a mile where his won't go a yard; when it will be: 'Thank you, officer, for the way you have done your duty in this case. I am glad to send this man up for a year'; instead of: 'Is that all you know against this gentleman? You policemen are always interfering with people. Why don't you let this gentleman alone? The citizen has no rights these days. The next time you come here I will put you in jail. Officer (to the court-attendant), see that the gentleman gets out.' And the 'gentleman' swindler, pick-pocket, or law-breaker goes off smiling."

This spirit, and the inherent belief of all the police force from top to bottom, that the press and public are prejudiced against them, and that the courts are their enemies instead of their friends, are working untold harm here in New York. Why don't somebody start a great big society, with the very best people in New York, called, say, "Society of Friends of the Police, for the Encouragement of Well Doing." Take up the case of a policeman who is obviously wronged by any one. A few sample cases, pushed to a conclusion by a society like this, would have a wonderful effect. Now, if there was a society like this, what greater work could they be engaged in than vindicating good men, and creating a healthy, intelligent, fair public opinion, and combating ignorance, injustice and prejudice and above all aiding in building of the force on the foundation of public confidence? Will we ever get such a society? I hope so—we certainly need it. Then, besides, it would balance things, because there are at least a dozen societies formed on the other line.

As I write, there is a murder case in the courts where all concerned have forgotten the alleged murderess and her victim and are on a fierce hunt for police infamy and corruption. So far as I can see, the woman might as well go home, as nobody is bothering with her. Why not try her first and the policemen afterwards? Heaven knows, if the police concerned are half as bad as the lawyers insinuate they ought to be convicted; but don't make even murder subordinate to a new police sensation and condemn the whole force. Procuring evidence against sexual vice is necessary, but it has terrible opportunities, especially for young men; and out of the whole force only four or five men preferred this work. It was a great statesman who said that a nation was as much ruled by its prejudices as by its laws, and the curse of it is that prejudices are harder to amend, repeal, or eradicate than laws.

XVII

DETAILS AND ASSIGNMENTS

THERE can be no question whatever that the system of details in the army, navy, and police can be frightfully abused. The analogy is almost complete. The law, for instance, here in New York, compels a lot of details, such as for boiler inspection, licenses, and many other things which are not at all police work. The reason for that is this: Those interested and the Legislature cannot agree as to appointing civilians. The same thing happens every day in Congress with the army and navy. Army and navy officers are put on all kinds of work far removed from that of a soldier or sailor. Congress has great respect for the sense of honor of army and navy officers. They hold a life tenure, with liberal pay on retiring, and are credited with a high sense of duty; so they are put on many commissions, made inspectors of all sorts of government work, employed in numerous bureaus, and given many purely civilian employments in addition to being attached to American embassies and legations in foreign lands, or having new inventions turned over to them for investigation and report.

The Japanese laid down the rule that a soldier was to be trained to fight. If they wanted a wagon driver they trained him to be a wagon driver—or a book-keeper, or whatever else. An ideal service condition would be—all army officers at professional work drilling and preparing for war, all policemen on post or at work as sergeants and captains in station-houses, and all sailors on ships.

Some people who object to details in the army, navy, and police service ask why should the government waste a lot of money educating a man at West Point to be a soldier, and then, at the end of thirty years of his career, find he had not even commanded a company, but, instead, was detailed this year to Washington and next year to Duluth or Brazil, in civilian or semi-civilian occupations, and so on, until he would not know the uniform of his rank if he saw it. The nearest contact he ever gets to the army is on New Year's Day, when, if he is in Washington, he puts on his neglected official clothes and calls on the President. Now the government has lost the money spent in educating this man for a soldier, because every year he is getting further away from the education it gave him; and then, too, the men in the service have no use for him. They say, "Why, Jones has never done any soldiering. He has hardly ever seen men lined up in a company formation since he left West Point. He has been detailed here and there, doing that thing and this thing, until he would hardly know a soldier if he saw one."

All the old chronic detail men bother the life out of Presidents, Secretaries, and Commissioners with political and personal pulls, letters, and abuse of social privileges and friendly relationship. Men get to be professionally detailed men, and really become good for nothing else—very good men in their way, and useful, and even necessary, but they are not soldiers or sailors or policemen. In Washington, Senators and Congressmen wear out their shoes trying to billet officers with a home pull at the capital or on missions to Europe.

In the army, navy, and police the first consideration in details should be to give them to the old, overworked field veterans; to them should go these places, if they are able to fill them. There are policemen forty years on the force who never had a detail, and good, honest old soldiers, getting congested livers in the Philippines, who never spent six weeks on a detail in all their lives.

On the whole, I do not think the details are as much abused in the police as, say, in the army or navy. The trouble about all details is just this: They make the men on the fighting-line discontented. The old policeman thumping the sidewalk for thirty years gets discouraged when he looks at these favorites, and the feelings of old, grizzled fighting officers in the barracks, on the drill-grounds, in the camp or at sea, can well be imagined when they meet these colonels, majors, generals, and admirals who have to be introduced to their uniforms, and don't know which side their sword buckles on, and are only soldiers or sailors in the eyes of credulous civilians who know nothing about army or navy matters.

To do them justice, there is no class of men so fully alive to all this illusion as the real soldiers and sailors of the United States, and the brave, tried, and experienced policemen in New York. Details should be made fairly, squarely, and on merit, and not influenced in Washington by five-o'clock teas, or in New York by clam-bakes at Guffey's Grove; not brought about because some one is first cousin to a Senator or brother-in-law to a member of Assembly. When on the police force an honest and upright policeman is punished by constant transfers for doing his duty, a grave crime is committed against the public interests. It is, indeed, the cruelest kind of persecution when a faithful officer feels that the political powers that control the department are bent on making it so humiliating and uncomfortable for him as to force his retirement or resignation, or else entrap him on some technical violation of the rules so as to dismiss him from the force because he refused to become the tool of the friends of law-breakers, or, in other words, a political policeman, and in the performance of his duty enforced the law against interests friendly to the administration. This is one of the causes that is sapping the life out of the force. It is wonderful that public opinion permits such outrages. The press has no consistent policy in this matter, and, worse than all, some newspapers back favorites who are very unworthy men. When gamblers and crooks can tell to an hour the time of transfer for an honest captain or inspector, and the press and public are indifferent, what can you expect of the police?

As it is now, in the matter of details, it is simply going up the hill and down again. A man is cut off from doing special work with more or less advertisement and restored to-morrow. Never believe that a detail has been really and honestly abolished unless you know from the records that the place has remained vacant at least six months or a year. It is a thing not unknown to announce a wholesale abolition of certain details, and then gradually refill the places with favorites of those who are running the police administration. For instance, you will read that all men detailed to this or that public office have been put on patrol duty. As a matter of fact, their places are not only soon after filled by men with a pull, but additional men are added to the quota formerly allowed such office. It is just a sort of grim joke at the expense of the poor, ignorant public. The motto is this: "The people know little, and what they know to-day they forget to-morrow." In any event, no money is saved to the city. Only a few months ago I appointed a commission from the uniformed force, including the chief inspector, the chief of the Bureau of Detectives, and the First Deputy-Commissioner, and authorized them to cut unsparingly into the details wherever they found one not absolutely necessary. After weeks of work, the present chief inspector, as head of this commission, reported to me that the best he could find was a very small number; that to cut off the others ruthlessly and without reason would only be temporary, as the exigencies of the service would demand their restoration speedily. I went myself throughout various parts of the city to look over the details and see what work they were doing in order that this reduction might be made. I was reluctantly compelled to agree with the present chief inspector that a wholesale reduction, governed only by what might be called the laws of chance, or made on impulse, would only disarrange the public and police business, and that the places so vacated would soon have to be filled anew. In this respect the courts, the Boiler Inspection, the License Bureau, the Charity and Street Cleaning departments should by legislation be compelled to furnish their own men. It is true that the Health and Charity departments both pay for the men furnished them from the police force, but even then a policeman ought not to be assigned to any duty which is not strictly police work. He should never drive a wagon, and if the city authorities were perfectly honest in dealing with the budget there would be no necessity for his being a clerk. I made a strong effort to get civilian drivers for the wagons so as to add to the men on patrol, but the proposition, after passing the Board of Aldermen, was beaten before the Board of Estimate and Apportionment, the then Comptroller, Mr. Grout, taking the view that these civilian drivers, if appointed from the civil service, would before long have a bill introduced at Albany to make themselves a part of the uniformed force. There was other opposition, and the matter died, much to my regret.

The chief inspector, whose powers should be increased by law, should deal with this matter of details, assignments, and transfers, and only from a police point of view. A large part of the time of the Commissioner is now taken up in hearing appeals by letters and otherwise for transfers, assignments, and details. If he is only a tool in the hands of others, he simply takes his orders and makes the transfers as directed. In such a situation some one man, acting for a sort of syndicate or coterie, gives the Commissioner his orders. Well, this, at least, saves the latter from labor, and can close out the people and the police themselves. The real powers are outside, not inside, the office. This is the last stage of outrage and maladministration. It is a great mistake for the public to suppose that this pressure comes entirely from politicians. Quite the contrary. I should say, on the whole, that nearly as many clergymen came to see me in regard to these favors as politicians or district leaders. As a matter of fact, all classes in the community—bankers, merchants, professional men, retired gentlemen, the lady who had her jewelry restored to her after a theft, even the children who get to be friendly with the man on post, and, above all, the clergyman who knew the officer's family—were constantly writing or calling or sending some one to the Commissioner's office to intercede for transfers, assignments, and details. The policeman who wanted the assignment or transfer was sure not to let the citizen rest or cease his pressure on the Commissioner.

In this matter of personal and political pressure on the head of the police, I do not think that it differs greatly from the same attempt to influence the heads of such great national departments as the war and navy. The methods are different, conditions of the service not altogether similar, but the "pull" is worked in Washington as well as in New York; and the worst of it is that it militates against the hard-working officer who possibly has no influence or political friends, and who, laboring away in some obscure quarter, does not get the benefit of personal contact with Commissioners and

Secretaries. These hard working, modest men are those one would really like to seek out and aid without any influence or suggestion other than that made by their merit and deservings.

In the matter of details, too, the present consolidated daily report as to form should be changed. It treats the Traffic Squad as a "detail," a word more or less odious in the public esteem. These men do the very best sort of police work. They do it openly, and they could not shirk it if they tried, and the Traffic Squad should not be carried as swelling the aggregate of details. The bulk of the details can easily be cut down by law as outlined above, and it should be done. Legislation is necessary, because the work now being done by policemen will have to be done by civilians, and their number, salaries, and qualifications must be established. Without this proposition, to withdraw arbitrarily the police now so employed would beget confusion and possible disaster in some branches of the public service.

The fact of the existence of these coveted detail places causes much discontent among the men. They sometimes see men who are not as deserving as others sent to these places, and they suspect, rightly or wrongly, that influence has been at work. The whole force feels a sense of injustice which tends to demoralization and discouragement. I tried in vain, during the two years I was at the Police Department, to get some active aid looking to legislation at Albany to effect this reform, but the Legislature was too busy with many great measures whose importance seemed to increase every year. Then, too, there is a vast amount of indifference and ignorance on these matters, and sometimes it must be confessed the law-makers themselves look with rather a friendly eye upon these detailed places.

When it comes to individual details, it is not as easy to make a decision which is at once just and fair as it would seem upon the face of it. Take, for instance, a large orphan asylum conducted by a religious sisterhood. On one occasion the life of the sister in charge was threatened by a young man who had entered there as a foundling. He had become crazed over his parentage and came back to demand information. Frequently, drunken and rowdy parents, who had left their offspring to perish, invaded the institution, which is supported in part by public revenues. In a case of that kind the safety of the lives of these devoted women, and the comfort of the establishment having the protection and health of so many helpless children committed to it, is to be gravely considered in the giving to it of special police protection, such as the detailing of an aged and veteran patrolman whose days of usefulness in active patrol are nearly over. Or in the case of one of the active markets on the river-front. Here, during all hours of the night, are arriving long trains of heavily laden wagons with produce from Long Island, New Jersey, and other parts. A whole army of pilferers, vagabonds, and petty swindlers are drawn to this place like rats. It is therefore a matter of public necessity to yield to the request of the reputable dealers to make a special post of this market between the hours of four o'clock in the morning and twelve noon, when it becomes a great distributing centre. The longer a man is there the more useful he becomes. The whole place is characterized by marked activity in the commercial dealings which take place there, and where great sums of money, in the aggregate, are handled. I withdrew a detailed man from such a place as this, but after I heard the argument of the dealers in the market I gladly returned him. In the case of piers, docks, ferries, and railroad stations, if the public safety demands the presence of regular policemen, should protection be wholly refused to the people because in so doing a private corporation may be incidentally benefited? Anything a corporation can do for the safety and protection of its patrons it should do at its own expense; but if it cannot give adequate security to the public with uniformed employés, where shall we draw the line between considering the place a public one or as a private enclosure? Is there a hard and fast rule, or must each case be governed by its own circumstances?

Now these two places may be taken as samples of many others so far as the principle is concerned. Men are detailed to such institutions as Randall's Island, the various protectories to which boys and girls are committed, and to places of amusement where nightly and daily the police have to look after the safety and comfort of great concourses of our citizens, where one uniformed man of the regular force, it cannot be denied, is equal by his very presence to at least five special officers paid by the establishment itself. In the case of a fire panic in a theatre, one policeman of the regular force will be better than any number of excited and unofficial employés. The same thing applies in summer to the public bathing establishments, the recreation piers, and those near-by resorts which have to be most strictly and carefully policed.

To sum it up: Cut down the details unsparingly wherever possible; adopt a policy backed by rule and system; don't approach the task as a kind of blind-man's-buff; don't slash around just to get a head-line in a newspaper; cut out all consideration of persons, politics, or "pull"; put it squarely up to the Legislature and the city authorities to co-operate; look out for the meritorious and make the detail an honor; consider all the public interests, and keep a good man where he is rendering the best service. There are men on detail in the army, navy, and police whose places could not, without distinct loss to the service, be filled by others in or out of the organization. In such cases rotation for the mere sake of change is a wrong to the public.

The vital importance of making wise assignments to important places and standing by those assigned against all possible pressure was well illustrated in the case of Captain Robert E. Dooley, of the Coney Island precinct. Under Captain Dooley a distinct reformation in the conduct of this great summer resort for the masses of our people was successfully inaugurated, and for these results infinite credit must be given him. There is no more honest man on any police force, and there is no policeman who has suffered so severely for his honesty and vigorous enforcement of the laws. Whenever the order of the day is for crooks at the front, look for him in disgrace at the rear—the place of honor under such conditions. Under his command Coney Island, from being a resort of thieves, thugs, prostitutes, swindlers, fakirs, gamblers, a field for indecent exhibitions and disorderly characters of both sexes, and of graft in all forms, became one of the cleanest sea-side resorts in this country. During the last two summers millions of decent and orderly citizens, with their wives and families, young girls and boys, a vast army of all classes, have enjoyed the daily outings there. Sometimes in one day the crowd will number hundreds of thousands, being much greater than attend most international exhibitions in a similar time, and yet during these two years scarcely a case of even petty theft occurred, very few arrests of disorderly or drunken persons, and there was not one gambling-house, poolroom, disorderly house, or assignation hotel on the whole island. The excise law was rigorously but reasonably enforced; all places closed at one o'clock, and the closing was no fiction. There were positively no all-night resorts. Under this police administration immense sums of money were invested by reputable corporations in providing amusements on a colossal scale, and Coney Island has become a pleasure resort not only for Greater New York, but practically for a big part of the country.

Better than all this, under Captain Dooley there was positively no police grafting of any kind. Every one obeyed the same law, and hence no one had to pay blackmail. Swindlers and thieves found no place on the island, and therefore there was no partnership with the police; disorderly men and women had to find other resorts; petty fakes and swindles were promptly suppressed. This style of administration caused very violent opposition in certain quarters, an opposition which begot for me an immense and continuous pressure from sources far apart. Coney Island, under a corrupt administration, would yield graft of immense proportions. One great source easily attained was to pass the word around through the various hotels, amusement places, resorts, and saloons that only certain brands of beer, cigars, whiskey, mineral waters, wines, and even food, would be allowed on sale without incurring police displeasure and persecution. How much does any one think a great brewery concern would pay for such a monopoly for one season?—or for an all-night license for their sole agency even in one place?

Captain Dooley was unfortunate enough, in the rigorous enforcement of the law and in the very vigorous cleansing to which he subjected the island in the regenerating process, to incur the enmity of a few of the men of the baser sort who attach themselves to great newspapers, misleading their editors and abusing their privileges, and taking every advantage of the opportunities of their position for their personal benefit. It would be an injustice to hold them as representative of the entire press, or, indeed, as fairly representing the newspapers whose police cards they held, until in some cases they were forfeited under arrest. If one of these men should prove himself corrupt or unworthy, his opportunities of blackmailing were even greater than that of a dishonest policeman, more especially if he had the run of the station-house and was allowed access to its secrets.

No newspaper should send a reporter as a permanent assignment to such important station-houses as Coney Island, the old and new Tenderloins, or other big precincts, unless they know him to be a thoroughly honest and reliable man and proof against all temptations, and free entirely from any bias or prejudice; otherwise its confidence is likely to be abused and its very name and power may be used for corrupt and extortionate purposes, and its influence for good in police circles entirely destroyed. If the man is lacking in these qualities, and is, on the contrary, corrupt, malicious, and deceitful, he will mislead his newspaper, constantly distort the facts, publish falsehoods, and prostitute the paper to his own uses; but beyond and above all this, he will be the instrument in doing serious injury to one of the most important bodies in the public service and to the public itself. In this connection it must be remembered that to suppress the truth is, if anything, more dangerous than to distort it in the telling.

In connection with this abuse of their claims and privileges by a few unworthy members of the press, I recall an instance of how a captain incurred the lasting enmity of three reporters and their friends under these circumstances. These men were in a concert-hall under the influence of liquor, and about the time when the law says a place of this class shall close. There was a woman singing on the stage, and they beckoned to the head-waiter and told him, to use their own language, "Bring that thing down here; we want to talk to it." He said it was against the rules and the law, and he refused. A few minutes after the closing hour they demanded to be served with drinks, and on being refused flashed their police cards, and told the waiter they would write up the place and put it out of business unless their demands were granted. They were ejected, and just at that moment the captain of the precinct with two policemen, a thoroughly fearless and honest man, came along. They drew their cards indignantly again, and defied the police and all concerned. The captain confiscated the cards and promptly locked them up, and the next day they were fined in the police court. I am in ignorance of whether the proprietors of the newspapers, some of whom I communicated with about these cards, saw to it that these men were never allowed again to report for any newspaper, or whether this outrageous conduct on their part was condoned. The likelihood is that the men who employed them never knew of the real facts, but the captain in question has not yet ceased to feel the vengeance with which these men and their friends have followed him.

XVIII

HARBOR POLICE. THE WATER-FRONT

GREATER NEW YORK has a water-front of several hundred miles, and there is more or less activity on every foot of it. On the North and East rivers, and in parts of Brooklyn, the piers are scenes of the greatest activity. Large steamers and sailing-vessels of all kinds and conditions, and under all flags, come to these places to be docked, to discharge and receive cargo. Every product of the earth, natural and artificial, is loaded and unloaded here. All the great railroad companies have numbers of piers where freight-cars are brought on floats. These cars bring an immense volume of freight to the city, and receive in turn an equally large amount. The traffic in and around these piers is intensely congested and has to be regulated by the police. West Street and South Street, especially in the vicinity of the railroad piers and those given over to the big coastwise lines and at the ferries, are often so jammed with trucks and wagons and stevedores that if left unregulated business would be brought to a stand-still. Indeed, this is one of the great problems the city of New York has to wrestle with in its competition with other cities like Boston, Baltimore, Philadelphia, and especially Norfolk and Newport News, Virginia. If New York is to keep her place, this traffic must be handled expeditiously and with order. These long lines of trucks laden with dry-goods must be able to get to the piers without too much delay, and good order must be maintained on the docks and piers; this is especially so on the North River side.

In addition to this, thieves are constantly invading this district. Cases of valuable goods and other property to the amount of thousands of dollars are stolen annually, and sometimes the whole outfit—horses and truck and goods—is stolen and driven off in the confusion while the driver is looking after a bill of lading. The very boldest and hardest thieves to catch work along the water-front. On many of the piers there is no doubt that the companies and those interested should have a sufficiency of watchmen with special police powers; but however well it may sound in theory, the uniformed, regular policeman is the only man that can handle the situation effectively. I have heard all that can be said on either side, and I have examined the thing personally time and again, and this is not only my opinion but is the conviction of old policemen and citizens generally who understand the subject. Of course, if they are not carefully watched, these men may abuse the trust reposed in them, and become more like servants of the steamship and railroad companies than of the city. I think the limits of police duty might be fairly drawn at the pier-line, the companies regulating the course of vehicular traffic on the pier or dock itself.

In summer, when hundreds of thousands of people are travelling by the river and day boats, policing the piers is simply an absolute necessity—that is, at the hours when these boats leave and arrive. At some of the piers the boats are constantly coming and going. This is one of those cases where it is hard to look after the interest of the general public without conferring a benefit on some individual or company. Here are a lot of helpless women and children crowding, pushing, and jammed on the end of a pier waiting for an excursion-boat. Well, suppose you say the company should look after them to see that their pockets are not picked or that they are not brutally treated by rough men, or insulted, or that decent and orderly citizens are not assaulted by toughs and disorderly characters. If the work of policing the piers is left to a few underpaid employés of a company, and the citizens suffer so that there is general complaint of lack of police protection, what should the Commissioner do? The company has technically complied with its duty. It has appointed two special policemen, probably good enough men to get a badge, but the rough element in the crowd understand that they are not really policemen in the sense in which they generally use that term, and they pay little or no attention to them.

In the hot weather the citizens want to get out of town for a breath of air for themselves and the children, and so go down to Coney Island or up the river, and they have a perfect right to demand that the police protect them going on and off these boats. As to any argument between the Police Department and the company, that is really a matter in which they take little or no concern; what they want is police protection from the regular city authorities. The Police Commissioner cannot say to a woman who has been insulted, whose children have been pushed and jammed and walked on, or an honest and decent man who has been assaulted by a tough, that complaint should be made to the company, which is supposed to look after their patrons more carefully. The citizens generally look upon these piers and docks as public places to be policed by the authorities. Once these boats have started, all this life on the water, whether for commerce, business, or pleasure, must also be looked after by the police so long as they are in New York waters.

The excursion that has been all day at some shore resort is now, with two or three barges laden almost beyond the safety-line with men, women, and children, coming back in the darkness to some pier on the North or East river to discharge its army of people, and has to be carefully looked after. The small rough element that went out with it in the morning has been drinking heavily all day. On the way home they begin to fight, throw bottles, probably fire pistols, assault men and insult women, and even terrorize the officers of the boat. The situation is dangerous and disgraceful. When the poor, frightened people have become almost desperate, and men almost helpless in contending with these ruffians who are revelling in their display of power and brutality, suddenly out of the darkness there comes alongside the police-boat *Patrol*, practically a small gun-boat or revenue-cutter in type. The big, brawny water police are on the barges in a minute, and the officers of the law are now doing the clubbing and shooting, if any is necessary. The tables are turned, and the terrified passengers thank God for the harbor police, and they are glad that the city has been wise enough to provide them with this boat and several steam-launches so that the whole water-front of Greater New York can be properly patrolled night and day. This squad is known as the forty-second precinct, and the steamer lies in at Pier A, North River.

The men work in platoons the same as on shore. They have nearly all been sailors or watermen before being policemen. They are great, big, strong men. They can handle a row-boat finely in all kinds of weather and under all conditions. They can all swim, and have saved many lives, and on the average they are better shots than the land force, because shooting at desperate dock-robbers who will return the fire is not uncommon. A man on the harbor police has to know how to shoot well if he doesn't want to get shot himself. A year ago, for instance, they practically cleaned out a systematic business of robbing coal from barges on the shores of Staten Island. Thieves from both the island and the Jersey shore would boldly carry off tons upon tons of coal from barges and floats. The fighting here was simply real war, both sides being armed, and there were many daring captures made at the risk of life and limb. There were no bolder or daring thieves than these. They would fight to the last, and then not even hesitate to plunge, in winter, into the icy water and try to escape. They also had made many original devices for taking the coal from the barges into their boats, and in some instances they had boats with motive power, capable of holding several tons, working in the trade. If it had not been for the harbor police the coal-trade of this part of the port would have suffered serious injury.

The dock-thieves, who make the big hauls of silks and laces or other valuable goods, are hardy, bold, and daring men. They are thoroughly reckless and brutal, and will stand up to kill or be killed. They almost invariably fire on the police, and it is a question sometimes of who gets the first shot. In one instance they got under the dock, and, by a series of borings, weakened the planking until they could chop it away and let two or three bales of goods drop down into their boat. The goods were worth several thousand dollars, but before they escaped they were captured by the police.

Then, on the water as on the land, there are a lot of small pilferers, sometimes under the guise of junkmen. These fellows hover around the piers like water-rats. They go down the bay and cheat the men or steal from the ships anchored there. They are restlessly prowling day and night, here finding a bit of rope, there some copper or other metal, and occasionally, if they get a chance, a little smuggling is added to the business. In summer a number of professional water-thieves hover around the small yachts, cat-boats, and sail-boats, like a lot of hungry wolves ravenous for food, pilfering and plundering, breaking into cabins, looting them, and sometimes actually stealing some of the smaller boats. In the summer-time, too, the whole water-front is alive, more especially with men and boys fishing, swimming, and boating; half-drunken young toughs in all sorts of small sailing-craft terrorizing the landing-places and insulting respectable people who are having a day's outing; dangerous characters prowling around the shorefront, looking for victims; and at night the big piers, especially on the East Side, are crowded with humanity, awake and asleep—all this calls for the outer guard of the harbor police, and their record is one of which New York may be proud. I do not remember, during my administration, of having one complaint against any of these men, and I have had great numbers of letters praising them and thanking them for special work they had done.

The steamer *Patrol* was condemned in 1905 as to her boilers, and other changes were found necessary. She is now practically a new boat and much improved. There were built during the last two years four steam-launches which are now in use. The river policemen take the rough and the smooth. Naturally, when things are quiet and orderly, or especially in winter, when the harbor conditions are such as to lessen life on the water-front and render navigation more or less difficult, they do not have to work so hard as in the summer-time. But the case is exactly parallel with that of the Fire Department boats. A fire-boat may lie at her dock for days or weeks without being called to a fire, but no one would think of putting the men ashore and making them hose the streets up-town because it so happened that they had not been called on for some days to fight a fire.

Taken all the year around, the harbor policeman works hard and renders full service for all the pay he gets. Then there is always something to do about the boats, such as scrubbing, a little painting, and making minor repairs, and, of course, drilling. And, besides, she is most of the time under way patrolling and directing the movements of the men in the smaller boats and visiting the water-side sub-stations. In this connection, too, it might be said that the *Patrol* is fitted up as a fire-boat and can put four streams on a fire, so that she is liable to be called on at fires just the same as the fire-boats. It is a fine service, taken altogether, and those who saw these brave, big, tender-hearted fellows the black day of the *Slocum* disaster, standing for hours in the water of the sound, and working tirelessly to recover the dead and render service to the living, felt proud of them and of the city they serve.

XIX

PERENNIAL AND SEASONABLE TROUBLES

Our benevolent friends in the United States Agricultural Department label many of their gifts of seeds as either perennial or annual, in the blessings of their usufruct. Some plants yield their perfumes and their fruits in the all too brief summer, and then pass away, but the hardier kind remain to remind us of the good-government Santa Claus all the year round. The Police Commissioner has some troubles that eat, sleep, and sit at his desk with him when blizzards drive citizens in desperation to the Subway and are just as vigorous when the open surface-car is none too open. All the year round the Commissioner is made to feel that he is under the ban of at least some courts.

These courts apparently guard with the most jealous care the rights and privileges of all policemen so far as affects their tenure of office; so that a continuous procession of dismissed policemen go from Headquarters to the courts, and by the latter are promptly returned to duty with pay for the time that they have been out of office; indeed, the longer a policeman who has been branded as dismissed from the force is out of office the greater amount of money he receives on his return, without having rendered any services therefor, the proceeding resolving itself into most delightful and restful vacations. If he is dismissed to-day and does not get back for two years, on his return he has presented to him two years' salary, with various costs and tearful judicial apologies for the possible injury to his feelings. This large amount of ready money makes it easy to employ the best legal talent, and where a great number of officers have been dismissed at one time, counsel is as easily procurable as in a good accident case against a railroad company. If one case will determine the principle at stake, it is customary for law firms to make contracts with a number of other officers affected, and by fighting the one case they dispose of all the others. The result of this is that a number of lawyers have become, by special training and experience, very able and clever in the obtaining of writs of injunction and mandamus against the Police Commissioner in the matter of fines and dismissals, and in all other cases where policemen believe that their rights have been infringed by the Commissioner, either individually or as representatives of a class. For instance, it was determined in one case that a man detailed to Headquarters for detective work was in law appointed a detective. This case was taken up and very persistently and cleverly fought out by the lawyers for the complainant. The principle, once established, forced the Commissioner to recognize a large number of men as detective-sergeants.

In a more recent case the Commissioner put an unusually large number of officers before the board of surgeons to be examined as to their physical capacity. The charter explicitly states that when the surgeons have in writing certified to the Commissioner that a policeman of any grade is totally unfitted for further police duty, from the physical stand-point, he shall dismiss and retire such officer on the pension allowed by law. In these latter cases the Commissioner, acting under advice as to form from the Corporation Counsel's office, presented a number of officers whom he had reason to believe were not physically fit for the performance of their duties. They were examined before the full board of surgeons, acting as a board, and the certification as to their unfitness was signed by the president and secretary of the board, as for the board. A test case was made as to this finding, and the courts held that the certification was not in proper form, but that the same should have been signed by the individual physicians who made the examination, the Commissioner having the right to designate by name the physicians to whom these cases were to be referred, and that the word "police" before duty had been omitted. This decision did not at all interfere with the finding of fact, as to whether the man was physically able to perform his duty. The court having decided that the form was improper, and that, therefore, no legal certification had been made to the Commissioner, reinstated those who had been thus retired, and at this writing the court seems inclined to the view that there is no limit of time within which all of the officers concerned cannot bring similar suits against the Commissioner to obtain a peremptory mandamus for their reinstatement.

This situation is a very interesting one both for the police and the public. An officer is sent before the full board of surgeons, who make a careful, elaborate, and painstaking professional examination. They certify to the Commissioner as a board, over the signatures of their president and secretary, that the officer examined is suffering from heart disease, or that his eyesight is such as to seriously interfere with his professional requirements, and that the disease is progressive and incurable. The officer goes to court, carries his case successfully to the court of last resort, which declares that the certification of the board of surgeons is not in proper form, and that therefore the action of the Commissioner on same was without justification in law. A peremptory mandamus issues that this officer shall be immediately put back on duty. This, of course, must be complied with, and a large sum of back salary paid to him, and the question as to succeeding promotions thrown into disorder and chaos; yet here is a man who a full board of surgeons deliberately, under their oath of office, have certified, was totally unfit for the performance of the police duty for which he is to be paid. Now, so far as the writer knows, the larger question of fact, as to his fitness or unfitness to perform his work, has not been passed upon by the courts.

In the army and navy the findings of surgeons or boards of surgeons, as to the question of fact regarding physical disability, are final and cannot be controverted in court. Indeed, in the matter of a cadet at the Naval Academy, the Secretary is not allowed by law to receive any outside medical testimony against the finding of the surgeons at the Academy. This is a well-established rule in both the army and navy, and from the wording of the charter it would certainly appear that the lawmakers intended the same procedure with reference to the Police Department. I have no hesitation in saying that, in my judgment, it should not be otherwise. Why should a policeman be given any more rights in this respect than an officer in the army or navy? I have myself known some very painful cases in the navy, where officers in all other respects eminently qualified to continue their professional career, have been retired to civil life, to the great regret of the service; but the board of surgeons were compelled, under their oath of office, to certify that they suffered from chronic and incurable defects, which brought them below the standard required. So far as the navy is concerned, there is no cause more frequent than that of eyesight, and while it might be true that a higher standard would be required for an officer in command of a battle-ship than for a captain of a precinct, still it must be obvious to any one that a man with marked and chronic defection of eyesight is not fit to perform police duty. There is no doubt in my mind that the surgeons appointed by the Police Commissioner, and acting for him, are the ones to fix the standard of physical requirements. If the courts have not decided that the certification of the surgeons as to physical disability is something which can be controverted by outside testimony, then it would seem to the ordinary citizen that it would be a singular state of affairs to have a man remain on the force whose physical condition, as certified to by a whole board of surgeons acting together, is such that he is totally unfit to perform police duty. It will, in my judgment, be to the public interests that this question be settled definitely and for all time; and in this connection it may be noted that there is a bill, at this writing, pending in the Legislature, apparently offered in the interest of those on the force who do not want to submit to physical examination, which is to be final and incontrovertible, and under the provisions of which the finding of the surgeons is a question of fact against which evidence can be offered before the Commissioner, and a hearing, with counsel present, be given, before he approves or disapproves the same. The rule and the law should be that the surgeons, with the approval of the Commissioner, fix the physical standard, and that the findings of police surgeons duly designated, that a policeman does not come up to this standard, and that he is permanently unfit to perform police duty, should be findings of facts, final in their effect and not controvertible in or out of court.

I think any one who has given this subject serious consideration will agree that it is much better in a service like the police, as well as for the army and navy, that men who are not up to the full standard of physical requirements shall be retired. Indeed, for the last twenty or thirty years, Congress has been constantly agitated by the younger men in the navy to open the way for retirement for older officers. The great incentive in a military or semi-military body is promotion, and where the city and the nation have their pick of the very best men for command, the law should be such as to facilitate the selection of the finest material, both physically and mentally. A policeman, even more than a soldier or sailor, is liable at any minute to be called upon to stand the greatest physical strain; he is likely to encounter at any time the crisis that calls for perfect physical strength and good health; and, indeed, many think that physical well-being in the police is a greater necessity than mental ability. I have but to say, in passing on these cases, that if a full board of surgeons certify that a man has an incurable disease of an organic and progressive type to-day, it would, of course, be impossible for them, without stultifying themselves, a year from now to certify that he had entirely recovered. Their original finding, therefore, made under their oath of office, must be accepted by the Commissioner as a settled fact.

At the beginning of my administration I had returned to me a great number of officers who had been dismissed by former Commissioners. The courts returned these on various grounds, such as the failure to produce or refusal to admit evidence, and other reasons common in the review of cases under the penal code. The judges of the higher courts, it must be said, are not so much to blame in the matter. They have before them but the printed record. They are bound under their oath of office to judge this by the strict rules of law, and the policy of the courts is that these police trials must conform to the strictest technicalities of criminal jurisprudence. An honest and conscientious Commissioner, acting for the public good, will have a better knowledge of the defendant, his merits and demerits, and his character and efficiency as a policeman, than any written record will disclose. As it is, an active Police Commissioner will have ample opportunity of becoming acquainted with the mandatory writs of the higher courts, as well as some extraordinary opinions of a few of the police magistrates as to the rights of the citizens and the police. He can, of course, solace himself with the idea that he is the best friend of the legal profession, even if he compels some of the judges to labor overtime in the signing of the multitudinous writs which flow in at Police Headquarters.

I believe it best that there should be connected with the Police Department, either independently or from the Corporation Counsel's office, a thoroughly competent lawyer, who should look after those cases in which the Police Commissioner is involved, and to advise with him on the legal questions of large public import constantly arising, and I am on record officially as advocating this course. I have not the slightest hesitation in saying that if during my incumbency of the office I had had connected therewith continuously such a lawyer, that he could easily have beaten down at their inception ninety-five per cent. of the injunctions obtained in favor of poolrooms and disorderly houses. It is utterly impossible to get the best results with one assistant from the Corporation Counsel's office detailed to-day and another to-morrow, and numbers of other assistants in charge of police cases in Brooklyn and other boroughs who are unknown to the Commissioner and ignorant of the customs and rules of the Department, and not one anywhere directly under the control of the Police Commissioner. The latter has to request all opinions, even in great emergencies, as a rule, by letter, with due regard to the conventionalities. In the case of required opinions, where the courts appear to be divided as to whether or not the law has been broken, sometimes a seasonable infraction of the law would have ceased before the opinion was rendered. An opinion on shovelling snow from sidewalks asked for in winter, might come along about the time the robins were nesting again; and hard-worked counsel could give a better opinion on Sunday baseball in midwinter than in summer.

It was the custom of most of the pool-rooms in New York to get their favorite writs in Brooklyn. For some reason which I could never ascertain, they seemed to think that the judicial atmosphere over there was more friendly, and their cases were generally taken to that borough. These cases could have been forced back to Manhattan for trial, and so long as one assistant was allowed to do the work pertaining to the Police Department, such was the practice.

As this book goes to press, the Appellate Division of the Supreme Court has rendered a most important and far-reaching decision affecting the police in dealing with pool-rooms and disorderly houses. In a case brought against me as Police Commissioner, the court decided that the granting of this great equitable remedy in behalf of alleged pool-rooms is improper and an abuse of the writ. This decision, coupled with that of the Court of Appeals, allowing the police to make special posts of suspected places, gives the Police Commissioner greater powers than hitherto, and unties his hands in the work of suppressing all pool-rooms and disorderly houses.

A dismissed policeman, a pool-room keeper, a gambler, an owner or lessee of property used for illegal purposes, and a confidence man, are the hardest fighters in the courts that a Commissioner meets. Whether it is because they get the ablest lawyers and those of most experience, who are thoroughly drilled in their specialty, I do not know; but while an ordinary citizen might fail fifty times out of sixty to get a writ to stop a nuisance, whether from smoke or noise, or to compel a railroad company to treat him as fairly well as the transported steer, he does not seem to get writs half as readily as these very able and clever people. There was one lawyer who, during my administration, got out hundreds of writs. When he missed suing me for one day, I felt lonely. He must have become very rich. My picture ought, at least, to adorn the cabin of his yacht.

The unfortunate Police Commissioner, if an honest man, is always between the devil and the deep-blue sea. If he doesn't prevent crime and repress vice, he must be crucified by public opinion, honest and dishonest; and if he infracts the law by even a letter in the act of prevention and repression, he is very lucky, in addition to the enemies he has made, if he escapes going to jail or being mulcted in heavy damages, which the very public who insist upon his enforcing the law will be glad to have him pay. Then, as the seasons roll round, each brings with it its own peculiar delights. As the bluebird appears in the hedges in the country, the small boy naturally takes to baseball in the streets, and as the weather grows more genial the older boys and young men hasten on the one day of the week at their disposal to the back lots and suburban commons to play the national game. Heaven forbid that I should get into any controversy with my Sabbatarian friends, but I must tell them that I almost regretted there was any summer at all, when they began to urge me to repress Sunday baseball among the four million more or less hard-working population of Greater New York. The fight for professional baseball on Sunday has been waged for some years past, and the Sunday law has been twisted and distorted in the higher courts, until just at present there is no thoroughly binding decision; and one learned judge has rendered what appears to be two distinct opinions on the same subject. The baseball people were also very ingenious, and, to avoid charges for admission, used to sell score-cards at arbitrary prices or accept voluntary contributions. In the courts, as high as the Special Sessions in Kings County, their attitude reminds me of that of a well-known labor advocate who was in my time a member of Congress. It was his custom, on the day given to the Labor Committee, to bring in a bunch of bills in favor of organized labor. He was nothing of a lawyer or orator himself, and as he advanced down the central aisle of the House, presenting a bill for consideration and addressing the Speaker, he would say: "The friends of the bill will keep silent; the enemies will do the talking. Let us vote." The minor courts seem to be all friends of the bill (or the ball), as they almost invariably acquit, without committing themselves to expressed judicial reasons on the law governing the case—and the enemies of the Sunday game do the most talking. I do not remember a case where any one was ever fined in a magistrate's court for playing ball on Sunday, and there has been an unbroken line of acquittals in other courts. I do not think that this crime got so far as the Special Sessions in Manhattan. The only way, therefore, that the police could suppress Sunday baseball playing was by continuous arrests of each individual player on the ground, and as they get a variety of judicial opinions, even where they are honest and well-intentioned in the premises, they sometimes fall back on the Commissioner and want something definite from him. The last official deliverance on this question was by the present Corporation Counsel, who gave a decision against the playing of baseball on Sunday, and under which the police have acted up to this date.

From the time the frost leaves the ground until football rages, no Police Commissioner will get lonely so far as this question of Sunday baseball and other out-door games on that day is concerned, for between disagreeing officials and discordant courts, the desire of human nature for amusement, exercise, and fresh air makes the conflict in its character irrepressible. Without venturing into the moral or theological domain, and premising it by saying that my early training in this respect was of the strictest kind, I feel compelled to propound this question: Whether it is better to have a large number of young working-men, on Sunday afternoon after church hours, seated peacefully and orderly breathing fresh air, watching a game of baseball in some remote suburban locality, without the slightest annoyance to the neighbors, than to have the same number of young men strewn throughout the congested and overheated districts of the city stewing in hot quarters of tenement-houses, standing in disorderly groups on street corners to the annoyance of every one in the neighborhood, or sneaking through side doors into saloons to drink liquor, possibly to break the peace, and pay all the penalties of dissipation.

In the winter the Commissioner's mail apprises

him of the uncleaned sidewalks, as to snow and ice, and the failure of the police to enforce the ordinance, when, as a matter of fact, all the police can do is to report the violation to the Corporation Counsel for a summons. Then all the out-door games of boyhood and girlhood come up in their season. In a great city like this, until plenty of parks can be had for this natural life of youth, one cannot help feeling sorry for children, and, yes, for dogs. A natural, healthy boy and a young, playful dog, with a narrow, hot, ill-smelling street congested with traffic for a playground, appear to be such hopeless, helpless prisoners, and more out of place than a bird in a cage. The police, however, must keep the streets safe for pedestrians and those dwelling therein, and cannot stop to admire that beautiful game of "cat," where a boy strikes the cat, or sharpened bit of stick, on the end and has it gyrate through the air into the eye of the pedestrian. Of course, in winter nearly every boy finds joy in throwing snow-balls.

With the first notes of spring the organ-grinder is on the streets, and with his appearance comes the complaint. One woman, poor soul, of course doesn't want him to play in her block, and the woman just across the street dotes on him. The Commissioner has to arbitrate the case or throw up his hands in despair. Then, long before the Fourth of July the fire-cracker complaints pour into the office. The nuisance reached the limit of endurance last year with the invention of a new explosive—something that sounded a little louder than the big guns Togo had on his battle-ship, and which gave ninety-five explosions to the minute. Some department of the city government had, apparently, generously given every kind of shop and news-stand license to sell fireworks. The evil became so great that I turned loose two or three plain-clothes men from Headquarters to repress it, telling them not to make arrests unless absolutely necessary. They did most effective work. They did so well with this, that when "cat," snow-ball, football, and baseball, and all the strenuous boy-life, including good, old-fashioned boy fights, followed fireworks, as they had preceded them in nearly every street, I kept these men at the work of repressing dangerous practices and restoring some degree of public safety. When it was concluded by a wiser authority that anything dubbed "squad" was a thing of evil and something to feel the official axe at once, this fire-cracker squad, so-called, was advertised as an all-the-year-round institution of vast numbers, and a most agreeable asylum for three or four battalions of policemen who did not want to work. Any one can see it was a huge joke. Just think of it! A fire-cracker squad at Christmas, and the squad numbering at least a hundred! I suppose these two men in plain clothes could do more and did more to break up dangerous games and practices on the public streets than any one hundred uniformed officers. Watch a bunch of real boys up to any deviltry, whether it is throwing baseballs through front windows, playing crap, or stoning an unfortunate peddler, "cat," "duck on the rock," holding up smaller boys, wrecking lamps; and could any herd of deer be quicker to scent the enemy than they to see the uniformed policeman? I was reading recently that certain species of deer signalled the approach of man to their fellows by wagging their tails, the white under-hair acting as a flag. That is pretty good for a deer, but in New York rarely does a policeman get near enough to a group of these spry, keen young savages to need signalling his presence. A small boy at one corner can see a policeman in the middle of the next block, and when the yell goes up, "Cheese it, here comes the cop," he might just as well try to catch the Empire State Express after it got fairly well under way, or to chase a fox in thick woods, as to lay his hands on the smallest and feeblest boy. In winter the congested in-door life produces its own crop of vice and crime, and the free out-door life of summer, with its excursions, games, and sports, and bright sunshine and sweet communion with nature, brings joy to many, but, as a consequence, sadness to the municipal scapegoat in the wilderness of Mulberry Street.

XX

MAGISTRATES

I AM not prepared to say that all magistrates are habitually antagonistic to the police; but, on the other hand, it is no exaggeration to state that as a body their attitude seems to be at all times one of suspicion, where the relations between them should, on the contrary, be confidential and founded on mutual respect. In practice, the attitude of the magistrates varies with the individual. Personally, I endeavored to lessen the friction between the magistrates and the police in every possible way. I have never criticised a magistrate where I believed that he was acting honestly and judicially, even if I thought he was wrong.

The large majority of the members of the force who have talked to me about magistrates trying cases without regard to testimony of the police feel that the magistrates are unfriendly to them, and that they do not treat them fairly in the courts. They say that some of the magistrates are more anxious to find fault with the police witness than to examine into the guilt of the defendant. In a great many cases I am told that corroborative evidence must be gotten beyond that of the police; in other words, police evidence is not considered sufficient. Often it is demanded that there shall be two police witnesses. If one is a liar, why two liars? In numerous instances the evidence of one policeman will not move the wheels of justice at all.

Some magistrates cross-examine the officer at great length, giving encouragement to notoriously professional crooked defendants by assuming a hostile attitude and making it evident to every one that they do not believe the officer. Unless the officer is a clever man, as well as an intelligent one, and knows something about law, a series of questions hurled at him in this way is apt to confuse him. When the magistrate gets through cross-examining he is handed over to a shrewd criminal lawyer, who gives him another turn. By this time the case of the defendant is sometimes apparently forgotten altogether and he is allowed to go, almost with an apology for being arrested. In saying this I do not want to condemn the magistrates as a body; I have great respect for some of them as honorable and upright gentlemen as well as efficient judges.

There seems in some quarters a disposition to believe that the policeman has some ulterior motive when he pushes a case, and that he is paid for it when he appears to falter in his evidence. They refuse to believe that he can be thoroughly honest and active, and with no motive other than a public and police one for pressing a case with vigor against a defendant; and, on the other hand, if he honestly and conscientiously hesitates in his testimony, either to hold or to convict, he is believed to do so for some improper reason. "Graft," politics, and women are supposed to be the main-springs of action with the policemen in giving their evidence. The very worst that comes from this state of affairs is that it encourages and aids crooked policemen to sell out to the defendants. The general attitude of the magistrates to the police gives a ready excuse for failure to hold or convict, when policemen are called to account by the Commissioner. When one magistrate advises law-breakers to shoot the police, and another says he would not believe any number of them in certain cases, what can a Commissioner do?

I do not know that the magistrates as a body assume that the sworn word of an officer of the law is worthless. If such a state of affairs exists, it is a positive public calamity and ought to be investigated thoroughly and at once by those charged with law-making or the administration of justice.

From the police point of view a large number of defendants are discharged who ought to be held, tried, convicted, and sent to prison. I have not found in my official dealings with the police that they as a body are liars; on the contrary, I have had some very strong examples of truth-telling where it required moral courage on the part of the witness. In putting up defences against their own delinquencies, they are, it must be admitted, ingenious and clever, to say the least. Human nature is such that, of course, some allowance must be made for the incentive of proper professional zeal on the part of a policeman against a defendant. The former, if he is honest, is naturally, after making an arrest, anxious to establish his case, particularly if he is morally convinced that the defendant is guilty.

I think the main chasm of difference between the magistrates and the police lies in this, that the police have a knowledge of the defendant, his mode of living, habits, character, and life generally, which enables them to reach conclusions with reference to his guilt, but which at the same time is not always susceptible of being reduced to absolute legal proof, especially when the rights of the professional crook are guarded so zealously; whereas the magistrates, on the other hand, look at the case from a purely technical point of view. This difference is a very natural one, and allowance should be made for it by the magistrate. An officer arraigns a prisoner before a magistrate. He says: "This man is a pickpocket; he is a vagrant; his picture is in the rogues' gallery. This is the seventh time that I have personally arrested him. I caught him on a Thirty-fourth Street crowded car with two or three other pick-pockets, who escaped. A great many citizens are having their pockets picked there every day. He has no honest means of support. Down at the Detective Bureau we all know him as a professed crook all his life. He is a dangerous man to be at large." The magistrate says, "Well, prove to me legally that he has no means of support." The prisoner thereupon hauls five-hundred-dollar bills out of every pocket, shows a large diamond, and calls up an accomplice, who swears that he keeps a small tailor-shop and that the man works for him. Thereupon the magistrate turns around and discharges the defendant and reprimands the officer. Every day in the year, like pouring water into a sieve, a great army of professional crooks are run through the police courts; they go in one door and come out the other. The police, as agents for the suppression of crime, believe these men ought to be kept perpetually in prison, so far as the law will permit, and that they have no more right to be at large in the city than the wolves up at the Zoological Garden. Only the other day I read in the newspaper that a magistrate in discharging four notorious pick-pockets reprimanded the officer and sarcastically told the defendants that hereafter they had better ride in automobiles and not go on the street-cars, as the police might arrest them, meaning that honest citizens riding on street-cars were in danger from the police.

The police are naturally very sensitive about this matter. The public look to them for protection. The man who loses his pocket-book wants to know what the police are doing, why the person who took it is not convicted and sent to Sing Sing, where he belongs. I think myself the law governing disorderly persons and vagrants in this State is not strong enough. The law in Massachusetts with reference to such people works well, does no injustice, and bars such people out of the State. I tried to have it enacted here, but some young lawyer objected, and it died in committee. The course of justice, like true love, never runs smooth. There would be no miscarriage of justice, not once in a thousand cases, if the law were changed. These people are as well known and marked as if they belonged to another race. I cannot understand why a magistrate with a notorious crook before him on the one hand and a policeman on the other, should not give his moral support to the officer. It renders the police problem here in New York very hard, and will continue to do so until some radical and far-reaching reform is attained.

In regard to the question whether the attitude of the general public here is antagonistic to the police, and why that should be the case when in other countries the public give every support to their police, I would say: The public here know the police through the press, and it is unnecessary for me to state what the general attitude of the press is towards the police. It is certainly quite true, in striking contrast with affairs here, that the police in great capitals, like London and Paris, are given every possible consideration by the magistrates.

The fate of the defendant hangs on the word of the policeman. A request for a remand even for eight days to get necessary evidence is at once allowed. The judge gives him every confidence, shows him respect, treats him as an impartial, honest, and fearless personification of the law of the land—practically consults him as to what he thinks should be done with the defendant in minor cases. In such cases and in dealing with professional criminals the opinion of the officer, and even his attitude towards the defendant, has weight with the court. I would be willing to wager that it rarely occurs that a professional crook will walk in triumph out of a Paris or London court-room with the officer reprimanded for arresting him. Here the policeman is the man on trial.

I told the police, and I insisted upon it as part of their duty, that they must pay no attention whatever to what happens in regard to defendants being discharged in court unfairly and unjustly. They must go ahead and arrest the men over and over and over again and unceasingly. The court may act as it sees fit. They must do their duty to society. For instance, if a man should be discharged fifty times a week, my orders were to arrest him the fifty-first time, where he is known as a professional criminal, and under such circumstances as to warrant the belief that he is intent on crime, and when they know that he has no means of support under the meaning of the penal code, and bring him back before the same judge and let him discharge him if he will. In other words, the police must not be discouraged, but go right ahead, taking the reprimands and discharges as they come and as a part of the day's work. If they did otherwise it would be useless to try to stem the tide of crime in New York.

To a certain extent the police themselves are to blame for the public attitude towards them. They believe the public are antagonistic. Naturally they fight back. They feel that no one appreciates them; they believe it is just as profitable to be crooked as to be straight, so far as the public is concerned; that the average man in the street does not respect them; that he is unfriendly to them. Here and there a sly, crooked, successful officer or administrator of police succeeds in getting power and wealth with the apparent respect of the public, but leaving behind him in the service a malodorous reputation; this discourages weak men and leads them to believe that crooked ways are better than straight ones.

The hardest thing that the head of the police has to do is to convince the men that honesty is the best policy, and that the successful crook who "gets away with it," to use the phrase, does not "live happily ever afterwards," as the story-book says, and enjoy the confidence of the community; that an honest policeman, living within his means, supporting his family in a decent way, giving his children a good education, seeing that they grow up with the respect of their neighbors because of the good character of their father, is better off and happier a thousandfold than the crooked one. That is the talk I gave the police constantly, individually and collectively.

The general conditions throughout the country are not the same as in New York. In Boston, for instance, the greatest confidence and respect exist between the magistrates and the police. The disorderly persons law there is better. The professional pick-pocket does not stand any show in Boston. He goes to jail at once and is kept there. Professional loafers and others, such as prevail in the Tenderloin, would be sent down the harbor to break stone thirty hours after they got to Boston. The same is true of Canadian cities. There the judges and police work together, both sworn officers of the law, both having thorough confidence in each other. That is a condition which must be brought about in New York. It is worth the effort of the best newspapers, the greatest reformers, and of every citizen. I feel it would be a good thing if an impartial committee of public-spirited citizens would organize themselves and go to the police courts frequently, or be represented there so as to watch all the cases, take notes, and make every possible endeavor to bridge over this chasm between the police and the judges. With hordes of defendants walking out of the court-rooms free men, with the department inundated every day with showers of writs, injunctions, mandamuses, and other powerful judicial embargoes, the condition is certainly not a good one.

The answer of some of the judges to all of this will be that the police are a lawless body; that they break the law at every opportunity and tell lies about it. This is distinctly not so; and if it were so, the largest contributing feature to it would be the attitude of the courts themselves. When a policeman finds that he can get no support in enforcing the law against a disorderly house, pool-room, notorious thief, pick-pocket, or loafer, the temptation is very great to resort to the law of force. The office of police magistrate, with the exception of the District Attorney, is the most powerful and important office in New York. It offers more opportunities to serve the people than almost any other public office, and when the people really and in earnest begin to demand the sort of government to which they are entitled, they will not for a day tolerate the prostitution of these immensely important courts by the appointment of men notoriously unfitted for such power and responsibility.

XXI

POLITICS AND THE POLICE

Politics ought to have nothing more to do with the police force than has the question of religious belief, and wherever it touches the department nothing but evil ensues. It paralyzes the police arm for the enforcement of the law; it puts merit to the rear, and incompetency and dishonesty to the front. The country at large has at all times been opposed to politics in the army or navy, but, after some experience with the Navy Department and the police, I have no hesitation in saying that I think politics are worse for the latter than for the army or navy. It is a greater crime against the public to transfer an honest captain from an important precinct and put in his place a weak or dishonest one, than to send an officer with a political or personal pull and no merit to some fancy assignment in Europe. Moreover, the police, as a political machine, is much more powerful than the army or navy. If a political organization were given the option of a large election fund, amounting to a very large sum of money, or complete control of the police machine, I am quite sure that an astute politician would choose the latter.

Aside from the fact that each policeman can control, if he exerts himself, certainly one vote in addition to his own, and sometimes maybe as many as ten, the police, from their numbers and influence, might determine an election. If in addition to this, for the political effect, some laws are enforced indifferently or half-heartedly, or not at all, under an agreement that the result is to show at the polls, the police machine can be made most powerful in elections.

The police of New York have time and again been used, so far as political organizations could control them, for politics both before and on Election Day. It has, however, not always followed that the political organization controlling the city government has been able to use the police successfully. The reason of this is because the rank and file of the police under a corrupt city administration are generally shamelessly used to gather in graft for the men at the top. They see the big fellows get rich; but clever and crooked men at the head of the force are very apt to be most severe against the smaller fellows getting any share of the plunder. It might, therefore, happen that where the men at the top, who control the police, would be thoroughly corrupt and reap large fortunes from systematic graft, that they would see to it that the rank and file did not share, in the slightest degree, in the profits of this nefarious business; and, indeed, they might go further and be strict disciplinarians. And it goes without saying that a crooked administrator of the police, himself in league with the law-breaking and disorderly elements, will know much more about the evils in the town than an honest man, and will be better informed as to the corrupt men on the force who might attempt to become grafters and bribe-takers on their own account.

In addition to this, a thoroughly corrupt administration of the police will not be satisfied with grafting on the public: they will also graft on the force itself. Every appointment, promotion, assignment, and transfer has to be paid for, cash in advance, and the man who does not pay must suffer. Under such a reign of terror the great body of the police, bitter at heart, will be found on Election Day secretly or openly opposing the party in power. If the administration of the department is aggressively honest, rigorously enforcing the laws, especially against paying vices, and is absolutely fair in making promotions, assignments, and transfers, on merit and for public reasons only, the dishonest element and the shirks and purchasers of favor will be in opposition. This opposition, however, is not dangerous politically, for it is sure to be offset by the votes of honest and appreciative citizens.

If all the dishonest elements in the police force were to be rallied under one banner, either for favors or a share in the plunder, and should go unitedly into action on behalf of a candidate or party, they would become a most powerful factor in all elections and a positive menace to free government. It is, therefore, absolutely essential to the public weal, to honest government and fair elections, to clean administration and an impartial enforcement of the laws, that the administration of the Police Department should be absolutely and wholly non-political.

Now the Police Department must be entirely non-political, or the reverse, because there is no middle ground. It is utterly impossible for an administration of the police to compromise with politics one way or the other. If the Commissioner makes one appointment, promotion, transfer, or assignment for political reasons only, he has vitiated the other ten which he may make for the good of the service and with honest intentions to better the same. The moment that the force understands that one transfer of a captain, for instance, of an important precinct, has been made to please prominent politicians with a pull, and in the interest, say, of the big gambling combine, the whole police administration is discredited from one end of the force to the other. It would be much better, therefore, for the police force and the public, if an administration was openly and avowedly political, rather than to be secretly and furtively political, while hypocritically pretending to be impartial, non-partisan, and influenced only by public reasons. A square and open partisan administration of the police would, in my judgment, of course, be dangerous to the public welfare, but the people are safer from an advertised and unconcealed danger than when misled by hypocritical pretentions as a cover for the carrying out of personal and political ends.

There are some inspection districts and precincts in Greater New York, especially in Manhattan, by which an administration can fairly be judged, as shown in the character of the officers assigned to these important places, such as the first, second, third, and fourth inspection districts of Manhattan; the twelfth, fifteenth, sixteenth, nineteenth, twenty-second, twenty-sixth, twenty-ninth, and thirty-second precincts in Manhattan, and the forty-ninth and sixty-ninth precincts in Brooklyn. If outside influences obviously make the selections for the commands in these districts and precincts, the worst can be expected and the best is impossible.

From the time I first went to Mulberry Street until I transferred him, intending to send him back in the spring, had I remained in office, there was an immense pressure on me to take Captain Dooley out of the sixty-ninth precinct. To show how important it is to those who want to thrive by the rich plunder of such a place as Coney Island in the summer, I need only say that at one time they went so far as to put up a job on Captain Dooley by planting a fake gambling establishment and raiding it from the outside in the hope of discrediting him, and they also endeavored to trump up other charges, finding that I was impervious to any outside influences in the matter.

A Commissioner who will agree to allow certain influences to name the inspectors, captains, and others for different assignments, or who will make such transfers on the suggestion of interested people and without any knowledge as to their wisdom, makes for himself a small army of powerful friends; but if he declares entire independence in these matters, he can look for the bitter enmity and unending hostility of those who claim to control the primal springs of government. Of course there are cases where a political leader of good character and with honest intentions to do the best for the people who support him, will ask to be upheld by the police in his own efforts to keep his district clean, and suggestions and information from such a man are not to be disregarded. But, on the other hand, I am perfectly frank in saying that I have seldom known a case where political reasons were allowed to govern in the direction and management of the force, especially in the matter of promotions, transfers, and assignments, that evil has not followed and the efficiency of the service been injured.

In saying what I have about the evil of letting politics have anything to do with the police, and asserting, as I do here, that it ought to be no more considered in the administration of the department than the question of religious belief, I know that I am running counter to the opinion of some very estimable gentlemen. It is eminently human for people to expect favors of their friends in office, and it is indeed right that the Commissioner should be apprised of the merits of men by his friends and those in whom he has confidence; and it is not at all unnatural that men in active politics, who have befriended policemen, should look to them for some degree of gratitude about election-time, or, indeed, in the performance of their ordinary duties. But all the arguments I have ever heard advanced in favor of allowing active men in control of political organizations to manage the police force, or to direct it either from the outside or inside, are to my mind utterly unsound.

Just before the last election I addressed the men on several occasions, especially those on probation, and endeavored to impress upon them that they should not vote as policemen but as citizens, and that they should keep their police duties entirely separate from their partisan predilections; and also to assure them that, so far as I was concerned, they could vote for any candidate they chose or any party they preferred with perfect freedom. In fact, it was their right and privilege to do so without any coercion from the Police Department or the city government, and without the dread of being punished in the future for whatever course they then decided to take. I think it an outrage for any Commissioner or other public officer to coerce a policeman as to how he should vote, and if he doesn't do as he is told, make him the object of revenge after election.

Why should not a policeman vote with the same degree of freedom as any other citizen? If he performs his duties honestly he is not under obligation to any party or politician. One weakness of the police force is this: they are frequently asking for legislative favors or lobbying the legislature or the city government, and very naturally, in return, the politicians expect them to repay this with their influence and their votes, or, worse still, to close their eyes to infractions of the law. It is pitiful to see policemen with honest intentions and impulses dodging and shirking the performance of their duty, cringing and cowering before every one that they think has a "pull," instead of walking out squarely and fairly in the middle of the road and executing the law without fear or favor.

When the police force is organized on proper lines and divided into two great armies—first, the uniformed force, to perform purely constabulary duty, insure order, preserve the peace, beget security for life, limb, and property on the streets, avenues, and highways; and the second a real detective bureau, organized on even stronger and better lines than the famous Scotland Yard, and acting entirely independent of the uniformed police, preventing secret crime, apprehending criminals, dealing with swindlers, gamblers, and all manner of vice, taking the place of the plain-clothes men in all precincts and districts, and acting directly under the eyes of the head of the police and the chief of the bureau—then the dangers of the police in politics will be minimized under any possible administration. Such a machine, well officered, will beget public confidence and respect, and will arouse an irresistible public opinion against any attempt to smirch it or prostitute it for political or personal ends.

Whenever a police captain, in an important precinct, begins to put the pressure of law on the disorderly and vicious elements, the cry at once goes up among a certain class of politicians that he is not fair, that he is a partisan, and that all they want is fair play, a square deal, etc. What they really mean to say is that he is enforcing the law against their followers, who are crying out against him, and they want him transferred, or made to let up, so that the profits of the business won't be interfered with.

When Inspector Schmittberger was transferred, for reasons which are not necessary to be stated in this book, to the third district, and Captain Dooley was sent to the nineteenth precinct, my intention being, after he had cleaned that place up, to return him in the spring to the Coney Island command, had I remained in office, these assignments aroused the most bitter, unrelenting, and malicious opposition in the whole history of the Police Department. The sending of these two officers to this district was accepted by the lawless element as a distinct challenge as to the continuance of their power. The rich, professional bondsmen, owners of property used for illegal purposes, Raines law hotels, gamblers, pool-room keepers, swindlers, and the law-breaking element generally, welded itself into one determined opposition. In wild desperation they ran around asking one and another, "Are Schmittberger and Dooley straight? Are they in earnest?" After they had been twenty-four hours at work the questions were answered in the affirmative. The heavy hand of the police fell on the "Bon-Ton," a mixed resort for negroes and whites run by an ex-convict—who had recently emerged from the Maryland penitentiary, where he had served five years, and who has broken his bond in the District of Columbia—and managed on the outside by the agent of one of the richest professional bondsmen in New York, who was the real owner. This place was not only a gambling resort of the lowest order, but was in itself a sample of the unspeakably vile and criminal mixed-race and mixed-sex resorts that have disgraced this city. It is shameful to say that politicians in both parties have time and again coddled these mixed-race places for the votes which they are supposed to influence or sell; and, up to the later arousing of public indignation by the exposures of the imprisoning of white girls in some of the worst of these dens, the Commissioner who undertook to deal with them had to expect the censure, strange to say, of some of the most eminent white clergymen in New York, and not a few newspapers.

These people, of course, are grossly misled and do any amount of damage, which I am quite sure they have never estimated. This colored element, when they feel the hand of the law, immediately appeal to the decent and respectable members of their own race, and cry out that they are persecuted by race prejudice. The spirit of racial fraternity is at once aroused, and white clergymen and politicians are appealed to as professional friends of the colored man to come to the rescue, which, apparently, they do without thinking or examining the case. Unless therefore, under great excitement, such as prevailed in the last notorious case, a Commissioner is very apt to find himself pilloried as favoring the persecution and even mobbing of respectable and decent colored people by white ruffians and loafers, and by brutal policeman, and being actuated only by racial and political prejudices.

Up to a few weeks ago there was no public opinion in New York against such hell-pits as the "Savoy" and the colored "Haymarket" in Thirty-second Street. The whole press of this city did not give thirty lines to my meetings with the defiant representatives of these doggeries, whose greatest outrage is against the decent, orderly, law-abiding, industrious colored people themselves. To get at these places effectively, the white and colored agitators and little, loud-voiced negro politicians must first be brushed aside and given no consideration. They swarm around these plague-infested caves of crime like hungry buzzards over unspeakable things.

This "Bon-Ton" dive was a most profitable place, and so the war was on. The next day, with surprising unanimity, the confederated reporters of the Tenderloin launched their inspired story of the alleged outrages — poor negroes beaten into jelly, costly clocks smashed, priceless bric-à-brac destroyed, numerous windows broken, valuable billiard-tables, ottomans, mahogany bar-fixtures, cut-glass chandeliers, costly paintings, all destroyed by the brutal, reckless, and lawless police. The Mayor was red-flagged. The continuance of such a Police Commissioner in office meant defeat at the polls. Schmittberger and Dooley must be court-martialled, disgraced, fined, dismissed or denounced, and transferred to Flushing, or some such place, at once. I made up my mind on the instant that no faithful policeman should be sacrificed, and that I would stand between two honest police officials and their enemies, if they included the whole press of New York and all the political organizations banded together. I thereupon placed myself in front of these two men and assumed responsibility for everything that they had done. Calling in David McClure, Esq., a lawyer of the highest ability and a citizen of distinction, I spent several days in a thorough, painstaking, impartial, and judicial investigation of this case, which resulted in not only exonerating the officers in question, but in commending them for their zeal, intelligence, and fidelity in the performance of their duty, which report was made to the Mayor.

Testimony disclosed that the place was a ramshackle, ill-smelling, unventilated den; that there were no clocks to smash or pictures to destroy, nor, indeed, windows to break; that it was a dirt-begrimed, unwashed series of lofts where poor, deluded, wretched humanity of both races and sexes gathered every day to hand up its money indirectly to the big scoundrels who get rich on crime and vice; that not a man was clubbed; that, on the contrary, crippled boys were helped out humanely by the police; that the number of police concerned was grossly exaggerated, being something less than a dozen. Of all the hundreds alleged to have been present, including the citizens of the neighborhood, and of all those concerned, only one witness turned up, and he was an unknown man who said he was a friend of the "bunch," as he called the reporters who got up this story. He acknowledged he had never been in the house at all, yet, according to him, the newspaper stories were based on his statements.

The indignation of the newspapers over the alleged original outrage was nothing as compared to their anger over the refutation of their stories. Of course they gave no great publicity to the denials, but made counter-charges of the suppression of evidence and all sorts of covert insinuations, but at heart they were no doubt bitterly and keenly disappointed. Baffled at the exposure of the "Bon-Ton" raid, and afraid to come forward and defend the ex-convict who had run the place, who was a notorious tool of the men higher up, they then turned their batteries on Captain Dooley. They must either make him a joke and ridicule him out of the precinct, or they must take him seriously and alarm the public with regard to him. The joke fell flat. Dooley didn't wear the best clothes, it is true. He had never taken any graft at Coney Island, and couldn't afford an expensive outfit, so his clothes were old-fashioned and a bit shabby. Of course, as he didn't know the big fellows in the Tenderloin, he was a countryman. The crooks and their friends were going to have a lot of fun with him, and all this would furnish columns for the newspapers; great reading, things that would make you laugh, and also show you how witty these men are and how sarcastic. It would please you when you read their stories, and would make them solid with certain other fellows who are handy to know in a pinch. It would also make the editors feel fortunate in possessing such brilliant writers; and, of course, no Police Commissioner could know as much as these people. Hadn't some of them been Tenderloin reporters for twenty years! This wild, absurdly honest countryman, Dooley, was going to really enforce the law and break dear old friendships, profitable alliances, and, in general, devastate the rich, juicy lowlands of graft.

The work done in those few weeks by Inspector Schmittberger and Captain Dooley was very great, as is shown by the figures. Did any one read in the newspapers credit being given for this? Was any apology made to Captain Dooley for the story about the curfew law? Was any notice taken, in a proper quarter, of this man's unusual honesty and ability? The rest is too well known to make comment on it. All the crooks, in and out of the police force, will profit by taking example of Dooley. The crop of Dooleys will not get too large in the future. The powers will see to that. How could you ever elect great statesmen to office when people like Schmittberger and Dooley are around; and of what use are fool Commissioners who will stand by such men, when they could make themselves everlasting friends of little men in big offices and be voted a good-fellow by those who make Mayors and Governors, and even Presidents.

The case was indeed desperate; given a Dooley in the Tenderloin, delightful customs and quiet little business ventures not allowed by law might be interfered with. Even by people in otherwise legitimate businesses, from chop-suey cafés to restaurants of national fame, from traders in diamonds and purveyors of rare wines to dealers in second-hand "dress suits," from the pious owners of property used for illegal and immoral purposes to the hackmen of darkness and night, Dooley was denounced as an outrage on a free and unbridled neighborhood, an impossible person, not amenable to good old commercial reasons, incapable of being driven by the "rulers of the darkness," ridiculously ignorant of business, and backed by a Police Commissioner under whom untrammelled government by the few at the expense of the many was seriously menaced.

The hired brains and ratlike cunning of the defenders of the old, profitable ways were on their mettle. The honest, ignorant public must be made to feel outraged. The heart of the community had failed to bleed for the alleged outrages on the pure souls and holy lives of the habitués of the "Bon-

Ton"; but wait until it heard the first peal of Dooley's curfew. With a suspicious unanimity, certain of the press, with due regard to big type, seriously informed the city that Captain Dooley had given an order that any woman out on the public streets unaccompanied by a male escort after 9 P.M. was to be arrested. In vain were the stenographic notes of the instructions given by Captain Dooley to his men offered in evidence, in vain the denials of the men of his command, in vain the results of a painstaking and thorough investigation of the charge, resulting in the admission of a police-court writer that he set it forth on imagination or rumor. Hotel proprietors wrote me as to the safety of their women guests, and one pastor of a church issued cards to the female members of his flock, certifying to character and necessity of being on the streets after dark. Indignant women inveighed against Dooley and the Commissioner as czars and tyrants, and learned judges tore their robes in just indignation, and the rough-coined lie stalked on its triumphal career, while howls went up that Dooley and the writer be thrown to the beasts, and every thumb pointed to the ground. If I went into public places my presence momentarily embarrassed impromptu indignation meetings, while the "ladies" of the pavements began again to throng the streets, objects of universal sympathy, the minute-women of civic rights, conscious that no court in the then state of the public mind would fail to recognize them as objects of police brutality and the personification of every virtue.

That no honest man or woman might be misled, I adopted the unusual course of going to the nineteenth precinct station-house, on a Sunday afternoon, and making in the presence of the representatives of the press an address to the outgoing and incoming platoons. In this address the curfew lie was exposed, the rights of women on the public streets carefully and explicitly stated, the captain and inspector assured of the support of the Commissioner, the men solemnly warned against disobedience, and threatened, in such event, with transference in a body and trial afterwards, and the evil powers in array against these officers defied and threatened; all this in the presence of the newspaper representatives, who were appealed to for square treatment and a manly display of fair play.

It may be that "truth crushed to earth will rise again," but I can certify that a good, healthy lie well persisted in can stand a good many falls, for there are people, I suppose, who yet believe in that deliberately concocted story, told with malicious persistence, that a curfew order against women on the streets was really issued and an attempt made to carry it out. And, after all, why should they not? The average man and woman depend almost entirely on the press as to what are the facts in the daily life of the city. They read of atrocious outrages by the dozen on innocent women, which, if true—and they were not—would have shown the Armenian doings to be mild and playful practices; and they have never yet, so far as known to me, seen one word of retraction.

Satisfied that Dooley and Schmittberger were to remain, despite the shrieks of the curfewers and the friends of the "Bon-Ton" law-breakers, bondsmen, gamblers, loafers, swindlers, and the leaders of the devil's old-guard in general, the logic of the situation pointed to but one solution—a Police Commissioner who had the audacity to challenge the very sources of government in the enforcement of the law, must go. Surely no sane, serious, and conservative statesman intent only on a business administration could stand for such a man. As a late popular public man would have said, such conduct was "indecent" and not "statesmanship." In speaking of politicians and the police, I am not, after a considerable career in the public service, inveighing against or condemning politicians as a body. Quite the contrary, and, indeed, to do otherwise would ill become me. I have always believed that there was much truth in what the late Mr. Reed said facetiously, but no doubt meant seriously, that "a statesman was a dead politician." All I insist on is that the control, administration, and direction of the police force of a great city should be even more removed from political influence than that of the army or navy, and that when this is not the rule the police cannot and will not be honestly efficient, and that under such a system crime and corruption must flourish; on such a soil nothing but poison-plants will grow.

The so-called bipartisan board is a sort of comic-opera idea. It never has worked well and never will. It simply provides for the two leading political organizations to run the police force on avowedly partisan principles in partnership and harmony and under a "gentleman's agreement." This precinct to you, that captain to me; you look after station-houses, I'll take care of the horses; if you won't let me promote Smith, you can't advance Brown; you make a bluff at enforcing the excise, I'll sound the siren to the gamblers. I'll be your wicked partner and you'll be mine, and blessed be the law makers; our responsibilities are beautifully divided, and yet we are so delightfully intertwined, and our interests so closely interwoven, that the party press and the party officers higher up cannot lay an unkindly finger on one of us without every bipartisan nerve of the whole board throbbing with indignation. The whole thing would be as harmonious as a sheriff's jury at dinner, nothing like as effective as Mr. Devery's famous pump, and would carry joy to all persons, powers, and interests with which a policeman is supposed to be constantly at war. No longer would we sing, "It was not like that in the olden days," for the olden days—in all their delicious ingenuousness, open-faced contempt for law, simple and childlike amusement at advocates of civic virtue, morality, and common decency and conventional respect for government—would be with us again.

I should think a bipartisan police board of good, old, hard-shelled politicians would be a delightful field for a man with a sense of humor. To listen with assumed gravity to the delegation of leading citizens denouncing some favorite form of law-breaking, while repressing well-springs of mirth at the gullibility and credulity of the people, and then to hear the merry wags burst with laughter after the "leading citizens" had reached the hall, would beat any farce, old or modern, known to the stage.

Until a Mayor can be found who has the courage and conviction to place the fearless enforcement of the law and the impartial administration of justice by the Police Department, of which he is the head, and the courts, of which he is the guardian, above political ambition or advantage, and who will show by his acts that he prefers to go down, even to defeat, fighting like a gallant soldier beside a faithful public officer, rather than insure his safety or conserve his personal comfort by cowardly compromise or shameless desertion, and until a failure to maintain this standard will arouse public opinion, hot, insistent, and irresistible, the era of good government in this and other cities is yet far removed.

"Ye shall know them by their fruits. Do men gather grapes of thorns or figs of thistles?"

When the best friends of a police administration are the enemies of the public, when its most ardent advocates are the breakers of the law, when its praises are chiefly sung by the beneficiaries of its infidelity or indifference to the obligations of its oath of office, then, indeed, the thistles and thorns of vice and crime have overgrown and overthrown the vines of civic virtue; the orchard is hidden and strangled by deep, impenetrable thickets of thorns, long breathing of the exudations of which beget lethargy, coma, and a stifling of the public conscience.

For you, my good masters, not grapes and figs, but poison-berries and thistle-burrs and much disappointment, until your present indifference is succeeded by larger, clearer, broader views, more intelligent and impartial investigation of this great engine of government; and until you have chosen wisely to heed your awakened consciousness and convictions, some man, fearless-hearted, earnestly honest, undeviatingly just, with capacity to command, knowledge of human nature, and who, untrammelled, independent, and grimly determined, will go into this dismal jungle armed with axe, spade, rake and hoe, and will not spare himself in the days' work until the good soil that yet remains is laid open to sunshine and air, where honest men, with honest ways, high intelligence, and devotion to duty can live and thrive, and on which can be built up a police machine worthy of this enlightened, powerful, rich, and populous city and its millions of people, to whom good and efficient police government is a question of transcendent importance, and which so built, will in turn repay in the greater security of person and property, in the advancement of public morality, in respect for law, and in the restoration to public confidence and respect of those clothed with its execution, and in manifold other blessings, all the labor, time, and sacrifice expended and made in this effort for the common good and the influence and honor of this capital of half a world.

THE END

www.ingramcontent.com/pod-product-compliance
Lightning Source LLC
LaVergne TN
LVHW020610110826
845149LV00002B/427

9781418188061